Let's Do Theology

Let's Do Theology

Resources for Contextual Theology

Completely revised and updated new edition

Laurie Green

mowbray

Published by Mowbray, an imprint of the
Continuum International Publishing Group

The Tower Building	80 Maiden Lane
11 York Road	Suite 704
London	New York
SE1 7NX	NY 10038

www.continuumbooks.com

© Laurie Green, 2009

First published 2009
Reprinted 2012

British Library Cataloguing-in-Publication Data
A catalogue record for this book is available from the British Library.

ISBN 978-0-8264-2551-5

Designed and typeset by Kenneth Burnley, Wirral, Cheshire
Printed and bound in Great Britain

Contents

Introduction

The first edition of *Let's Do Theology* was written in 1989 and, much to my surprise, twenty years later it is still being read and used by Christians around the world who are intent on using the wonderful gift of theology as a tool for liberation and transformation. But as I pick up that first edition and re-read it today, it seems lacking in many ways and I have therefore been grateful to Andrew Walby at Continuum, its present publisher, for allowing me this opportunity to rewrite the text substantially and introduce into the book a considerable amount of new material.

Let's Do Theology began its life after twenty years of ordained ministry in the British industrial city of Birmingham. Building on my experience of studying theology in London and New York and my abiding interest in adult education since working for an educational psychologist in a mental hospital, I began to formulate a method of doing theology which kept context very much in mind. I honed this methodology among the laity of my working-class parishes, and later with theological students when, for seven years, I had the honour of training them for ordained ministry. The methodology had already resulted in an earlier book, *Power to the Powerless: Theology Brought to Life*,[1] which was my account of how our small group of inner-city Christians had come to make for themselves a theology which was vital and relevant to their urban experience. My Brazilian contacts assured me that they felt that the book described an authentically British example of what they were calling in Latin America, 'Basic Ecclesial Communities', for the group's theology was reflective yet active, committed yet thoughtful, questioning yet substantial. For me, that book raised some basic questions that were demanding an answer. What is the nature of theology? What is actually going on when we do it? Why has theology become the preserve of specialists? Why can it sometimes appear so distant from the worship and devotional life of the Church? *Let's Do Theology* was, in part, my attempt to answer those questions.

At that time there was also an impenetrable reluctance on the part of academic theologians to mix it with ordinary Christians, and that had been giving theology a name for being remote, erudite and book-bound. It was assumed that theology was the preserve of white, Western, male academics, and any theology produced by women, black, Asian or working-class Christians was looked upon as an interesting oddity. How far we have travelled in just a few decades.

The first chapter of the first edition of this book was therefore arguing into a context of bookish theology that seems so different from where we now are. The Asian theological voice is being heard at last as never before in the West; African and African-American experiences are all generating new theological insights; and feminist theology is now considered by most thinkers as crucial and mainstream. Liberation Theology, so fundamental to the first edition of this book, has helped us on our way to the deeper insights of the new Post-colonial Theology, and we no longer have to fight against those who portray theology as a corpus of revealed information – most know that theology is an activity rather than a substance, even if some theological teachers still find it hard to get their heads round that. It has therefore been a great delight to rework this text substantially, with all these developments in mind, and I have taken opportunity to introduce some of these insights and newly developed methodologies into the body of the book. In this I have been substantially helped by the opportunities I have had to travel to other continents and to survey the scene for myself. I have been invited to run seminars on theology in the United States, Brazil, India and Europe, and, in the process, I have been introduced to new thinking and have been in awe of the work being done as the practical outcome of doing theology contextually.

Since publishing *Let's Do Theology* twenty years ago, many others have now published their thoughts about how theology should be practised and I have introduced a brand-new chapter into this edition which surveys the new scene, carefully describing and critiquing the new contributions, and revising my own model in accordance with the best of their insights. I have been surprised, nevertheless, to see how rarely new writers have substantially deviated from the model and style of theology I proposed all those years ago, and perhaps that is why the first edition of *Let's Do Theology* ran to so many reprints and remained in the catalogue for twenty years, despite its many obvious deficiencies.

But there remains a long and challenging journey ahead, and that is why this second edition of the book, which is so thoroughly reworked and updated, is important to me, and I hope it will be welcomed by its readers.

The first challenge which this book seeks to address is the fact that the term 'contextual theology' is still being thought of by some to mean that theology should be understood to be a body of crystallized truth which can then be 'applied' to various contexts as required. I have seen many a seminary or college syllabus offer courses in 'contextual theology' which merely teach students the best ways of introducing old wine into new wineskins, rather than how to look in the new wineskins – the new situations – and find exciting new theological insights already there. Theology from the roots up, which actually derives from the context in which it is set and incarnated, and which is discovered and mined out by those already experiencing the full subtleties of that context, is the stuff of the model I propose. And it is because this theology is so imbedded in the culture and fibre of the locality, that it resonates there with the felt experiences of the place, the time and the people, and leads them to new awareness and to new exciting possibilities. When we look to the life of Jesus himself, we see there precisely this incarnational model of deep engagement, and so we can have every faith that we will find transformative theology if we do our theology in this same way. It will uncover local truths that speak of eternity. As I am fond of saying, 'Act locally, think universally!'

This leads me to the second challenge which this book seeks to address, for I do believe that any theology worthy of the name must be transformative theology. Good Christian theology is able to change us and change situations. The style of theology which this book proposes is designed to integrate action and reflection, and yet all too often theological reflection alone is offered as the full content of theology. I believe theology to be a spiritual exercise through which we are brought to awareness through the process of reflection, but then the theological process continues by challenging us to repentance and empowers us by the Holy Spirit for our own transformation, the transformation of other individuals involved, and the transformation of the related societal structures. Good theological reflection should raise awareness, but if the theological process ends with reflection, then it is only doing half of what transformative theology is intended to do. In this book I make a clear distinction between 'theological reflection', which is largely a cognitive exercise, and 'doing theology', which involves the whole of our being. When we consider that central tenet of the Christian faith, the Incarnation, we are reminded that to be fully human, as in Jesus Christ, we must, like him, be an integrated unity of body and spirit. So it is that our contextual incarnational theology must likewise model an inextricable unity of action and reflection. It is theology which seeks to serve humanity holistically through theological reflection and responsive transformative action. Theology is a much more powerful and transformative instrument than many give it credit for, and this book sets out to explore the extent of its possibilities.

Third, although we've come a long way in twenty years, in the United Kingdom, theology has not yet been sufficiently democratized. It does not yet fully belong to the people, the whole 'laity' of God. If we ask where we see theology presently being done, our answer will almost certainly be – theology is being done in the universities among academics, in the seminaries and colleges among ministers and ordinands, and in those courses designed for laity who will be moving into specialist, accredited lay ministries within the institution. But I dream of the day when we will see women and men doing theology in order to decide each and every church policy; see it being done by young Christians as they plan drug addiction or outreach programmes; see theology driving our budget planning, our vision setting, and the actions of every Christian group and organization. We see the first exciting glimmers of this in our churches, but we still have so far to go. As it is, most of the crucial elements of our Christian corporate life are decided on the basis of pragmatic expediency or the latest bright idea. When a way forward is offered which is clearly and overtly based in theological analysis and reflection, it is welcomed with open arms as strikingly unusual and refreshingly faithful. This book seeks to offer a way of doing theology which can become second nature to every Christian.

I believe that the reason for such a dearth of everyday theology among Christian people is that we are still not quite sure how to do it, and we still feel that theology is for those who have special skills who will, after they have done it for us, feed us with their resultant insights. Even the clergy are not exempt from this reluctance to do theology for themselves. I recently attended a seminar for clergy who were within three years of retirement age. Most had been ordained all their adult lives and so we expected that the session entitled 'theological reflection' would open up all sorts of fascinating insights into the theology of the ageing process, physical diminishment, transition, loss and recreation. Instead, these experienced clergy simply did not know what to do or where to begin. It became clear that their ministerial formation had occurred almost 40 years ago when it was not expected even for clergy to make the connections between the theology they read and the realities they faced. It was therefore doubly difficult for them now to make the faith connections with the reality of the retirement which was looming up before them. Doing theology, making the transforming connections between our real-life issues and the fundamentals of our Christian heritage, is not something that the older generation of church leaders was trained to do naturally and easily, and it is only through their own later determination that any have made that transition to a more dynamic use of theology. My hope and prayer is that this book, and this new edition of it, will continue to help that transition for those already in ordained or lay ministry, and that it will be of substantial service too for those who are just starting out on this wonderful adventure of 'doing theology'.

So, although theology has come so far since the first edition of *Let's Do Theology* was published, many challenges still remain. I hope therefore that this new edition, so substantially revised and enlarged, will continue to help make the doing of contextual theology an essential and natural instrument in the toolbag of every Christian, ordained or lay. It will always be a work in progress and I hope that readers will take the ideas in this book and develop them further as their own situation demands. I will always be pleased to hear how their group experiences have progressed and where improvements can be built into the ideas developed here.

Countless people have helped me to write this book, and some will never know how much they have influenced it. Many have been group participants, some have asked of me really penetrating questions at conferences, so that I have been made to go home and think again. Some have been close associates and friends. Special thanks must go to the Revd Joe Duggan, the Revd Michael Allen and Joanna Cox for their helpful critique of the old edition, and to Becki Green and the Revds Chris Mann, Martin Wood and Frances Drake for their invaluable IT skills. Thanks, as ever, are due to my work colleagues and my family for their encouragement and practical support. But I want to register my especial thanks to the Revd Dr John Vincent, the founder of the Urban Theology Unit, who has, through many years, been a source of inspiration for those of us here in the UK who have sought to do theology with contextual integrity.

Laurie Green
www.lauriegreen.org
July 2009

Note

1 Green, L. (1987), *Power to the Powerless: Theology Brought to Life*. Basingstoke: Marshall Pickering.

Dedicated to
The Revd Dr John Vincent,
without whose encouragement, friendship and inspiration
this book would never have existed

Part 1

Describing the Process

In this first part of *Let's Do Theology* we will describe a dynamic way to do theology which allows this precious instrument to be used by all members of the Christian Church, not just academics – although they too will have an important part to play in the process.

We will explain where this model of theology originates and offer some exciting examples of its use to help the reader see how it brings theology alive in a transformative way.

1

Transforming Theology

Why do theology?

Most people in the West today seem to believe that the Church is out of touch. It does not touch their everyday lives, it does not touch their concerns, their routines, or their struggles. When asked whether or not they believe in God, however, many will say that they do, and many will go further and witness to an experience of the nearness of God in their own lives. Some feel that the Christian faith especially holds out a promise of meaning and value which they yearn for, and of which they have had some glimpse within their own experience. But ask them about the Church and it's a very different matter. I am often struck by the church noticeboard slogan which reads 'Christ is the answer'. I suspect that many would be prompted to respond, 'I agree! But does the Church know what the question is?'

Christianity is a transforming and vibrant faith which holds the key to our deepest concerns, and yet we are beset with the constant difficulty of trying to find a fulfilling way to integrate our Christian belief and our daily life; instead, we hear this wonderful Christian faith being smothered by churchy arguments, complicated theological jargon and what sound like contrived explanations. We have to admit that we, the Church, do not really do the Christian faith justice. At its best, of course, the Church does try to address the world, and faithful Christians up and down the country and around the world work away at the front line, binding up the wounds of those who suffer, engaging in the struggles of the day and offering profound worship; although much of that Christian faithfulness is hidden from the public gaze, it does, I am sure, bear witness to how faith and life are constantly being brought together in the lives of ordinary Christians. It seems to me, however, that this sort of Christian witness to the relevance and vitality of the Christian faith could be greatly assisted if Christians had better tools for understanding the faith, and for seeing how very clearly it does relate to their joys and their struggles. Those outside the Church would then be able to look at the lives of Christians in the Church and feel that they were on their own wavelength, witnessing to a faith that does indeed ring many bells consonant with their own experience of God in their lives.

I have always had a deep conviction that theology can be transformed in such a way that it can become a very productive tool in this endeavour. It was in that spirit that I wrote the first edition of this book back in 1989, for, by then I had had experiences of being with groups of Christians who had found a way of doing theology which brought together the crucial experiences of life and the abiding truths of the Christian faith. The problem was that, at that time, much of what passed for theology was a rather arid turning of academic pages in theological colleges by students who were advised to keep well away from the world 'out there'. So the transformation of theology was an ambitious enterprise, especially when even the word 'theology' itself was being used as the ultimate put-down by those who were out there in the world of issues and decision-making: 'Now your arguments are moving into the realms of fantasy,' they would say to opponents, 'you are just talking theology!'[1]

But I had seen theology revitalized in the hands of groups of ordinary Christians, where it had proved itself to have an amazing potential for the re-creation of integrated Christian living. It was putting the faith back 'in touch' with life. Even then, there were stirrings around the world which indicated that theology is capable of turning the world upside-down. In parts of Latin America, Africa and Asia a new interest in theology had blossomed and had so empowered those Christians involved in it that their whole lives had been transformed, so that they felt liberated by their discovery of it.

Since the writing of the first edition of this book, an amazing transformation has occurred in academia too. Time was when students would go to college or university to 'read' theology rather than 'do' theology. Their expectation was that the tutor would tell them where, in all the great tomes on the library shelves, they would find the answers to the great philosophical problems of the world. They were to digest the arguments set out in the books and learn the content of them so that, later in their lives, when out in the world, they could apply all those answers to any problems that came along. Paulo Freire called this the 'banking theory of education',[2] whereby you make multiple deposits into your wisdom account during your time of formal theological education so you can withdraw your credit later when you wish to apply it to situations in life. This approach assumed that there was in the college a store of 'pure' theology which could be 'applied' to any situation, even though life might be throwing up all sorts of new and unique complexities. No wonder some accused theology of being irrelevant fantasy.

However, this 'banking' approach to education was beginning to frustrate many academics themselves and they too were looking for new ways in which the treasures of theology could be put to the service of Christian life. At the same time, Christian women and men were leading active and creative lives, running churches, engaging in community projects and seeking to influence society, but often without the benefit of thoughtful Christian reflection upon their activity. Some of them felt they were missing the important assurance that their activity was fully consonant with their faith and beliefs. On the other hand, more conservative Christians felt that any theological appraisal of their activity would not have been 'living by faith', and so had decided to carry on without too much thought. Yet others simply found the old-fashioned 'book-bound' theology too intimidating. There are many in all societies who find reading difficult, and there are those who can read but simply don't. In what ways could a theology, so weighed down by books, be relevant to them?

It is the aim of this book, therefore, to propose a far more ambitious way of doing theology, whereby the very best of what the traditions of theology have to teach us can be fully integrated with our daily lives and with the issues that are now impacting upon society. I hope that in this way both camps of 'activist' and 'academic' theology can find a common mission and serve one another in the quest to transform people and the society in which we live. This will, of course, call for a substantial reformulation of what we consider theology to be, and will require that those who currently engage in academic theology, and those who reject that whole enterprise as unnecessary, may come to see theology as a far more wide-ranging activity than they might have expected – an activity in which all will have their own indispensable part to play.

Participating in theology

By searching for a kind of theology that is inclusive of all types of people, we will enrich it tremendously. No longer will it be implied that books are the only carriers of spiritual wisdom, but now stories, films, popular music, spir-ituals, poetry, handicrafts, computer-gaming, dress, dance and so much more, may turn out to be carrying people's expression of spiritual and profound experience, and may be doing so on behalf of that part of our culture that is especially enamoured neither of the classroom nor of the chapel. If all this wealth of expression is brought to the theological task, then theology begins to break out of its verbal captivity, using all the liberating avenues of culture and body language to express the wisdom it seeks to focus. After all, the Church has known for generations that the great truths of the faith will be confined and crippled if limited merely to erudite statements. This is why it has sacraments, Christian art, music, church architecture, community projects, missionary service, worship, care, fellowship and so on. St Francis put it succinctly when he advised his followers in the art of evangelism. He said, 'Preach the gospel to all you meet. Use words only if necessary.'

So we will not be espousing a more participatory and practical way of doing theology just because it is educationally more sound (although it is), nor simply because it will help people to grow personally in the faith (although it will), but because it will address today's issues and allow the Kingdom of God to beckon us forward, so that we might participate in the transformation of society. It will invite all God's children to become the subjects of their own history, deciders of their own fate, rather than just pawns in the hands of ungodly forces. For Christianity should not be allowed to lull people into a false fatalism but, on the contrary, should be an agency for promoting active commitment for justice and peace on earth, 'as it is in heaven'.

This transformed theology, being open to all, will demand that theologians really engage with the world in the quest for God's transformation of it and of ourselves who inhabit it. The word that has become a shorthand way of describing this sort of active theological work is 'praxis'. Sometimes it is misunderstood to mean simply 'practice', but this specialist word means a great deal more than that. It stands for that reflection which, of necessity, involves action, and for that sort of action that demands reflection. 'Praxis' is the intertwining of action and reflection, of commitment and spirituality, reminding us that any action without reflection may well be irresponsible, but reflection without action is sterile. As St James put it in his epistle, 'Faith without good deeds is useless . . . faith and deeds working together' (James 2.20, 22) – that's 'praxis'.

Let's do theology!

Freda is an ordinary Christian woman faced with a problem. She is sitting in the office at the back of the shop where she works. She has just learnt from the boss of the chain of stores that employs her that she must make one of her staff redundant if the shop is not to close. She has good relationships with her staff and knows their personal stories – but she's been told that one of them has to go. First of all, she decides that the best thing to do is to read up on the law relating to employment, redundancy and so on, and then to check the facts of the case carefully with her boss and her colleagues. Being a committed Christian, she might soon start praying about the situation, but this will not be the only thing that she can call upon to help her to work out the answer to her problem. She may also find, for example, that she is helped by reflection with local Christians, perhaps at a Bible study group if there is one. Or maybe, as she worships the next Sunday morning, she finds herself singing a hymn that somehow puts her choices into better perspective. A talk with her vicar may prove helpful, or maybe she takes a Christian magazine and happens to read an article about the choices that Christians have to make in today's world. All this activity may help her in all sorts of ways to come to a decision about how she is going to cope with her work situation. She then talks with her colleagues at the store and they devise a strategy and implement it together.

The question before us now is, 'Has Freda been doing theology during this process?' Much of what she has been doing – studying employment law, praying, worshipping and making decisions, for example – might not fit neatly into an old-fashioned definition of theology as 'reasoned discourse about God'; but my own inclination is to say that she has indeed been involved in the theological endeavour – perhaps unknowingly – because she has been reflect-ing in her mind and her heart upon the nature of God and upon what God would have her do in her situation, and then she has attempted to respond faithfully. She has been engaging in a praxis style of theology – action and reflection working together. She has not simply relied on common sense or pragmatism, but has attempted to work carefully through the question of how God wants us to operate in the world. She has opened herself up to the prompting of God through worship and her relationships with the Christian community, and the outcome of all this has had profound influence upon her behaviour at work. She has not been content only to be pious about it, but she has carefully questioned and critically judged the situation and thought about God's values in relation to it. Let us take a moment to check through precisely what she has been doing so that we can learn from each of her actions.

One of the things that Freda did was to pray. I suspect that it was the sort of prayer with which every human being is familiar – the prayer of anguish when we feel overtaken by experience and cry out, 'Dear God, what on earth can I do?' It is an immediate attempt to put ourselves before God and have our minds and wills inspired by God's nature and presence. This mode of prayer has an attitude of adoration about it – we feel out of our depth, but know that God is over all and above all. I suspect that whenever I am overwhelmed by God's power and beauty in this way, something is going on in my mind and heart which will affect what I think and feel about God and will influence how I make my life respond in future. And is not this to do theology?[3] The Eastern Church has always held that the theologian is primarily a person of prayer, and

I will certainly be maintaining in this book that prayer and spirituality lie at the very heart of all honest theology.

The Bible study group which Freda attended would surely be an ideal place to do theology. Bible study is about God because it is God's 'word' that is studied, and the group engages in careful thinking about that word; so, according to most definitions, it must surely be theology. Of course, not all Bible study groups remain all that well focused. I once attended a parish Bible study group on the parable of the sower where the group allowed the rural setting of the parable to lead them into a long debate about lawnmower problems! To be 'theological' we would certainly hope for more self-discipline than that. On the other hand, does the intellectual rigour of the participants have to be of a particular standard? Does it have to be 'clever' in order for it to be deemed 'theology'? I suspect not.

Freda attended worship the next Sunday. Does this count as theology? Immersing ourselves in the experience of the worshipping community is to put ourselves in touch with the worship of God through the ages, and seek to be in communion with God's Church on earth and in heaven. It is also to drink in the gracious Spirit of God and to offer ourselves to God with all our heart, soul, mind and strength. Is theology being done within such an experience of worship? When an insight in a sermon stirs us and makes us rethink or take our thoughts about God to a deeper level, then is that not a theological experience? When we find ourselves making connections between the Gospel stories and our own experience, is that not pushing at the very threshold of the theological endeavour? And what are we doing when we state the Creed together, if not giving assent to formulae about the faith that were worked out by theologians centuries ago as they grappled with the issues that faced them? Are we participating in their theological work as we stand and recite their words? And what is happening when we feel ourselves seized by the power of the sacraments? Their symbolism can speak to the very depths of our being, in potent dialogue with our souls. Can that be part of what it is to be a theologian – allowing that dialogue to seize us and take us to another spiritual plane of awareness?

Freda then went to have a word with the vicar. What was happening in that conversation? Is not one of the minister's tasks to help her to put her own problem alongside the wisdom gained by the Church over the centuries? The vicar will have studied the gathered wisdom and experience of Christians who have gone before, as well as Christians of different cultures. In that conversation with her minister, Freda will thus be helped to check out where her experience resonates with the gathered Christian wisdom and experience. Reading a Christian journal is another means of entering into dialogue with that wider Church community, this time through the written word rather than the spoken witness of her local minister.

Another thing that her minister may offer her is the all-important questioning critique which helps to translate her experiences of the faith into the hard stuff of theology. For while much of our Christian religious experience in prayer, worship and so on allows for wide and liberal use of symbolism, poetic language and licence, she will also be in need of some hard-headed and precise Christian critique if her decisions about work are to be made upon firm ground. Doing theology should bring together the best of heart and head.

Freda's theological activity did not end when she had done all her thinking at church. She then had to remind herself of the intricate details of the problem at work and, no doubt, as well as reading up on employment law, she talked through all the practical implications with her work colleagues. Checking the hard facts of the case was part of her theological work, which did not finish when she stopped using the word 'God' or thinking about 'religious' matters. We might even suggest that she was still doing theology as she spoke with her workmates; for she was seeking to make faithful Christian decisions and act responsibly. It could have been that the decision at the store was that they would all band together and refuse to make a colleague redundant, but instead try to negotiate with the bosses for an alternative policy to be implemented. In that event she would have needed all her Christian wits about her, and care would have to be taken that she received strong support from her church congregation; being in constant touch in that way, she would have been more sure that her thinking and acting remained in conformity with God's will. If she managed to accomplish this complex task of keeping her actions properly integrated with Christian understandings and the Christian community, we could then judge that even her resultant actions were in some sense 'theological'.

We must take care, however, not to define theology so broadly that it loses all meaning. There is a strong temptation to do this because theology is better understood by doing it than by trying to define it very precisely. Theology is not so much a thing to be described as a way of life to be experienced. I am therefore going to spend most of this book describing how it can actually be done in an exciting and creative way. My expectation is that the true meaning of this tantalizing word 'theology' will thereby become clearer and more precise for the reader as we journey together through these pages.

Before I describe how theology may actually be 'done', let me share a little of my own context so that you may discern something of the provenance of the style of 'doing theology' that I will be offering.

Living through exciting times

1. Salvation and the Kingdom of God

I was born at the end of the Second World War in a poor neighbourhood in London's East End, the son of a bus-driver and a factory worker. Proud of my working-class heritage, I was schooled in the family's socialist beliefs before becoming a Christian. I was particularly enamoured of that prayer of Jesus that God's will should 'be done on earth as it is in heaven'. By 1968, however, I found myself living as a young man in New York City where the Civil Rights Movement was clamouring for the freedom of Black Americans. Women too were just beginning to reconsider their identity in society and some were asking what this new awareness of themselves might say about the nature of God. They were showing me that personal experience and identity were bound up tight with how society impacts upon us, and that God is intimately concerned about all that. All these insights into society resonated with the experience that I was bringing from the UK and I began to learn from my new colleagues that God's gift of freedom is not only for individuals, but that it works also and emphatically at a structural and societal level – at a Kingdom level. The African proverb, 'A person is a person because of other people', reminds us that to be fully human, one has to be in relationship to society. We are so much partakers one of another that my freedom and salvation cannot truly be complete unless my brothers and sisters are also free. St Paul himself acknowledges, 'who is weakened and I am not weakened, and when anyone is made to fall, I burn in agony myself' (2 Corinthians 11.29).

The implication of all this for me was that theology must focus upon the issues of human freedom and fulfilment at the personal, communal and structural levels so that people can become the active subjects of their situations and not just pawns in the game of life; for while structures have the potential to liberate human beings and enable them to live in fellowship, these same structures also have the capacity to hold whole groups captive (cf. Colossians 2.15). God's promise of this liberating freedom for individuals and for society must impart a strong, joyous element into our theological adventure. There will be lots to celebrate when we do theology well.

2. Theology includes action

When I left school in 1963, I had the good fortune to be offered a post in a Birmingham mental hospital as an assistant to Dr John Locking, who was then researching ways to assist those who had very severe learning difficulties. He was working with the theories of Jean Piaget, a Swiss philosopher of epistemology,[4] translating those theories into practical learning systems for our own adult patients. Dr Locking would undertake an experiment and then we would reflect on that experience in order to set up the next experiment until we arrived eventually at something which seemed to work well. It was action and reflection, doing and thinking – the two continuously interweaving in the pursuit of excellence. Today, this 'action–reflection' model – what we earlier called 'praxis' – has been taken up by all the major professions, but it is still not the default mode among professional clergy, nor in the Church at large. Social workers, medics, lawyers, teachers, all have their mentors and groups where they are helped to reflect on their experience in order to better their work practice. Likewise, good practice in theology should utilize this action–reflection mode of human learning.[5]

Jesus was clear that belief was important, but in the last analysis he told us to judge by a person's actions – 'By their fruits you shall know them' (Matthew 7.16, 20). Theory is fascinating, but the danger is that it tempts us to forget the real world from which it springs. However, theory is useful when it helps us stand back from a situation and view it more objectively, allowing it to instruct our action so that it is informed by our Christian faith. If action is part of theology in this way, then we are enabled to judge theology not only by its erudition, but also by the way in which it generates faithful lives.[6] If we are to create a really good theological process, it must therefore clearly have a place for both theory and practice – we will be 'doing theology', not just 'theological reflection'.

3. The question of power

After some time in the United States, I returned once again to work in Birmingham and met Bob Lambourne, the University's first lecturer in Pastoral Studies. He introduced me to the work of Anton Boisen who, in the 1920s, had been a patient in a mental hospital. Boisen found that his doctors believed that his own insights about his illness were of no account. As a 'patient' he was expected to be passive, but he passionately believed that he had a part to play in the power dynamics of the therapeutic relationship, and so spent the rest of his life devising methods to enable power to be shared between professionals and their clients.[7]

While Boisen was working at the question of power at the more interpersonal level, in the 1970s an advertising agent working for American Express invented the word 'globalization' and the world was suddenly more aware that new power dynamics were at work around the globe. We knew already that missionaries around the world had sometimes imposed their home culture upon native cultures, never stopping to think what power-games were being played. Now, however, scholars such as Benjamin Barber were explaining that when one culture seeks to dominate another in this way, we can eventually expect a significant backlash from the recipients. The title of his paper, *Jihad vs. McWorld*, summed up his theory very well.[8] In today's world, the great powers – be they nations or corporations – seek to impose their cultures and ideologies around the globe, threatening the peace of the world and the sustainability of the planet. They seek, in Barber's terms, to create their own 'McWorld'. But as they squash local cultures and identities in this way, so there builds a justifiable backlash on the part of local people who resent the power of the dominating incomer. So it is that at interpersonal and intercultural levels, the same question surfaces – 'How should we deal with power?'

God is the all-powerful one, and yet, unlike us, uses that power only in the cause of love. I have, therefore, come to believe with all my heart that to wrestle with the question of power is to wrestle with the character of God.[9] Power is a spiritual question in that it relates so intimately with questions of love and hate, good and evil. Yet Jesus confounds all our human understanding of power, by suggesting in the Beatitudes (Matthew 5.3–12) that it is the powerless who are especially blessed of God.

Therefore, this mysterious, spiritual question of power, its nature and its exercise, must always remain a prime concern of theology, since to wrestle with the question of power is to wrestle with the Divine. We must forever be asking who it is that has the power in each situation and who will most benefit from what is going on there. Even in the actual *doing* of theology we must be alert to questions of power – it must itself be a shared community affair, open to all and not in the hands of any elite group, academic or clerical. Theology must become public domain material, and all the more powerfully vulnerable for that.

4. All theology has context

Mones Farah is a Palestinian Christian and a good friend. He invited me to stay awhile with his family in Nazareth, and his father Anton, a highly respected Palestinian teacher, walked with me around the ruins of Sepphoris, admiring a city which had been just an hour's walk from Jesus' home. As Anton showed me the streets, market place and palaces of Sepphoris, the world in which Jesus lived came alive with astonishing clarity. In recent years so much has been learnt from archaeology and historical research about the context in which Jesus lived and moved, and this has enabled us to understand so much more about his life and teaching.[10] Just as Jesus' incarnation had been quite specifically in one geographical and historical context, study of that context helps us understand more of his revelation to us. So we are reminded that every theologian thereafter has been rooted and grounded in a particular place, time and culture, and to understand that culture will likewise help us understand that person's theology.

I have had the privilege of living through a period of unprecedented discovery in cultural studies. I had only just been ordained when Clifford Geertz published, in 1973, his seminal work, *The Interpretation of Cultures*[11] which heralded a new respect for others and offered tools to understand our cultural differences. This realization of the importance of context[12] not only alerted us to the dangers of cultural imperialism in mission, but it also liberated some Christians to begin to speak about God from within their own experience and context, and that freedom spawned the exciting new developments of Black theology,[13] feminist, liberation and urban theology,[14] and similar movements, and, in so doing, the face of theology has been changed.

Christ, at his incarnation, puts himself right inside the cultural context, alongside the people's experience. We must therefore be sure to devise an incarnational theological method that allows for the careful critical reading of each context so that our theology can derive not from abstract assumptions, but is instead substantial, pertinent theology that speaks from, and is relevant to, real people in their specific culture, place and time.

5. God's concern for the marginalized

Being with the Church in Latin America and Asia has had a profound effect on me. No Western person can imagine the reality of the slums of Rio de Janeiro or Madras/Chennai. But to see the people of God in those degrading places, loving and caring, is profoundly humbling. In the Hebrew Bible (2 Kings 7.3–20), the story is told of four lepers who are locked out of the besieged city and who decide to try their luck in the camp of the invading army – for they have nothing to lose. It is they who bring back to the city the joyous news that the enemy have fled. The shunned lepers turn out to be the bearers of the Good News.

For many years, as a parish priest in deprived areas of the UK, I experienced first-hand how the deprived and marginalized would be the ones who could open up truth to me in a way that the more secure and self-sufficient were simply unable to do. It seems that it is only from the perspective of the most downtrodden and 'heavy laden'[15] in any society, that a society may properly be judged. This is because the poor, being unprotected from the harsh realities of a society, can see those realities only too clearly, while others, who are protected from life's harshness, simply cannot see what the poor can see. Jesus chose to ally himself with those who were most oppressed and who saw society from the underside. In the parable of the sheep and the goats he speaks directly of himself as being found in those who are hungry, thirsty, strangers, naked, sick and imprisoned (Matthew 25.45).

In framing our best method for doing theology, we must therefore hold fast to God's prior commitment to the downtrodden.[16] But there's a big danger here too, for as Kwok Pui-lan[17] warns, so often well-meaning church people become fascinated by the suffering of the poor, and it is noticeable that Western theologians in particular 'use' that suffering in their thinking and writing, but do not actually work alongside the poor so as to change the power relationships which cause the suffering. Our theological method must bring us into solidarity (*koinonia*) with the poor, not simply make their grinding poverty our focus of interest.

6. Courageous spirituality

André and Almir both spoke in Portuguese. Through an interpreter, Bishop André of Angola shared with me a deep concern. 'I know from the writing of St Paul that we should rejoice and give thanks for everything that happens to us in our ministry. So I'm struggling to find a way to thank God that next year there will be no money to pay a salary for me to work and care for my children.' Almir, a missionary bishop from Brazil, prayed movingly for him, himself due to return to his very dangerous ministry in the deep forests of the Amazon. Courageous spirituality is difficult to define, but when you are in its presence you certainly know it.

Let us remember that the best theology is not so much talk *about* God, as attaining the habit of knowing we're always in God's presence. To make ourselves 'present to the presence of God' was the whole concern of theology during the earliest times, for you can read theology without praying, but you cannot be a theologian yourself without the habit of prayer and devotion. Evagrius of Pontus in the sixth century even defined a theologian as 'one whose prayers are true'. To become a theologian will therefore require that we discern that 'mind of Christ', as St Paul calls it (1 Corinthians 2.16, cf. Philippians 2.5), which will allow us to throw away the garbage of status, listen attentively to the depths of others' experience and have the tenacity to act bravely when action is called for. There are tremendous forces ranged against justice and peace, and to combat them together we will need the empowerment of the Holy Spirit (Ephesians 6.10–20) – and a courageous spirituality.

We will rely too on the Holy Spirit being with us if we are to make those imaginative links between faith and life which are at the core of doing theology. For example, at Holy Communion, as we look at the bread on the altar, the Holy Spirit allows us to see in that simple thing the very presence of Jesus, and with our eyes thus trained we can then go out into the world ready to see God in everything. Without this Spirit-filled attentiveness, we cannot do theology, and so we must develop a method of doing theology which opens us up constantly to the very presence of that Spirit.

In this first chapter we have considered why we are ambitious for theology to become a tool for the transformation of our own lives and the society we seek to serve. I hope I have given you a picture of some of the experiences that have influenced me as I have developed a model of 'doing theology' that may help us attain our goal. Let us now move on to describe that model and see how it works.

Notes

1 It was in 1989 that I heard the highly respected and very learned British politician, Dennis Healey, say precisely this in a BBC Radio interview.
2 Freire, P. (1972), *Pedagogy of the Oppressed.* Harmondsworth: Penguin, p. 46.
3 On the experience of God in overwhelming situations, see especially Ford, David (1977), *The Shape of Living.* London: Fount.
4 See for example, Piaget, J. (1953), *The Origins of Intelligence in Children.* London: Routledge & Kegan Paul. Epistemology is the study of how we know things.
5 See Foskett, J. and Lyall, D. (1988), *Helping the Helpers: Supervision and Pastoral Care.* London: SPCK. Also see, Hawkins, P. and Shohet, R. (2002), *Supervision in the Helping Professions: An Individual, Group and Organizational Approach.* Buckingham, UK, Philadelphia, USA: Open University Press.
6 We can also see action and reflection working together when we observe how much doctrine and theology is derived from the experience of worship. We find many examples in the Bible of theology being generated from liturgy, for example, in the letter to the Hebrews and the book of Revelation. In the Hebrew Scriptures the great festivals likewise gave rise to theologies of Passover, Exodus, and so on.
7 Aden, L. (1990), *Turning Points in Pastoral Care: The Legacy of Anton Boisen and Seward Hiltner.* Grand Rapids: Baker Books.
8 Barber, B. (1992), 'Jihad vs. McWorld'. *The Atlantic Monthly* and reproduced in (1996), *Jihad vs. McWorld: How Globalism and Tribalism are Reshaping the World.* New York: Ballantine Books.

9 Cf. Genesis 32.23–32. When Jacob wrestles with God at Jabbok he is wrestling with questions of power, authority and blessing.

10 See, for example, Crossan, J. D. and Reed, J. L. (2001), *Excavating Jesus, Beneath the Stones, Behind the Texts*. London: SPCK. Also see Sawicki, M. (2000), *Crossing Galilee: Architectures of Contact in the Occupied Land of Jesus*. Harrisburg, Penn: Trinity Press; and see Herzog, W. R. II (2000), *Jesus, Justice and the Reign of God: A Ministry of Liberation*. Louisville, Kentucky: John Knox Press.

11 Geertz, C. (1973), *The Interpretation of Cultures: Selected Essays*. New York: Basic Books.

12 On the matter of all theologies being contextual, see Schreiter, R. (1985), *Constructing Local Theologies*. London: SCM Press, pp. 93ff. See also the further arguments of later chapters of this book.

13 See for example, Beckford, R. (1998), *Jesus is Dread: Black Theology and Black Culture in Britain*. London: DLT; and Reddie, A. G. (2008), *Working Against the Grain: Black Theology in the 21st Century*. London: Equinox.

14 See http://www.urblog.typepad.com.

15 Words taken from Matthew 11.28, 'Come unto me all that travail and are heavy laden, and I will refresh you'.

16 On God's prior commitment to the downtrodden, see Bishop David Sheppard (1983), *Bias to the Poor*. London: Hodder & Stoughton. A more systematic survey of reasons for taking this stance is to be found in Leonardo and Clodovis Boff (1987), *Introducing Liberation Theology*. Tunbridge Wells: Burns & Oates, pp. 44–6.

17 Kwok, P-l. (2005), *Postcolonial Imagination and Feminist Theology*. London: SCM, p. 74, quoted by Graham, E. (2007), 'Power, Knowledge and Authority in Public Theology', *International Journal of Public Theology*, 1.1, p. 57.

2

A New Way to Do Theology

Developing a method

Since my early days working at the mental hospital alongside Dr John Locking, I have retained my fascination for how adults learn. So it was in 1978 that I began to meet with a small group of parishioners in my working-class parish in Birmingham, to see if we could learn to do theology together in a way that we could all enjoy and benefit from. Some years later I published the story of what we did in a book, *Power to the Powerless*.[1] What best suited that particular group was a dynamic mixture of action and reflection – the 'praxis' model which I described earlier – and so, as we were reading the parables of Jesus together, we decided that we needed to act on what we were reading. Before we embarked on a project, we undertook a rigorous exploration of our community, its issues and its joys, which we then put under the microscope of the Christian faith. After months of reflection, we saw what seemed to us a way forward and put our resultant project into action. But it did not stop there, for we continued to learn from our project by scrutinizing that too, in the light of the Christian faith, before moving on to new actions based on that new theological learning. We called it our 'Parables in Action' group.

Some time later I came across a book by Daniel Kolb which had been published in 1984 called *Experiential Learning*.[2] Kolb was an educational psychologist who had studied the philosophical work of John Dewey[3] and the writings of the Swiss philosopher, Jean Piaget – whom we mentioned earlier. Kolb produced a diagram that was intended to describe a method of learning which paid due attention to the experiences that adult students brought to the classroom. The diagram attempted to display how elements from experience could be brought together with elements of theory. I remember how I began to play with the idea of substituting into that diagram new words and phrases which could convert it from a conservative learning model into a theological method for personal and social transformation. It was a diagrammatic picture of what we had been experiencing in our Parables in Action group. After much trial and error with a number of back-street theological groups with whom I was then working, I ended up with a spiral diagram which also owed much to my previous reading of Paulo Freire and Juan Luis Segundo, two fascinating thinkers from South America.[4]

Most of the descriptions of theology that I had met before had made the whole theological process sound more like a method of control, rather than an open system of discovery and transformation; however, the more I developed my spiral diagram, the greater my conviction grew that here was a style and approach that would serve people who were more concerned to be open to the Spirit's operation in the world, than merely learning theological constructs from the past. It was not until some time later that I realized that what I had been doing was trying to reinvent the wheel! For it was on meeting a number of Roman Catholic friends, who had recently returned from Latin America, that I learnt that there already existed a circular model of doing theology, which they referred to as the 'Pastoral Cycle', and the similarities between that and my home-grown spiral were remarkable.

Some people believe that the Pastoral Cycle was first invented by the Liberation theologians of Latin America, but this is not entirely true. They had developed a model which had in fact originally been created by their Roman Catholic cousins in Europe. Father Joseph Cardijn, a Belgian priest who had been the inspiration of many Catholic workers and students between the two World Wars, had found ways for Christians to make a careful theological analysis of their situation by asking them to 'See, Judge and Act' upon their experiences. So it was that Juan Luis Segundo published *The Liberation of Theology* in 1977,[5] in which he refined the European model considerably. In 1983, the focus moved to the United States where Joe Holland and Peter Henriot inspired a movement for Social Analysis there by publishing, in 1983, *Social Analysis: Linking Faith and Justice*,[6] while in Europe, such organizations as the Ecumenical Institute for the Development of Peoples (INODEP) sponsored similar routes into theology.[7] I was intrigued to find so many parallels between all this work and what we had spontaneously been developing here in the UK. I was therefore even more convinced that we were mutually on the right track.

Although my spiral diagram conforms largely to the Latin American Pastoral Cycle, the way of working which will be described in this book is very much home-grown, and has been developed from many hours' experience of using the model with a variety of Christian groups in Britain, and latterly on my travels around the world.

The Doing Theology Spiral

Let me now present, in diagrammatic form, how I think we should go about the business of doing theology. As I have suggested, I have found it most helpful to think of the process as a circle, cycle, or even better, a spiral, which moves around continually from action to reflection and from reflection to action; it is this constant interplay between the two that I have earlier called 'praxis'. To earth my description it may be useful to make reference to an example so that we can see how the spiral works in practice. Freda, whom we mentioned in Chapter 1, presents an ideal example, because her situation of having to make a decision at work about a staff redundancy is a typical starting point for doing theology. Thus the spiral starts with experience.

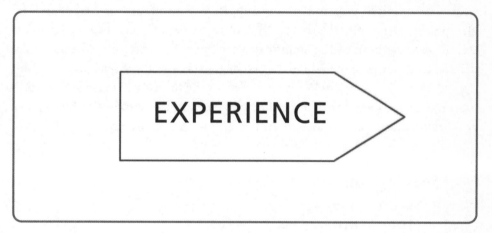

Figure 2.1

The encounter with experience is fundamental to any earthed theology, so we begin by trying to become as conscious as we possibly can of the real situation that surrounds us. We will not be wanting at this stage to engage in a thorough analysis of that situation, but instead simply make sure that we really are conscious of the feelings, emotions and impressions that the experience engenders in us. It is therefore best to choose an experience which really does concern us. It may be a very active experience, like running a rowdy youth club evening, or it may be more passive – more a predicament than an activity. It may be best if it is a situation demanding a response, like that of Freda hearing that an employee has to go, for it seems true that the best raw material to work with is a situation which has an element of worry or anguish about it. 'How are we going to cope with this?' or 'What on earth can we do about that?' This may have something to do with God's special concern for those who are marginalized or otherwise in trouble; but, in any case, it is a fact that good theology is more likely to derive from a problem than a statement – just as the New Testament epistles were more likely to be written from a prison than a palace.

At this stage of the Doing Theology Spiral, we simply share with one another how the experience feels, and hear from others in the theological group how they are feeling and what sort of experience it is for them. Of course, no one comes to the experience as if from nowhere and so, at this early stage, opportunity is also made to explore some of our prior feelings and prejudices, for good or ill, about the issue in question. As Christians, we will also want to express something of our inner understanding of what meanings and values lie behind our immediate perceptions of the situation and, as Freda found, this can often be done by joining in prayer and worship, as well as through discussion or non-verbal exercises in a group. In any event, at this first stage, the group needs to identify clearly just what the experience is, and begin to develop a feel for something of the significance of the experience. Already they may discern what some of the issues are that are at stake, and the questions that are begged by the experience. When the anecdotal work of the Experience phase is complete, they can move quite naturally around the spiral into the Exploration phase, where they more carefully explore the experiences.

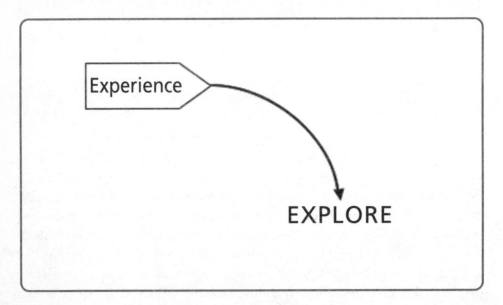

Figure 2.2

Exploration is key, and yet it is a stage often skipped by those who are too hasty. Having first, in the Experience phase of the cycle, shared how they feel about the situation they have chosen to address, in this phase, group members now seek to bring more precision to their understandings. They do this by immersing themselves in a thorough analysis of the situation to go alongside their preliminary anecdotal evidence. Here, the group gathers factual information to put alongside their stories and allows their early feelings to open up new lines of factual enquiry. If Freda had heard only the first couple of words that her boss had spoken to her and had addressed her anxious feelings, but had not taken time to read up on employment law, she would never have registered the wider implications of her predicament. So, like her, we too have to use all the means at our disposal to get right under the skin of the situation about which we are endeavouring to do theology. It makes very good sense to use people from the fields of sociology, psychology and the humanities, who are often surprisingly keen to help. They mustn't be allowed to let their own agendas dominate the group's life however, for it's the local group that must always be in control.

This is a phase of the circle which groups usually love. It brings them together and is so illuminating. They itemize, analyse, search back through the history, and gain perspectives from all sorts of other sources, always remembering to ask the 'power' questions of the situation – 'Who decided it should happen?', or 'Who benefited most from that?' They may even be able to put the experience into a national or global perspective if they ask the right questions. It will be important to see what values are or are not operating, and in what direction the whole issue seems to be heading. The group will find that, if they can excel at this Exploration stage, then the more their later theological reflection and activity will go to the jugular of the experience.

Having 'Explored' the 'Experience', the next stage is to 'Reflect' about it all (see Figure 2.3, page 22).

At this stage in the cycle the group works concertedly to see how the Christian faith directly relates to the experience at issue. They check all that they now understand about the situation, including the major issues that are standing out, to see how the treasures of the Christian faith might relate to what they've found. Bible study, prayer, worship, hymns and songs, the creeds and councils of the Church, the theologies of times past, the present social teaching of the Church,[8] the great themes of the faith like salvation, creation, sin, thanksgiving, and so on: all these and much more will be at the group's disposal as it engages in theological 'Reflection' upon the Experience and Exploration phases of their work. Just as Freda went to her church to worship

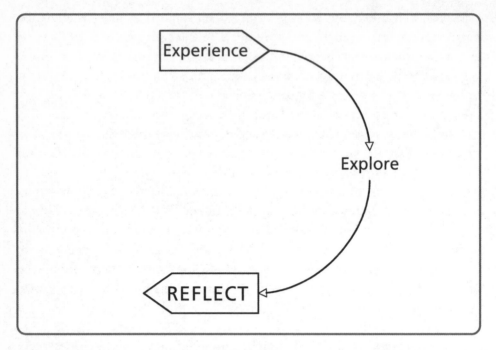

Figure 2.3

and to her Christian house group meeting, and talked it through with the vicar and read some literature about the subject, so the group will need to reflect carefully upon its experience in all manner of ways. Freda may well have considered some of the Old Testament prophets' injunctions about the nature of justice in society, or been helped by hearing a prayer about human responsibility and God's grace. The stories of Creation and the Garden of Eden in the book of Genesis may have thrown light on the difficult balance that must be struck between being productive and being responsible stewards in God's world. Jesus' discipleship group may well have modelled to her something of the sort of solidarity that she and her colleagues were striving to emulate at work. Just as Freda did, so the theological group will try to bring into the light those treasures from the Christian heritage which seem to resonate with the experience that they are currently exploring. This is the Reflection phase of the Spiral.

Many people will not, of course, have all this 'religious' information at their fingertips and this is one of the reasons why theology is best done in a group. The group helps in a whole variety of ways and not least because – although at first sight it may not appear to be the case – the theological depth of most Christians is quite astounding, and the group is there to help each member find their voice. This is not to say that a group is an absolute necessity when doing theology, for sometimes a theologian has to work alone, whether they wish to or not. But a group is a great boon as we shall see, and it is always good practice for the individual theologian to also be in a group if possible in order to gain from it all the advantages that we will later enumerate.

After the Reflection phase comes the moment to 'Respond'.

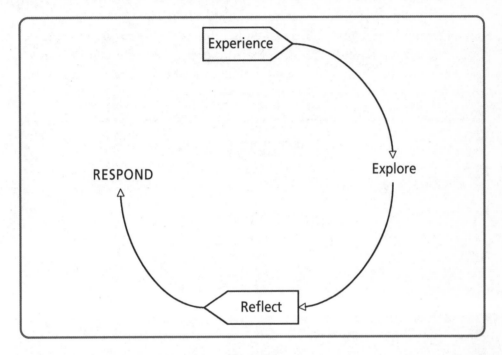

Figure 2.4

We can sit and reflect till the cows come home. If that's all theology is ever going to do for us, then we would be right to ignore it, for, as St James writes, 'do what the word tells you and don't just listen to it' (James 1.22). To this end, the group asks itself, at this point around the circle, 'in the light of all the Experience, Exploration and Reflection about this issue, how does God want us to Respond?' This is where faith and action really do go hand-in-hand as theology becomes concrete again, and cashes out in experience. The group sets about experimenting with a range of different responses to see which one works best in practice, given the new insights derived from all their theological reflection. Freda, you will remember, had many options. She could choose to sack one of her staff, or reflection may have prompted her to try to engage in new negotiations with her employer. Like Freda, a group's responses can take a whole variety of forms, from tough action to silent presence, or indeed it may even be that a group will determine to continue doing what they had been doing in the first place, but this time with much more insight and understanding. Whatever the choice of action, it will be a response based in the faith, and therefore worthy of being called a 'spiritual' activity, because however practical and down to earth, it will derive from a hunger to see God's will done. Indeed, all around the circle, the activity will have been under-girded by that same spiritual quality – an openness to the presence of the Holy Spirit throughout.

Once round the Doing Theology circle, things are never the same again. Even if the group have decided that their Response will be to continue much as before, now they will be doing so with new insight and understanding, and so, in fact, they will have arrived at a new situation.

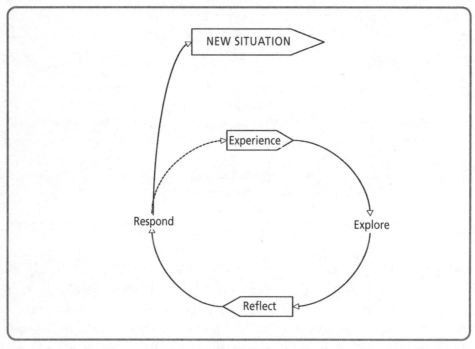

Figure 2.5

This New Situation is itself worthy of exploration and reflection, just as the first situation prompted them around the circle the first time. Like a wheel on a bicycle, the circle itself can continue around time and again, but by doing that it propels the bicycle to a brand new place at every turn. So the theology group makes its journey, and as the wheel continues to turn, new insights move them to new actions and ever greater fulfilment. In view of this, it seems best to no longer refer to the process as a circle or cycle, but rather as the Doing Theology Spiral.

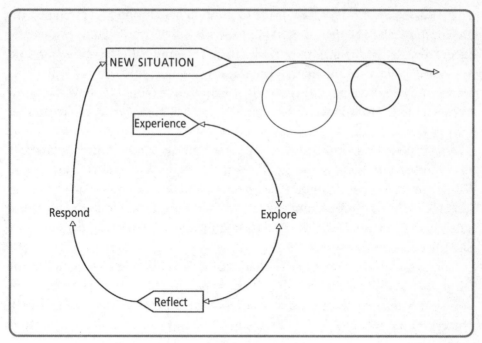

Figure 2.6

Some health warnings

Any diagram will have its limitations, and I am all too aware that this diagram shares that problem. In reality, the process it seeks to express is far more free-flowing and natural and much less prescriptive than a line drawing can express. Also, the diagram does not take account of many detailed matters – but to make the diagram more complicated by adding more details would simply exacerbate the problem. For example, an obvious thing which is not included in the diagram is celebration. Some have thought to add a fifth 'celebration' phase to the cycle, but that would simply not be true to experience. Groups find that they are celebrating at all points around the process, not just at the end of the cycle – indeed, parties seem to be a constant feature of all the groups I've belonged to. In a similar manner, the important matter of evaluation is not specified on the diagram, for again, it is integral to each phase of the process.

We must also be aware that the distinctions between each phase of the cycle are certainly not always as clear in practice as the diagram might imply. For example, the diagram makes the distinction between Exploration and Reflection much sharper than it is in reality. However, if we had not separated them out clearly in the diagram, it would be all too easy to forget the importance of analytical exploration. We are prone to jump to conclusions, leapfrogging the Exploration phase, much preferring to work only with preconceptions and ideologies that we bring with us rather than engaging with the observable and 'awkward' realities of the matter. Having stressed how important it is to experience and explore, I nevertheless find it helpful sometimes to draw the arrow between the Exploration and Reflection phases as a two-way link to remind us that as long as we do both, the order is not cast in stone. The diagram is drawn as a logical circle, as if during one phase the group is not allowed to venture into another, but this is simply not the way of imaginative groups. The diagram is there to make sure we undertake each task and don't do too much leapfrogging about, but the group must live its life naturally, trying to keep to task but not getting too worried if imagination and unexpected creativity lead in a slightly different direction.

This brings us to another factor that cannot adequately be represented in the diagram, but which will certainly become apparent in the subsequent chapters. It is simply that experience can play a very significant role in *all* the phases of the cycle and not only in the first phase. The work in each and every phase must constantly refer to the lived experience. Also, the work that is done through every phase of the spiral can be 'experiential' when that is appropriate because, by using the insights of adult education and learning theory, there is no need to limit ourselves to a distanced or theoretical style of operation at any time, as I hope to make clear as the book proceeds.

It is also important here to clarify further my use of the terms 'doing theology' and 'theological reflection'. I like to reserve the term 'theological reflection' for that aspect of theological activity which is centred upon the Reflection phase of the cycle, where the explored experiences are brought into engagement with the great traditions of the faith. I save the phrase 'doing theology' for the whole process. You'll find that many commentators call the whole process 'theological reflection', but my reason for keeping them separate is for clarity's sake and also, as we'll see, the disharmony between activists and academic theologians may have been worsened by a confusion of terms and definition.

Finally, you may have noticed that the Parables in Action group that I mentioned earlier actually started their work not in the 'Experience' phase of the cycle but with a Bible Study – the 'Reflection' phase. Yes, it's possible to bite into the spiral almost anywhere – it's as flexible as that – but it is essential that we allow the diagram to remind us that there are phases which work pretty well in logical order and certainly must not be missed out altogether, lest we ride slip-shod into action which is not theologically sound.

Our aim is to become so acquainted with the spiral progression that it becomes second nature to us and we find ourselves following the cycle quite happily, without having to make constant reference to a complicated blueprint. The cycle moves along into new discoveries and new places at each turn of the theological wheel, and in this way it reminds us that theology is a vehicle on a Christian journey, which never allows us to remain in one secure place for long. The Doing Theology Spiral is just one more supportive tool for following Jesus *in the Way*.

I hope the diagram is helpful, but let us now get away from diagrams for a while, as I offer a few examples of how this style of doing theology actually operates. The first example comes from South Africa.[9]

An African example

A small group of young South Africans, black and white, decided to do some theological work together, and decided upon 'the Church' as the focus of their interest. They had no formal theological education, so where were they to start? We could imagine them starting from the models of the Church to be found in the writings of St Paul or the Early Fathers. They could have read expert expositions in scholarly books on the subject. But instead they chose simply to describe to one another their own concrete experiences of the Church. They described the Sunday services that they had attended, sermons they had heard, doctrines they had been taught, Christians they had met, the church buildings and different denominations they had come across. Everyone of course had plenty of raw material to offer because it was concrete, here and now experience, and far from abstract. It soon became clear that their feelings about the Church were full of ambiguity, and in their group they were forthright in expressing some very negative feelings of anger and frustration about the Church they had experienced. They were very critical, and yet they also felt that the Church was of very great value and significance for them. From this experience they realized just how full of contradictions their Church was. So much for the 'Experience' phase of the spiral.

Next, they moved to the 'Exploration' phase, and set about enumerating, listing and analysing the grounds for the emotions they had expressed, to see if the contradictions they had sensed were fair and appropriate to the facts. They explored a whole range of contradictions: the Church's disunity despite its aspirations to be one and catholic; its fine words about justice and yet its lack of action in the matter; divisions within it between its professionals and its uneducated members. They lamented the fact that there were certain people of status who adopted autocratic attitudes in the Church despite Jesus' words of admonition, 'It shall not be so amongst you' (Mark 10.43). Even the grand church buildings came in for criticism when compared with the tiny shacks in which the people themselves had to live. So it was that in the Church, and in the preaching of the clergy, the whole group recognized that the facts of the matter vindicated their initial frustrations and angers. They had 'explored' the issue which they had 'experienced' and so were ready to move to the Reflection stage of theology.

Some of the group wanted to skip this reflective work and rush headlong into a response by setting up their own 'pure' Church which would have none of the contradictions they had exposed. Other group members suggested that before they acted out of impatience it would be well to sort out what their picture of an ideal Church might in fact be. The agreement was made to look to the Scriptures. They looked first in the Hebrew Scriptures and saw in the book of Exodus how God called the people of Israel to become the chosen people of God. Moses' initial hopes were high but, as the biblical history unfolded, they read that the nation had not lived up to that ideal at all. So the group moved its attention to the New Testament, and found there the picture of Jesus and his group of disciples – twelve, to replace the twelve tribes of Israel. It was this discipleship group who were to become the first Church. But even here the group could see the same contradictions and failings emerging. In the Gospel accounts, the twelve disciples seem always to be arguing and, eventually, Judas actually betrays his master. So it began to dawn upon the South African group that they had, perhaps, been looking in altogether the wrong place for a picture of the perfect society. They should not have been looking at the Church, 'the discipleship group', for perfection after all, but rather listening to the teaching which Jesus offered to that first group of disciples whenever disputes arose among them. Jesus had then spoken to them and preached about the Kingdom of God and pointed to that godly society as the ultimate aim of all their endeavours. So, from their reflection upon the New Testament, they could see that while the Kingdom offered perfection, the Church was made of human disciples in the here and now, doing their best as part of our struggling, failing, hoping history. It was this realization that sobered the group and made them more self-critical, and more aware of their own imperfections, as they compared their meagre responses with the perfection of the Kingdom of God vision which they heard in the teaching of Jesus. They too, they now perceived, were involved in the same contradictions that they had noticed so glaringly in others.

But the group's theological reflection did not confine itself to the Bible. The group decided that they would need to get to the root causes of the Church's problems if they were ever going to play a responsible part in overcoming its contradictions. They therefore felt it right to obtain some books about the history of the Church in South Africa in order to discover the historical causes and processes which under-girded the contradictions. However, they got nowhere. They found themselves struggling with the history books. They certainly sensed that there was something here worth following up, but they themselves could not fathom it. So they opted to invite along to the meeting a specialist in Church history – not to give a lecture, but to answer a set of very specific questions that they had worked out. 'When is the first time in history there was a contradiction in the Church?' 'How did they handle money when they set up the South African churches?' They asked questions about ideologies, economic systems and vested interests. They heard answers about influences in the Church from the time of the Roman emperors through to the establishment and maintenance of the South African Church itself. They were particularly interested in the relationship they could now see between the missionaries and the colonialists. And they interpreted the information they heard from the specialist in a way that made sense for them. They felt that ever since their Church had been brought to them from Europe and America it had found itself caught up in a 'top-down' model of decision-making. It had imbibed a deep-seated conviction that the white approach was good for Africans and that it was godly to see the world in terms of 'us' and 'them', since some people were born to be employers in charge and others were destined to be underlings. Through the years there had been repeated attempts to shake off this old colonialist infection, but the colonized had themselves internalized the ideology.

The outcome of this process of reflection was a new appreciation in the group that the contradictions within the Church were extremely dangerous. They could be destructive of persons if they were to continue to be ignored and hidden from the people's consciousness. These same contradictions could, however, become creative and productive of change if brought into the open and realistically faced up to by Church members. This consciousness, if faced squarely, could produce a very creative repentance and determination to reform the Church so that it could more resemble the Kingdom of God for which the group members so much yearned.

The historical facts they had unearthed about the Church were true in themselves, but they then began to realize that those facts were also symbolic of the wider community and its leadership. Their discoveries could, therefore, be used to help explain why problems exist today in the wider South African society. What was needed were people who would speak out plainly about the contradictions so the Church could become realistic about itself, be seen to be so, and emerge as a visible sign of hope and honesty for the whole wider society – a community of people on their way to God's promised Kingdom. This they decided was to be the thrust of their 'Response'.

They set about explaining all that they had discovered about the Church whenever and wherever they were given opportunity. They invited the clergy in and asked them to allow group members to preach about their findings in their own churches. They asked the clergy to work with them in their con-sciousness-raising activities. Many searched the Gospels to see how Jesus had chosen to proclaim his message, and this helped them find ways of sharing what they had discovered about the Kingdom and the Church's struggles to achieve it. Some of the group's teaching made the poor whom they visited feel more confident and hopeful, and this was reminiscent of the New Testament accounts of how some of Jesus' evangelism was received by those in especial need. At other times, the group's actions and teachings were rather resented, but this failure resonated with many passages in the Gospels too.

The group had started their work by acknowledging their own experiences of Church, they had worked their way round the theological spiral, only to find that as they carried out their responsive action they were confronted by new challenges and opportunities – perhaps even an emerging new identity for them-selves. The Doing Theology Spiral was propelling them into an exciting future.

This example highlights a number of points about how the cyclical method of doing theology may be facilitated. First, as I have already stressed, the group had a clear preference for starting from their own experience – their actual, concrete experience of the Church – and not from some abstracted concepts about what the Church might have been. They came with a whole range of preconceptions about the Church and, starting from experience, made sure that all these thoughts and feelings were laid bare.

Second, we notice that it was obviously a communal effort. A people's theology cannot be the result of an individual working alone. Obviously, there is more chance of a group being creative than an individual, given the old adage that two heads are better than one, but additionally, and perhaps more importantly, if risky responsive action is expected of group members, then two things are essential. First, they must have the support that comes from group solidarity, and second, each member must have had a hand in the reflection that has led to the responsive action – otherwise they might not be convinced enough to see the action through. Thus it was essential to work as a group. The Doing Theology Spiral can certainly be used by theologians working alone but the theological endeavour will never be quite as successful and generative of liberation if it is always done in isolation.

Notice too the South African group's preparedness to ask questions honestly and fearlessly. It may not have been thought polite to ask the Church institution about its financial relationship to slavers and merchants of the past, but in the end it was certainly more productive and theologically creative to ask straight questions. This questioning had to be thoroughly self-critical too, and it was good to see how they eventually came to the realization that they were themselves responsible members of the Church they had been criticizing. In addition, their critical questioning approach made sure that any pre-packaged answers and authoritarian posturing by teachers or leaders would soon be cut down to size. In this regard it is instructive to notice how this South African group seems to have gone instinctively to the question of power in their discussion with the Church historian. When I was studying political theology in New York some years ago, my professor, Nile Harper,[10] had the irritating habit of thumping his open palm onto the table and demanding, 'Power! Who's got the power? If you don't know that, you'll never make theologians!' I have since come to see just how right he was to push the point home.

That leads to a fourth major lesson to be learnt about theological method from our South African example, namely, how knowledge should be used by the group. Wherever the process of doing theology makes it necessary to find out more about history, sociology, economics, biblical interpretation, or whatever else, the experts may well need to be consulted and the information they are able to provide has to be drawn out from them. But the power must at all times remain within the theological group itself. Any amount of information can be drawn from people, books, the Web, or other resources, as long as that information truly throws some light on the questions that arise from the group experience itself. The use of information for any other purpose – to maintain privilege or to avoid the real issue – would be an abuse of the power of information and would detract from the integrity of the enterprise. We must be careful, then, how information is shared in the group, for it can be a powerful put-down or means of control.

The fifth and final point to draw from this South African example, is that it acknowledges the importance of the practical. While engaging reflectively, good theology nevertheless begins and ends with the practice of Christian faith. Our example begins by looking at what Church members do in practice and it works its way towards love in practice. Some Christians seem more intent on making sure that people think correctly about their faith than that they should live out their faith in practice, but the South African group seemed to me to get the balance just right.

A British urban example

I share now an example of working around the Doing Theology Spiral which was undertaken in the UK by a small group of elderly women who had been meeting together for some years to knit garments and which raised money for the Leprosy Mission. Over the course of years their numbers had dwindled, but faithful members still met once a week to share a cup of tea, to knit and raise money for the charity. I therefore suggested that they might like to engage in some thinking about their knitting and I described the theology spiral to them. They quite liked the idea – perhaps because they knew that not everyone took them seriously, and here would be an opportunity to be recognized as women with purpose. They began by giving me a simple knitting lesson and, as we sat knitting, the women spoke of the sheer enjoyment and satisfaction they experienced through the production of knitted garments. This creativity was enjoyable, and so too was the companionship engendered by their meetings. Next, they showed me the brochure that came from the Leprosy Mission, and confided how concerned they felt for those poor people who had to suffer in that way. After sharing these feelings, we moved on to the next phase of the cycle – the detailed exploration of what we were about. We looked analytically at the mechanism of knitting, in which a long woollen thread is manipulated by means of needles into complex patterns and garments which offer durability, warmth and beauty. Then, after exploring this creative process, we moved on to consider the composition of the group itself and began to appreciate the variety that was represented there. We then explored the issue of leprosy, and shared a slide presentation all about the subject.

Then came the time to Reflect on the whole Experience and Exploration. The first issue that had arisen in discussion was that of creativity. We all knew there were creation stories at the beginning of the Bible, so, as we read the stories of creation in the book of Genesis, the women reflected on how much joy God must have felt during the world's creation, for they themselves had little glimpses of what joy and satisfaction creativity can bring. Some of the knitting patterns which the women were able to work with were of the highest complexity. This, they felt, mirrored the measured and disciplined forms of the first Genesis creation account, where God is pictured as taking a steady and stately six days of creativity to bring complex order and beauty out of chaos. The second creation account, recorded in the second chapter of Genesis, mirrored for the women the other aspect of creativity they had experienced – the spontaneous and effervescent bubbling over of the creative act. They seemed to be able to knit at extraordinary speed while talking about an altogether different subject – it just spilled out of them. The second creation story had this same quality – creation just came bubbling from the generous creativity of God. Now they could appreciate just how much God had enjoyed the process of creation, and I must admit, I had never thought of the biblical account in quite that way before.

From there, they moved on to reflect upon the second issue that had surfaced for them – the make-up of their group. As well as elderly white women, the group included two from St Kitts and another who had arrived in Britain many years before from northern India. This diversity, they felt, had produced a much more interesting and buoyant group and they recognized the extent to which they relied on the variety of gifts that such diversity afforded. They felt that this mutual reliance upon the creative gifts of others in the group was mirrored in what St Paul had written about the Church. Each spiritual gift was important, he said, for each was the distinctive offering that a member makes to the well-being of the whole body (1 Corinthians 12). A knitted garment was much the same, they suggested, because if just one stitch should be dropped, then the whole garment would be at risk of disintegration. Every stitch counted, just as every member mattered. The Gospels spoke affirmingly to the group – each individual was of infinite significance to Jesus, however lowly they might be in the world's eyes.

The final issue that had arisen in their reflections together was the matter of leprosy itself. They were soon able to make the connection with the fact that Jesus had taken especial trouble to reach out to those whose bodies had been spoilt and marred by disease. In those people, creation had come to grief, and Jesus had bound those lepers back into the body of society; no longer outcast – no longer an unimportant dropped stitch. How pertinent the connection was between the group's creative knitting of single stitches into whole, complete garments, and the healing and inclusion into society of those who had experienced the separation and disintegration that leprosy wrought. It was this reflection that prompted the little group to do something further. They decided to move to the Response stage. Their decision was that they would try to enlarge their knitting circle and offer membership to those who, like the lepers, were usually barred from society. They sought out the house-bound and frail and visited them regularly in order to sit and knit with them where that was possible. They went out of their way to contact past members who had become too old to attend and pressed local car-owners to gather them in for the weekly meetings. Interestingly, the group also brought their learning to the attention of other Christians by setting up a display stall in the church entrance hall. They took responsibility for a service of worship where hymns and readings told stories of creation, of lepers being healed and society finding new wholeness and completeness. As a consequence of doing theology together in this way, the group had grown, not only numerically, but, from having been a rather lack-lustre gathering, they were now a vibrant and inspired group determined to continue the search and make their contribution towards a better society – they had become participants in the promised Kingdom of God.

This example of the little knitting group illustrates how exciting even the most minimal theological activity can become for those involved in it. The group had no formal theological training and knew themselves to be well past the age where great projects were any longer manageable. And yet they accomplished great things!

Getting stuck

One final example may help to illustrate another facet of the Doing Theology Spiral. This example is once again a British one, the full story being already told in my book, *Power to the Powerless.*[11] As I've already mentioned, the book tells the story of a group of working-class Christians in Birmingham who, in 1978, set about the study of the parables of Jesus only to find themselves propelled into the Doing Theology Spiral – and they did that before we had ever developed the diagram. The outcome of their Exploration of their neighbourhood and their Reflection on the parables of Jesus, was the establishment of a Community Advice Centre at their church. But having once got the whole project up and running, and after years of preparation, they found to their horror that nobody came to their Centre for advice. Had they been only a church 'action' group, the whole project might well have faltered and collapsed at that point. However, they dutifully continued round the Doing Theology Spiral into a fascinating Exploration and Reflection upon their new situation of failure. It looked and felt for all the world as if they had come to nothing, with a project that had fallen flat. But rather than close the project there, they reflected on how it felt to be underused, ignored and dejected. From the basis of that experience of failure they developed an amazing 'spare-part-on-the-shelf' theology – a theology of unemployment, old age, disability and marginalization. In addition to this, they found that the Bible could point them to more positive ways of understanding their waiting and 'stuck-ness'. The Gospels showed them that Jesus himself had been led out into the wilderness for a period of waiting. After his baptismal anointing, when everything seems ready for an active ministry, that expectation is stalled as the Holy Spirit leads

Jesus into a wilderness time of deeper reflection on his future ministry. Following Jesus' lead, they could use their waiting time constructively in preparing themselves more carefully for the ministry that lay ahead. This waiting time of reflection led the group into new responses that prompted them to make significant changes to the Advice Centre project, and visitors began at last to flood in. Thus, both they and the wider community found empowerment.

But things did not end there for them. They decided that, since they now knew the benefits of continuing their theological reflection when things were failing, they should now do their reflection on their new experience of success – and they found that much of what had counted as 'success' was in fact only superficial. Their Advice Centre was easing symptoms in the community, but it was not touching the underlying causes of those symptoms. On one occasion they had rejoiced at helping an elderly woman gain the health care she had so eagerly awaited; but at the next moment they wondered why thousands of others were still waiting in the health queue. Had they helped one person at the expense of those who would still have to wait at overcrowded local clinics and hospitals? Such insights brought home to them just how powerless they remained in the face of such issues. Such powerlessness led them to look carefully at the trial scenes of Jesus and at his crucifixion. They read magazines and newspaper articles about power, saw films, and heard what the theologians of old had said about powerlessness. From all this reflection they were led again into new commitments to their community and a deeper awareness of the power of God's self-giving. It was all so significant for themselves and their community that it issued in the publication of their story in *Power to the Powerless*.[12]

Above all, this final illustration emphasizes the crucial realization that doing theology is not a one-off event. As the theology cycle turns again and again, so the Doing Theology Spiral becomes a Christian way of life, not just a helpful theological tool.

Mind the gap!

In each of the examples we have considered it is quite evident how doing theology moves us from experience and practice into reflection and then back again into practical outcome. This dynamic of action and reflection we named earlier as 'praxis'. But we must beware of an important danger. As the following diagram shows, the action part of the cycle is easily separated from the reflection half, and a gap is created.

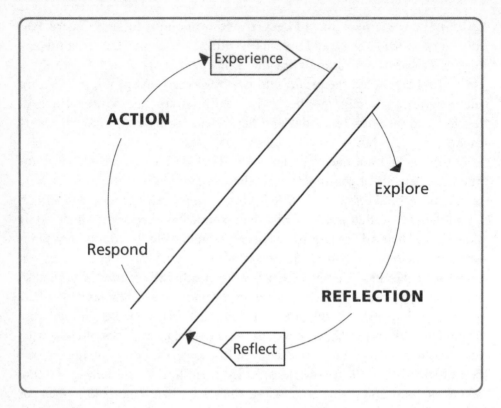

Figure 2.7

This division of the cycle into two is a constant and real danger, for many theologians have started out with every intention of completing the whole cycle, but have become so immersed in fascinating reflection that they have forgotten to return to the action half of the diagram and they finish their theology with just theological reflection and fine words. On the other hand, many parish churches fall for exactly the opposite temptation. Their church and church hall may be teeming with active groups throughout the week – everything from day centres and toddlers' clubs to unemployment drop-in centres. But all that activity may be completely separated off from the reflective worshipping community. The congregation do their theological reflection on Sunday mornings, but maybe do not even know the people who run the active programmes that flourish during the rest of the week in the church hall. This is anything but a united cycle of action and reflection. The worshippers may be lulled into thinking they are part of an active and integrated church, but in fact they are just one half of a fractured cycle. If those who were active would only engage in theological reflection about their activity, and if those who were worshipping would take the risk of also venturing into responsive action together, then the whole parish enterprise would have more faithful theological integrity. The cycle would be made whole again.

These examples have been chosen to illustrate particular points about the process, but they also show how the Doing Theology Spiral, although not offered as an infallible blueprint, has in fact proved successful in an extraordinary variety of situations. It is appropriate for use at a Church Council meeting when an important decision has to be made. It has proved a helpful tool in enabling local churches work out their strategies for future mission. It can encourage little groups to find their feet and their purpose once again. It can help those who are suffering to make a little more sense of their plight and restore courage. It can help the already stretched small congregation set its priorities. It can be used by the highly articulate or by those who are yet to find their voice. It can be used quietly on retreat by an individual; it can be energetic in the cut and thrust of the workplace. But the Doing Theology Spiral really comes into its own when it is used by groups who have a deep commitment to transformation. Then it becomes more than just an educational method – it becomes an instrument of the Kingdom. I have known it used by people who have had no such prior commitment, but the Exploration and Reflection phases of the process have so opened their eyes that they have found themselves becoming more committed to transformation as the process has excited them.

Stephen Bevans has noticed that some who extol this praxis model of doing theology do not seem able to follow it in their own work. He writes, for example, that Leonardo Boff 'is certainly aware of the importance of praxis in the theological enterprise, but several of his books do not immediately reflect the method of praxis at the heart of their construction.'[13] I would therefore recommend to the reader my own *Urban Ministry*[14] as an example of a book which is deliberately constructed according to the Doing Theology Spiral. It will offer yet another example of how the method can lead us into new insights and transformative action in our ministry.

Notes

1   Green, L. (1987), *Power to the Powerless: Theology Brought to Life*. Basingstoke: Marshall Pickering.
2   Kolb, D. (1984), *Experiential Learning: Experience as the Source of Learning and Development*. New Jersey: Prentice Hall.
3   Dewey, J. (1920), *Reconstruction in Philosophy* (2004 edition). Minneola, NY: Dover Publications.
4   See for example, Freire, P. (1972), *Pedagogy of the Oppressed*. Harmondsworth: Penguin. Also see Segundo, J. L. (1977), *The Liberation of Theology*. Dublin: Gill and Macmillan.

5 Segundo, J. L. (1977), *The Liberation of Theology*. Dublin: Gill and Macmillan.

6 See, for example, Holland, J. and Henriot, P. (1983), *Social Analysis: Linking Faith and Justice*. Maryknoll: Orbis. Also see the work of the Center of Concern, Washington DC 20017, at www.coc.org.

7 The Paris-based Ecumenical Institute for the Development of Peoples (INODEP) facilitated programmes of training in the techniques of education developed by Paulo Freire. The Center for International Education at www.umass.edu/cie/index.html continues the work.

8 See, for example, Bishop, R. L. and Guilly, S. J. (1988), *In Pursuit of Human Progress: An Outline of Catholic Social Teaching*. London: CAFOD. Christian denominations produce their own synodical papers and special published reports. Such teaching will be particularly interesting for groups wishing to find out what various denominational authorities are saying about the theme they have chosen to study.

9 This example is drawn from the South African Institute for Contextual Theology which is now at 8th floor, Auckland House, 185 Smit St, PO Box 32047, Braamfontein, AFRIQUE DU SUD 2017. It has published a whole range of material drawn from their own African experience.

10 See Harper, N. (1999), *Urban Churches, Vital Signs. Beyond Charity, Towards Justice*. Grand Rapids: Eerdmans.

11 Green, L. (1987), *Power to the Powerless: Theology Brought to Life*. Basingstoke: Marshall Pickering.

12 *Ibid*.

13 Bevans, S. (1992), *Models of Contextual Theology* (revised edn). Maryknoll: Orbis, p. 79.

14 Green, L. (2003), *Urban Ministry and the Kingdom of God*. London: SPCK.

Part 2

The Four Phases –
The Doing Theology Spiral in Detail

In the first two chapters of this book we proposed that theology could become a vibrant and exciting tool for those who want to connect the traditions of the Christian faith with the issues of daily life, and we offered a process which asks us to experience, explore, reflect and respond. I hope that the reader now has a picture of the skeleton of the process and is keen to try it.

This second part of the book offers more detail on each of the phases of the cycle of theology and provides a large 'toolbag' of practical things to do in order to help the process along. Do feel free to adapt these suggestions as you will, so that you can make the Doing Theology Spiral your own.

The following four chapters will therefore detail each phase of the cycle of theology, so that in the final part of the book we can discuss the full implications of the method and ask critical questions of it.

3

Starting from Experience

Making the experience come alive

Many churches are fearful of doing theology because they feel that they already have so many drains on their time and energies that the thought of setting up yet another group fills them with dread. I have explained already that the Doing Theology Spiral can very helpfully be used by an individual working alone, but it comes into its own when it is used by a group working together. Usually the group that undertakes the process will be a new one, coming together specifically in order to begin to do theology, but the method does not necessarily require brand-new groups to be set up. It does, however, demand that we take more time in planning the deliberations and actions in the groups we already have. Once the method is fully implemented, group participants often find themselves empowered to do things of which they would never before have felt themselves capable and so, in the longer term, the load on any one person or group eases considerably. In the short term, however, it is an extra commitment. Other people may be fearful of utilizing the method because they sense that it may lead them into areas where answers are difficult to find and where they feel out of their depth. As a poor swimmer, I have to confess to knowing how that feels, but I would never have learnt to swim at all had I allowed myself to be disabled by my fears. In any case, Jesus tells us that we will only gain our life if we risk the possibility of losing it (Matthew 10.39).

Let us look more specifically now at how the first phase of the Doing Theology Spiral can be approached. This is the part of the cycle where we own the experience and try to get inside it as much as possible in preparation for a later and even more thorough analysis at the Exploration stage. Let us recall first how the Experience phase stands in relation to the whole exercise, by reference to the cyclic diagram.

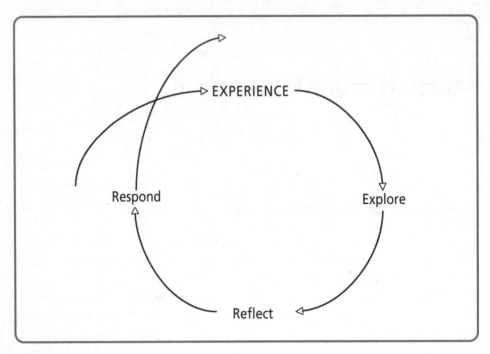

Figure 3.1

There are three elements or tasks to accomplish within the Experience phase.

First, it will be necessary for group members to get to know one another quite well and begin to share something of themselves in the group. Obviously, as time goes on, the group members will become close associates, but right from the beginning it will be important for them to get used to the group and to begin to feel that they can trust it and open themselves up within its circle. Next, it will be necessary to focus upon an issue or theme around which the theological work will be done. This focus may relate directly to the locality in which the group lives, or it may have to do with a common piece of work in which all the members are engaged. It could, on the other hand, be a fresh theme that the group has never thought to focus upon before but which clearly fascinates the group enough to devote time and attention to. Third, when the group is clear about its focus, the members will then need to share their first impressions of the issue or theme that they have chosen. They will not at this stage need to be scientifically precise about the theme, but rather the intention is that they should share their feelings, inclinations and preliminary thoughts together so that the theme is sufficiently identified among them.

Let us take each of these three elements in turn and describe in more detail how we might go about achieving each one.

1. Getting to know the group

Our spiral diagram tries to indicate that we never come to an experience as if from nowhere, but we bring with us a whole range of prior experiences, reflections and beliefs, and all these will affect how we initially respond to any situation. By sharing of ourselves at this early stage, the group is better prepared to appreciate that each participant will be coming at things from a different perspective and will have different things to offer during the development of their theology together. It will also be important to build up a team spirit in the group so that all the members know they have something worthwhile to share and the team values all their gifts. A pleasant room to meet in, a warm welcome and a friendly atmosphere will be important to the success of the group, and time should always be taken for plenty of 'getting to know you' opportunities. There is no need to rush this important aspect of the group's life, for time taken now will pay great dividends when the time comes to share deeply together and to support one another during the later phases of the theological enterprise.

Sharing my story

It might be helpful to describe one such sharing exercise in order to see how the more informal 'Hellos' can be supplemented by opportunities to go much deeper. The exercise I will describe is best done once the group has been drawn together, but participants do not need to know one another all that well. It gives opportunity for the members to share with one another in a non-threatening atmosphere something of their own faith and the values they hold dear. I have described this exercise in detail in a small worksheet entitled 'My Faith, My Story'.[1] Each participant is provided with a piece of paper on which to make some personal jottings or drawings which, it is explained, will remain confidential to them. Then, in a meditative way, they are asked to think slowly back to some early memories and take time to recall where they grew up, the first school friends they remember, what it was like to leave school, their first job, their early loved ones, their first encounter with the faith, and so on, right up to the present. They are then asked, while still in this meditative mood, to decide on two or three major turning points or factors in their life story and to consider whether they feel God was present in those moments or not. By this time in the process there is usually quite a lot of quiet reflection going on in the group. We can either end the exercise there and have everyone share how it went, or we can take things further by remaining in a meditative mood and asking the members to select in their minds a couple of stories or people in the Bible that mean something to them – Bible stories they warm to in some way. They are then asked to reflect on what it might be in their own life's experience that has led them to select these particular stories or passages. All sorts of groups find this exercise quite liberating, especially if everyone gets a chance afterwards to chat about how the experience felt for them – but their personal jottings remain confidential.

The life-line

There are many variations on this same theme. One is to ask people to draw a line which represents their life journey, and to place upon that line simple drawings or words that remind them of events, special people or places in their life story. Sometimes music can be played so that participants relax enough not to have to keep interrupting other members while they are still completing their pictures. Then everyone gets a chance to introduce their picture to other members of the group and, after this, members are asked to think together what place each feels God may have had in their life picture. It is a simple method but very effective. After such a faith-sharing exercise it is helpful to have a short time of quiet prayerful meditation in the group so that each life experience can be treasured and valued before God.

The tree

Some groups may find it more helpful to have the picture introduced to them of a tree with roots, trunk and branches. The roots represent a person's past and background, the trunk represents their present, and the branches represent their aspirations for the future. When each participant has had a few minutes to draw their own tree, they spend time drawing or writing onto it the appropriate things about themselves at each level. The group can then share it and chat it through together. It is always a joy if similarities can be found in the various stories, and the group may wish to draw a combined tree symbol for the whole group if they feel that they already share enough common experiences or hopes. They may even want to draw onto their tree a few early blossoms. All such exercises, and there are many variants upon these themes,[2] help to weld the group together, introduce members one to another and also get them into the habit of valuing their own experiences and making connections between that and God's activity in their lives. All these things will be very important in these early stages of theological endeavour.

Implicit religion

During the course of these preliminary exercises, it is to be hoped that the group members will be trying to express the values that they hold dear, and this will all help uncover something of the innate theology with which they come to the group. For although few, if any, will call themselves 'theologians' as yet, they will all be carriers of an implicit theology by which they already operate their faith in the daily routines of life. Even members who would not normally call themselves Christians may find that they are imbued with some sort of 'popular faith' or 'folk religion', which is their attempt to express something about God which they feel, but perhaps have great difficulty in articulating and defining.

They might therefore use superstition, community wisdom, corporate activity and the vestiges of Christian stories and symbols, all wrapped up together, to try to express something of the flavour of their experience of the Divine, and it will be good if the group can help its members express something of all this at an early stage. Many regular churchgoers will be more reliant on this 'folk religion' than we might expect, but all this is best given a chance to surface at this early stage so that it can be utilized and properly transformed as we progress through the various stages of the theology cycle.

A group identity

When the group feels it is beginning to create its own identity by means of these 'getting to know you' exercises, then it is usually helpful for members to give their group a name. If the group members know already what the direction and focus of their concern is going to be, then they may build that into their name, but often a group name will originate from the feelings the members have about the group itself. I have known groups call themselves the Mustard Seed, the Seekers, the Salt and Pepper group (when there were an equal number of black and white members), and so on. The team name gives members a sense of identity and belonging. A name helps members own the group and its process, and begin to take responsibility for it.

This whole process of getting to know ourselves as a group may only take a couple of meetings if members know one another well already – but there is no substitute for an outing or common activity to really weld the group together in these early stages.

2. Discerning the focus

The next task for the group to accomplish in this early phase will be to choose a specific focus around which the theological work will be done. Now that they are getting to know one another better, it will be easier to be sure that whatever focus is chosen really does appeal to all the members of the group and is not just the personal interest of one or two of the team. It must be a shared choice if the enthusiasms of the whole group are to carry them through to the accomplishment of the whole process. The more commitment the group can have to the chosen theme, the more vital will be the theology that will flow from it.

It may be a very church-centred concern that strikes them as important, such as the experience of sitting in church Sunday after Sunday and becoming increasingly bored by the worship. Members may decide that they all share an interest in trying to find out just why they are so bored and are sufficiently committed to do something about it. It might, on the other hand, be a very positive experience about prayer that they choose as their focus. Some members may be very gifted in prayer and so the theme will interest them, while others may be committed to the theme for the very opposite reason and want to find a way to get them started in prayer. Alternatively, perhaps there has been a lot of illness and death in the community lately, and the group feels that it is time that they really got to grips with the difficult question of why God allows suffering to happen. It may be, however, that the group has come together around a previously agreed focus because it is not a new group at all, but a group that already meets regularly for a particular purpose. It may be a Leprosy Mission knitting group, as in my earlier example, or a youth group that is worried about a recent drug craze that is hitting their town. Or maybe they are the Parochial Church Council which has some crucial decision to make about the parish.

Whether the group has chosen the theme themselves or whether it has already been decided, it will be very good if it relates in some way to the concerns, struggles and predicaments of the marginalized, for my experience is that the theology that such a theme will engender will be even more likely to issue in a transformative and exciting group life.

We may in the end be spared the trouble of having to search for a theme because it comes to us of its own accord. I remember being involved with a Parent and Toddler club where a number of the mums began to talk about their fear of becoming boring and nervous people. They worried that the outgoing energies that they used to have when younger had somehow atrophied now they were tied to the home. They even said that they could understand parents who ended up beating their children, because they themselves had sometimes felt those uncontrollable emotions of frustration and panic at being totally at the beck and call of their toddlers. We decided to meet again the next week with this important issue in mind, and to do some serious Christian thinking about the problem. Even though these mums were not regular churchgoers, they were very pleased to do some experience-based theology for a few weeks around this difficult issue because it was one that was of great importance to them. Very often indeed, issues will come to the group from the community in which it is set, and one only needs to be on the local grapevine for a short time before the issues and concerns are being very loudly articulated.

It is often the case that a number of themes begin to surface and the group has to decide which one they would like to take as their major focus. As we've said, the most important criterion by which to judge which to go for, is that the theme or issue should be one that engenders the strongest group commitment, but this may have to be weighed against which issue represents the most pressing problem. The group will also want to choose one which feels manageable for them, given their resources. Through this process of elimination, one issue or theme is discerned as a front runner.

There is no reason, however, why a theme should not be changed and redeveloped if, in retrospect, the team begins to lose interest in the original focus. Even in the process of taking the chosen theme round the spiral once or twice, all sorts of implications and depths will be unearthed of which they were not at first aware, so that the original theme focus may change and reform as the process unfolds. In general terms, then, the rule seems to be, start where the group feels it is possible to start and let things develop naturally. Let down our bucket where we are and we will surely find water.

3. Sharing first impressions

Having begun the process of getting to know one another and feeling some sense of group belonging, the team has then moved on to discern a focus for its theological work together. It must now move to the very important third element of this Experience phase of the cycle – sharing of participants' first impressions of the subject that they have chosen to study.

A broad outline

The group should try first to describe in broad outline what it is that they have chosen to look at. If the members are asked to gather up pictures, newspaper cuttings, photographs, magazine articles, videos, songs and so on, which they feel relate to the theme in some way, then a very interesting session can be spent sharing these preliminary findings. Outings to plays, films or places that have something to do with the theme are ideal experiences for opening the group up to further awareness of the feelings related to the issue. If it is a church-related issue, then there may be another church nearby that has taken an interest in the topic, so an exploratory visit may be helpful. As the group gets into its subject, so members will tell lots of stories that relate to the theme – stories from their own experience and stories from friends or relatives. As the stories are shared, time can be taken to check out how other members feel about the stories, and the story-teller should be helped by the group to be aware of how the story makes them feel as they tell it. All this activity will help the team build up a general picture of their experience of the theme or issue.

At this stage it is good if the theme can be given as clear a name as possible. This gives the group a specific sense of direction for its future work and sharpens its focus.

Sharing feelings

The group may now find it helpful to select some key words that have arisen so far in the discussion. Write each word at the centre of a large separate sheet of paper and then let the group spontaneously shout out any words which, for them, relate in some way to that central word. Groups usually call this 'brain-storming' or 'word-association'. Doing this can helpfully open up some of the wider implications of the theme, but will also help the group discover their initial feelings about the subject. If the chosen theme word is 'race', for example, if the words they naturally think of are black, white, immigrant, soul, hatred, police, and so on, this will alert them to some of the associated feelings they have about the subject. In this way, the word-association exercise helps the group share something of their preliminary feelings and thoughts about the theme in general and about the various aspects of it. It is well to bring these feelings into the open at this early stage, because group members will inevitably already be harbouring ideas, emotions and prejudgements about the theme. Such feelings are not always easy to specify or to own up to, and so it is often helpful to have groups draw in chalks or paint what they think of when the subject is raised. They should then be given plenty of time to share their pictures and discuss them together. Photographs, stories, role-play and so on may also help to trigger the feelings with which the group members come at the issue.

All this activity should help the group to move to the point where they can express in some way or other just why it is that they feel a commitment to the theme – why it grabs them. Just to sit quietly and meditate on the issue for a moment can often help at this point, allowing members to sense where God might be in it all. To place a candle before a picture that represents the issue for them can be a great aid to meditation of this sort.

By the time the group has finished this first Experience phase of the work, they should, to some extent, have begun to discern what is involved in the issue and who feels affected by the situation they are studying. They should be able to say how they feel about it and how it touches them, and why it is that they feel gripped by the subject. They should also have a notion of what thoughts, feelings and experiences they have had about it all in the past and, more significantly, intuitively they may already be sensing something of where God is present in it all. If this is the case, the group may wish to celebrate this first phase in worship and song together.

4. Explaining the process

If all this has been accomplished, it will be time to move on from the Experience phase to the phase of the cycle that we call Exploration. But before going too far round the spiral it is important that the group has some notion of what the aim of the whole exercise is, and some agreement about how they are going to set about this endeavour of 'doing theology'. It can be very disconcerting to be a member of a group and be asked to engage in various activities without having any notion of why you are being asked to do so. Someone, therefore, should have the responsibility of explaining the Doing Theology Spiral at this early stage so all the participants can decide whether this is the approach they want to take. The power must be left with the group to determine their own agenda and they may decide to vary the spiral in some way to suit themselves. It is to be hoped that the action–reflection emphasis will always remain, but the spiral diagram must be open to the group to modify as they will. It's their group and their theology!

Getting the best from a group

Having described in more detail the first phase of the Doing Theology Spiral, it will be good now to take time aside for a moment to consider the style and ethos to be found in those groups that have worked most successfully around the spiral. For those who are highly skilled in group process and adult education methods, then much of what I have to say here will be second nature, but it is important to record some basic points nevertheless – and especially for those who are engaging with this sort of process for the first time. I have, in addition, included what I hope will prove to be a helpful list of additional books, websites and resources in the Bibliography at the end of this book.

The group

It will be evident already that I make the assumption that this sort of theology is preferably a group exercise rather than the pursuit of private individuals. Fundamental to the theological cycle is its affirmation of the mutual sharing of experience and reflection and the honouring of the experience of others. There is also implicit within it an acceptance of the fact that theology belongs to the whole Body of Christ and that a collaborative and co-operative style will therefore serve it best. We have our best example of that in the way Jesus called together an intimate fellowship to be his first discipleship group. As fellowship and mutual understanding emerge in the group, so the quality of the sharing and the preparedness of its members to be vulnerable to one another will also develop. The pooling of experience and spiritual insight which is then possible in this sort of sharing atmosphere far outweighs any advantages that an individual theologian working alone may have. Therefore, when an individual does theology alone it is best to give them as much support as possible by having them belong to a theological group at least at some stage in their development, when it proves possible. Sometimes enforced isolation means the theologian cannot be with their group and they must of necessity do their theology by themselves. But their memory of the group will be a fundamental support even in their isolation. A Christian wrote from her Argentinean prison, 'Every time I am threatened by bitterness or anguish, I feel the presence of God and all of you supporting me, and then I want only to rejoice.'[3] A theologian can of course work alone, but the experience of having been in the group will be a wonderful resource for them, just as the Apostles, moving out on their individual missions, must have been glad to remember their early time alongside Jesus in his discipleship group.

Groups may be of any size – although experts in group dynamics say that the optimal number is only eight. A very large group may therefore best be split into smaller sub-groups for much of the work, coming back together as a large group as and when desired. I would hope that our groups can always include some people from marginalized situations, or at least those who are not in positions of power or advantage in our society. This will encourage a more down-to-earth and experientially centred theological style in the group, and will also help us to focus our understanding of society more sharply. Often in the Gospels we find Jesus teaching that it is the outsider or the socially marginalized, like the Samaritan, the leper or the poor widow, who becomes the catalyst for the deepening of insights, and so we need to attract into our groups those who are at the margins of society. But if such folk are going to feel ready and able to articulate their experiences and feelings in the group, then it will be even more important that a great deal of trust and honesty be engendered within it in the early stages. Unfortunately, many church meetings unintentionally exclude the contribution of black and working-class people by making them feel on alien territory, rather than at home among friends. Luckily, some Christians have a powerful gift of hospitality and really help a group to be warm and welcoming. Groups will need to be alert to this if they are not to be unwittingly exclusive.

Most groups in today's society will of course have some mixture of classes and sub-cultures within them and so the enabling task will be to keep an eye on where the power lies in the group. The group itself will need to be very aware of its balance of black to white, male to female, Methodist to Anglican and so on. And when newcomers or non-church people arrive, again care has to be taken that they are truly included by the group and not overwhelmed by any exclusive Christian jargon or excessive 'fellowship'. I have especially enjoyed groups which include people of other faiths, since they are able to open up to us significantly different perspectives and share stories from their own culture. There are some groups now operating which have equal numbers of Muslims, Jews, Hindus and Christians within them and this certainly creates a fascinating new dynamic and introduces fresh ways of understanding how God reaches out to us.

Personality differences

Daniel Kolb, who has been mentioned earlier, undertook some informative research into how different people responded to his action–reflection learning circle. Honey and Mumford followed up this study[4] and discovered that activists enjoyed the practical engagement in the group, while those of a more theoretical turn of mind revelled in the exploration and analytical aspects of the work. Pragmatists were very good at planning and organizing sessions while those who were drawn to careful listening, observation and making creative connections were very helpful when it came to the Reflection phase of this learning cycle. It is clear that any really good group will have a great variety of personalities and gifts within it, but it is most creative if those differences between people in the team are understood and appreciated. Short courses for groups, such as the Enneagram or Myers-Briggs[5] workshops, can stimulate mutual understanding of these factors and help each member to flourish and play their part to the full, whatever their personality type. I will speak more about this in Chapter 8.

The place

The group usually finds it helpful to have a home base to call its own – somewhere it can feel secure. This all helps to build the self-confidence of the group, and the right kind of confidence is a key to success in doing theology. I would suggest that the meetings of the group should never be known as 'classes', which may, for some, be reminiscent of painful school experiences, but rather be described as groups, teams, meetings or workshops or whatever the members prefer. The home base needs, if possible, to be within walking distance of people's homes and the obvious safety precautions have to be taken if the meetings are to be held in the evenings. These points may seem insignificant but are essential if people are not to be inadvertently excluded. There is no substitute for personal invitation and coming along with a friend, especially if participants are wary of 'churchy' things, and the most successful groups may be those that work on the principle of personal invitation. In many British cultures today the group is more likely to be well attended if the meetings do not occur every week but are scheduled for, say, four consecutive weeks at a time, with a week or two off between each group of sessions. This allows those with other responsibilities to fit everything in to busy lives. The venue may be a room at the local club or pub, the back room at the Parents' and Toddlers' Club, the unemployment centre, the church, or the front room at a neighbour's house – there is a whole range of venues that may be appropriate. But groups should not confine their activities to classroom-type venues. There must be time for outings and visits to places that are especially related to the theme that is under discussion. Visits to other groups, project work, worship celebrations and so on may happen in many different places and will not be confined to the group base. Feel free to experiment.

The leadership

Most church groups will find it fairly easy and even comfortable to become passive in the company of a designated or ordained leader who seems to know all the 'answers', and it is often easier for the leader to conspire with that wish. It saves the group having to do any tough theological work for itself and it feeds the leader's ego wonderfully well! It is a very real temptation for all concerned. But if the group is to work, the leader will need to guard against this temptation, and instead become a vulnerable learner among fellow learners in the group. This will allow us to talk not so much of 'the leader', as of 'shared leadership'. It used to be that a Bible study would consist of the group sitting round listening to the vicar speaking eruditely about each verse from the notes he had copied out of his commentary the night before. That may have made everyone think that the theology they were imbibing was strong and secure, but it was something of an illusion, and such groups learnt little. One way to get away from this style is to rotate the hosting and leadership for each session, or ask different members of the group to be responsible for different aspects of the group's life. One member can be the timekeeper, another the host, another the 'memory' who takes a note of events or decisions and recaps for the group if it feels itself getting lost. Worship will constitute an important part of the life of the group, but a style of worship must be found with which members feel comfortable and which is appropriate to the focus of their theological investigations. Very often it is here that certain members of the group, if given the opportunity, will prove to have liturgical gifts, and may lead prayer, hymns or worship presentations with great flair.[6] It is always desirable to have some moments of prayer during each session, and it has been my experience that the sharing of the Eucharist has been a very important occurrence too. But all this will depend upon the wishes and preferred style of the group itself.

Another way to remove the focus from one leader is to make sure that any meeting papers are available for all, and if video or electronic presentations are made, then no one person should be constantly in charge of preparing material. Large pieces of paper, pinned on the wall or put on the floor with felt-tipped pens provided for all, are an old-fashioned but more reliable way to encourage a democratic atmosphere. Whatever arrangements are used, do make sure that the power of information and leadership is shared by all participants as much as possible.

Confidence building

It is important to cultivate a group awareness of the resources that are within it, so that participants do not look constantly outside themselves or to the clergy for some secure authority from which to receive ready-made answers. Those who are responsible for hosting or being group leaders must know and use the names of all members and use some simple exercises to encourage people to trust one another in the group. Asking people to share about very safe subjects is a simple way to engender trust. For example, a helpful starter exercise is to have a number of pictures or articles around at the start of the session that relate to the theme. If people are asked which they prefer of the objects or pictures displayed, then it will not be difficult for anyone to get into the conversation and it will lead helpfully into the subject in hand. Most leaders will remember to do some such thing to help the group at its very first meeting, but we are inclined to forget that each and every time we meet, we need a 'starter' exercise of some sort to help the group re-form. If we forget this, we may realize only halfway through a meeting that some more nervous member has not really got started in this particular session, but by then their nervousness has escalated and it has become doubly difficult for them to begin to play their full part in the group. So we help everyone to 'break their duck' and say something at an early stage of every meeting, not just at the first session. Simply asking everyone to share briefly what has happened to them since the last meeting will suffice. Time spent in this way always helps the group to share more intimately later, for it can feel very intimidating to be asked to share an important thought or feeling when you've not spoken yet at all this session. Others of course must be encouraged to stop hogging the limelight, be still and listen.

Above all, we need to make sure from the outset that everyone knows that their contribution is valued, and we must therefore offer a wide variety of styles of operating in the group so that everyone has a chance of expressing themself in a way with which they are happy. Some people will be helped to express themselves by having the group draw or act, others by chatting in twos or threes. Others respond well to pictures, others like lists on a flip-chart or drawing diagrams (that's me!), while others will prefer straight discussion. We must try very hard not to have most group sessions based on the style that the leader prefers – and this danger is easily alleviated if the leadership rotates around the group for each meeting. There is an amazing wealth of material now available which offers helpful advice and ideas for getting groups started and making sure that the group style remains open, interesting, inclusive and to the point. Again, the Bibliography at the back of this book should prove helpful.

It is absolutely crucial to be aware of the degree of literacy in the group or we can frighten people off straight away if they are suddenly expected to read. My rule is never to pounce on anybody expecting them to read even a small section of text, however erudite and confident they may appear on the surface. I was fifteen before I could read in front of others and I remember the trauma and embarrassment which that created for me. If we want to ask for volunteer readers, then I think it is best to photocopy the text and divide it up into very manageable short sections, and then only let it be read by those who readily volunteer. Bibles can always be made available later on for those who want to see the whole passage in context.

Despite all our emphasis on groups, there are some who find groups a frightening and intimidating prospect. Such folk need very gentle encouragement and the security of knowing that there will be no pressure on them to do things or say things that they do not want to do or say. Many people express concern about groups but, once they have experienced them, find membership a delight and a liberation. Clearly, though, patience and sensitivity must be exercised if groups are to be experienced by all their participants as facilitating and not intimidating experiences.[7]

Those of us who live and work in the so-called 'urban priority areas' know that urban group attendance will often fluctuate because people who are living on the margins of society will constantly have crises to deal with. One evening Mrs White couldn't make it to the meeting because her daughter was having difficulties with her husband; the next meeting she was absent because some lads were making trouble in the street and she was fearful of venturing out. The next week she got a little evening job, and so it went on. But Mrs White was still a member of the group and the group knew it. They told her about the meetings each week and she sent messages about her points of view. Commitment is not always expressed in the way we might expect, but my experience is that when a group is working on the Doing Theology Spiral, then there is a remarkable degree of commitment to it on the part of its members, however that may be expressed.

Tools to encourage the theological process

As the group journeys through each phase of the Doing Theology Spiral in turn – Experience, Exploration, Reflection, and Response – there will be certain tools that can be used repeatedly to enhance the process of theological discussion, analysis and group life. Let me briefly describe some of them so that we can make reference to them in future chapters.

Stating the problem

Raising creative tension through critical questioning is known by adult educators and group theologians as 'problematization'.[8] It is a rather ungainly word, but it is an essential ingredient if the group is to move forward with its theme and at the same time save itself from becoming too self-regarding. Put simply, problematization is the process by which we take any common statement and turn the sentence around so that it takes on the form of a question. This allows us to see what the problem is that has been hidden by the statement. The South African group that was the subject of our earlier example, instead of constraining their work with the statement 'the Church has contradictions', turned that statement around and asked, instead, 'Why are there contradictions in the Church?' 'What are these contradictions and where did they come from?' Likewise, the little group that met to knit for Leprosy Mission were not content simply to state that lepers were outcasts. Instead, they turned that statement into a problem and asked, 'Why are lepers outcast?' 'Why should anybody be set aside by society?' Quite often, when doing theology, we will get stuck and not know which way to go. One straightforward way out of the impasse is to 'pose the problem' and ask 'What is the problem that lies behind the statement?' In this way, critical questioning will carry us forward to the next step. Dom Helder Camara offered a wonderful example of this process when he said, 'When I give food to the poor, they call me a saint. When I ask why the poor have no food, they call me a communist.'

Word-association

We have already made mention of this very helpful tool that facilitates the group's theological process at every turn. This is a process where the group agrees for a short period of time not to block any notion that may come to mind. The group settles on a word that most describes what they want to think about together, and then one of their number draws an appropriate picture or writes that word in the middle of a sheet of paper for all to see. The members of the group then call out – just like in a word-association game – any words that come into their minds when they think of that keyword, and a member writes those words on the same sheet of paper. It is very free association that is called for, and the rule is that no one questions a contribution, even if it seems unrelated or even bizarre to their mind. It is a chance for the group imagination to run wild and come up with all sorts of leads, some of which, it is true, may on later reflection turn out to be dead-ends. But to question a contribution at the early stage stops the imaginative flow and, what is more important, makes that member feel their contribution is not worthy of inclusion in the group's life, and that is a cardinal group sin. Once the paper has enough contributions written or drawn on it, then the group can look at each suggestion in turn to see what it makes of it. When the group has an idea of what each contribution means, then a coloured ring can be drawn round just a couple of the very best suggestions which the group feels it wants to follow up. Word-association is one of the easiest of group exercises and yet is so useful when the group is not sure quite what to do next, for it really does free the imagination in a most refreshing way and clears the log-jam.

Keeping a record

I have already mentioned in passing another helpful group tool, and that is 'the memory'. It sometimes happens that a group may function really well for one of its sessions, only to find later that no one really remembers what it was that was said. My experience is that the keeping of a confidential group record of events can prove very beneficial. A simple audio recorder can be used to this end with great success. A group member is responsible for making the recording during the session and then listens to it once again just prior to the next meeting so that they can remind the group of some of the important phrases, statements or happenings that struck them as significant as they listened. The group may want to write some of those points up for the beginning of their next session so that they can be owned and developed. Photographs and pictures of previous sessions and events can also act as a fine 'memory' for the group and can ensure that one meeting builds upon the last without boring the group members with the reading of minutes of the previous meeting. If the group finds it acceptable, it can be very helpful and affirming to create a scrapbook history of the group's life and work.

Multi-media

Throughout our description of the phases of the theological cycle we will also be referring repeatedly to the use of the expressive arts as a way to enliven and open up the group's theological work. Using a multiplicity of media gives opportunity for all types of people to express themselves at levels that they may not have explored before, and in addition, it limits the degree to which those who are verbally articulate can dominate the group. Painting or chalking pictures, working from TV and DVDs, slideshows, photographs, dance, cartoons, tapestries, banners, clay modelling, murals, and so on, may all have their part to play. I was once in a group which included Julie Harper, an accomplished artist. She helped us first to get the feel of expressing ourselves by drawing shapes, but then she let us loose with paper and poster paints. We had

had a number of discussion sessions on the theme of 'suffering' but it was not until we were given the paints that our deeper unexpressed feelings began to surface. We may be really surprised at the depth of expression and discovery which the use of these media engenders.

In this chapter we have taken time to consider what style of group life is most conducive to the doing of theology; the Bibliography that I have included at the back of this book will direct the reader's attention to more detailed and technical material on this question. Our brief sketch should, however, have given a sufficient flavour of this participative group style, and we can therefore turn our attention now to the next phase of the theological cycle.

Here the broad-brush observations and the concentration on stories and feelings, which were our focus in this Experience phase, can be scrutinized more precisely in the Exploration phase. Those earlier impressionistic sketches of the group's chosen issue can now be focused by more detailed description and the group's anecdotes can be supplemented by finer analysis.

Notes

1   This process is written up in a very simple worksheet entitled 'My Faith, My Story' by Laurie Green, *UTU Worksheet no. 4*. Sheffield: Urban Theology Unit.
2   See the Bibliography for more resources.
3   See Gutierrez, G. (1984), *We Drink from Our Own Wells: The Spiritual Journey of a People*. London: SCM and Maryknoll: Orbis. On page 119 he quotes this letter as dated 8 August 1975, Argentina. See *Praxis de martirio ayer y hoy*. Bogata: CEPLA, p. 29.
4   Honey, P. and Mumford, A. (1986), *Using your Learning Styles*. Maidenhead: Peter Honey Publications.
5   Bergin, E. and Fitzgerald, E. (1993), *An Enneagram Guide: A Spirituality of Love and Brokenness*. Dublin: SDB Media; and for a good introduction to Myers-Briggs, see Keirsey, D. and Bates, M. (1978), *Please Understand Me: An Essay on Temperament Styles*. Delmar, CA: Promethean Books.
6   See Bibliography for resource suggestions.
7   On adult resistance to learning groups, see Goodburn, David (1988), 'Needs', *British Journal of Theological Education*, Volume 2, Number 1, Summer 1988. Also see Hull, J. (1985), *What Prevents Christian Adults from Learning?* London: SCM.
8   On the problem-posing concept of education or 'problematization', see Freire, Paulo (1972), *Pedagogy of the Oppressed*. Harmondsworth: Penguin, especially Chapter 2.

4

Exploring

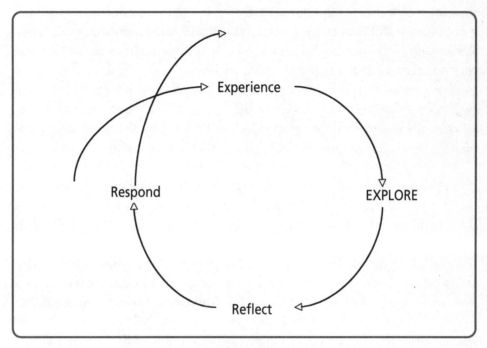

Experience

EXPLORE

Reflect

Respond

Figure 4.1

From anecdote to analysis

During the Experience phase of the theological spiral, the group got to know one another, decided upon a theme that was to be the focus of their theological work together and, after owning up to their prejudices, hopes and fears, they then considered the theological or faith commitments with which they came to the theme they had chosen to study. To help them do this they shared stories and anecdotes, drew pictures, gathered magazine and newspaper clippings, and so on, until they felt they had a broad-brush impression of the subject that they had chosen as their focus. But at this Exploration stage of the spiral, the group must now move from those impressionistic anecdotes into factual analysis – from generalized sketches to specific description. In any action–reflection 'praxis' there will be a need to stand back a little from the situation in order carefully to analyse the hard facts of the issue, while at the same time it will be important to keep well rooted in the experience of it all. To this end we will need to move constantly back and forth between the feelings raised by participation in the issue, and the more clinical and systematic investigation of it. In this way it will be easier to judge both its critical and its felt nature.

The importance of moving from experience into analytical exploration is illustrated by thinking for a moment of a typical television documentary. Such a programme will include many emotive pictures and suggestive camera shots designed to give expression to the feelings the issue evokes, but the programme may not necessarily have offered much hard factual information to the viewer. I often come away from a television documentary feeling that I need some way of checking that my emotions about the issue have not been manipulated by emotionally charged images. This is indeed the danger of story. Story is very emotive, but it does not, of itself, give very much opportunity for a more objective verification. Some would say that one story can be judged by another if it is placed over and against it, but it remains difficult to know on what basis one judges one story as valid and another as false if there is no factual information to go by. The opposing myths and stories of Northern Ireland are very often of this emotive nature, but they are rarely to be taken as the basis from which to determine the rights and wrongs of the situation in that grief-stricken land. To do that we need hard facts, statistics and the objective evidence that stories were never intended to provide. And yet, without the stories to back up the facts, the statistical information remains cold and clinical and gives no impression of the importance of the people who lie behind the facts and figures. The attendant human emotions are as real as the clinical data, so both the Experience and Exploration phases of the Doing Theology Spiral are crucial.

We need to gather facts, but we also need to listen to the stories in order to keep our balance during this Exploration phase of the cycle. If, for example, the group should be considering the issue of freedom, then as well as collecting data about slavery and captivity, it would be well for the group to visit one of the old slaving ports such as Liverpool or Bristol. There have recently been some very fine booklets published that will guide the group round the old slave buildings and enable them to visit the pertinent sites. Similarly, a visit to a play or a film that relates to the questions of slavery or freedom would help to round out the picture derived from the group's gathered statistical and historical information. If a visit is out of the question, then the same purpose might be served by having one or two members experience for themselves what it is like to be tied up for a brief period during one of the meetings. This would serve the same purpose – to allow the data to be made human, and the felt experience to be complemented by objective facts.

A group visit to the planning department of the city or town can prove to be a more interesting way of gathering community statistics than hours spent reading through statistical data or, if the group is studying homelessness and destitution, it might be helpful to engage in an exercise known as 'the plunge'.[1] This method invites participants themselves to sleep rough in the city for a night or two with just a few pence in their pocket and find out at first hand something of the reality of destitution. These sorts of exercises and visits can easily be developed around the chosen theme so that the Exploration phase of the cycle can be interspersed with fresh experience of the questions at issue. Not only does this help to make the detailed exploration more exciting for the group, but it also liberates them from too clinical an analysis and helps to broaden the base upon which the analysis is founded. In this way we do not fall foul of what Martin Luther King called 'the paralysis of analysis' – getting so stuck into the complexities of analysis, and so overwhelmed by the data, that we become divorced from the felt realities of the experience and lose all our enthusiasm for transformation.

Using the analytical tools

When a theological group engages in exploration, they will be gathering as much precise information about the issue or situation as possible. To this end there will be a wide range of tools at their disposal. They will look, listen and use all the natural inquisitive interest of their senses, but they will also need to utilize checklists, research, and other analytical and observational tools that derive from the social sciences and the arts.

Since sociology has been so heavily influenced by Marx, and psychology by Freud, participants may fear that in utilizing techniques from these disciplines they will be buying into Marxist or Freudian philosophical assumptions as a consequence. But we need have no great fear of this because, as we move round the Doing Theology Spiral, there will be ample opportunity for questioning and criticizing all our findings in the light of the insights that come to us from our Christian faith. This critical approach will help us to utilise other disciplines without being subservient to their ideological assumptions.

The Arts will likewise present us with a whole range of material to help focus, clarify and interpret the issue we are studying. We will be reading novels, looking at videos and works of art, attending cultural events, and so on. Once again, we will want to remain alert to the cultural and class derivation of such material. If, for example, we confine ourselves only to 'high brow' classics, we will skew our explorations and be left with a very lop-sided take on the issue under investigation. Great care has therefore to be taken to use insights that come to us from popular culture, television, pop music, trade unions and rap poetry, as well as from the Tate Gallery, Covent Garden and the classical poets.

Whenever we begin to use the disciplines of the social sciences or the arts, those who are well acquainted with these approaches will have an obvious advantage over those who have never before looked at sociology, history or classical literature. It takes confidence and an attentive ear on the part of those who know their subject if they are to enable the group, rather than disable it by their knowledge. The South African group that we referred to in our second chapter got around this problem by inviting the experts in to answer only the questions they themselves had prepared during their preliminary investigations of the subject. The expert was allowed to answer these questions and do nothing more, in this way the group were not overwhelmed by biased experts.[2]

Gathering analytical information

Sometimes, masses of data about the issue at hand will emerge from within the group itself but, more often than not, the group members will have to unearth information from other sources. This can be a lot of fun and include group visits, interviews, searching for documents and pictures, descending on the local library, and all manner of new experiences. The internet is a wonderful source of information but if members can web-search in small groups this safeguards against the small screen isolating members one from another.

Areas of analysis

There are six major areas to investigate (see Figure 4.2, opposite), but most groups will be working within certain time constraints and thus have to select those areas where they can most usefully concentrate their energies. If we can at least touch on each area in some small way, it will be helpful.

There are many ways of coming at each area, and there follows a whole range of ideas from which to choose – but no doubt the group will find for themselves ways best suited to their issue and their own membership. These are just suggestions.

```
┌─────────────────────────────────────────┐
│                                           │
│         Areas of analysis                 │
│                                           │
│        1    Historical                    │
│        2    Geographical                  │
│        3    Social                        │
│        4    Economic                      │
│        5    Cultural                      │
│        6    Religious                     │
│                                           │
└─────────────────────────────────────────┘
```

Figure 4.2

1. Gathering historical information

There is a Chinese saying: 'If we do not know where we have been, we will not know where we are going.' It is only when we appreciate the history or the story so far, and understand the social trends, the myths and expectations that surround the issue, that we can set about writing the next page of the story ourselves.

If the chosen issue is rooted in the locality, then we will probably be helped by the use of maps. The local library is usually full of old maps and it is possible to have them photocopied. By buying sheets of transparent acetate and the right marker pens, it is quite easy to draw from later maps onto the acetate sheets and then overlay them onto the oldest map that the group can find. If this is done in large format and in colour, then a clear visual picture begins to emerge of how the neighbourhood has changed at different times in its history and how the issues have developed over time. If the group contains the right expertise, a fine display of this sort can be produced on the computer screen with moving images and graphics. Local people very often show great interest if they hear that the group is to mount a mini-exhibition of old local photographs, and the meetings of the group begin to bubble once a sense of local identity and pride develops. And it is not only among the older folk that enthusiasm is evident. Younger people can also become excited by this historical analysis, as if thirsting for a sense of their own historical identity and for their roots. Visits come into their own at this point, because many of us have an extraordinary ability to live in an area for years without getting out and discovering all its nooks and crannies. Even in the cities, many citizens have never walked along some of the old industrial canal footpaths, for example, even though some of our cities are riddled with them. Some groups enjoy inviting in outside speakers to give presentations about the history of their community, while others love to draw historical charts and diagrams. Some will record interviews with elderly residents, or create photographic, tapestry or video presentations of their history – the story of their communal identity.

It may not be the locality that is the focus of interest, but rather a theme or issue such as racism, schooling, running a youth club, or trying to make the Church Council more relevant and decisive. Thinking up new ways of exploring the history of these issues can be quite an exciting challenge. How long has the issue been around? How did people first think about it? Collecting cuttings from old newspapers and magazines sometimes helps to fill out the background. On occasion, specialists can be brought in who have read the books on the subject and they can be quizzed to see what the history has to tell. Again, even with an issue-based group, a pictorial and sometimes mapped history can be drawn and displayed on the walls of the meeting-room so that it is more comprehensible to all. It is also helpful to plot on our maps and in an accompanying loose-leaf scrapbook the major stages through which the issue has passed.

The group should by this stage be in a position to highlight the major turning points in the story and begin to perceive certain patterns of change emerging. They will perceive how major external events, such as war or government policy, have played their part in the story. As the history emerges, it will become necessary to look at the past not only from the perspective of those who gained from it, but also from the point of view of those who suffered as a consequence. The group will need to work out who and what were the major agents of change and, if they can, where their power in the situation came from. All this will help us appreciate and understand the trends and patterns that carry through into the present.

2. Gathering geographical information

Our checklist directs us next to the gathering of geographical information. If our concern is with the locality, we can once again start with maps. This time it is worth obtaining a reasonably large-scale Ordnance Survey map and marking on it all sorts of social features. If the group cannot obtain a map of its own, one can be borrowed from the library or the internet and a copy drawn that is adequate for the purpose. The group can go into as much or as little detail as they have time for, but it will be helpful to draw onto the map at least something of the following. The locality and approximate age and type of housing can usually be simply colour-coded, as can different types of industrial or farm distribution. Buildings of special religious interest can be labelled, such as churches, chapels, mosques, temples and so on. Public amenities, shops, pubs, clinics, parks, schools, etc. can be located, but it is important to keep the map clear – too much detail can muddle the picture it seeks to clarify. Again, if there is a lot of complexity in the area, the detail can be drawn onto acetate sheet overlays so that significant trends or coincidences can be discerned and noted. Computer graphics are the best way to display this information, as long as the screen is big enough for all to see easily. The dates of the development or rehabilitation of the different areas can all be plotted, as can those areas that show a dominant ethnic group in residence or ownership. The age of the population in various locations very often relates to the historical development of urban regions, so it is helpful to plot age trends in various streets and districts if they can be determined easily. All these statistics should be readily available from local government offices, the planning department or simply 'Google' it. However, on one occasion I came up against extreme reluctance to let our group have figures relating to the amount of lead in the atmosphere in the area of the city in which I was then living. But opposition like this can indicate that we are on to something of real significance! The group should get into the habit of following leads and ferreting away until it has the information it requires. This sort of exercise also helps to build group confidence and solidarity, which may become quite significant when more formidable obstacles are met later.

We may have chosen to look at an issue that is not easily mapped, such as the health service or the quality of local education, but a little imagination on the part of the group will pay ample dividends. Mapping local health authority areas, local surgeries and ambulance distribution may help to pin down the more abstract issue of public health, while mapping of fair-trade networks may help broaden our perspectives on issues that have to do with global economics or industry. Geographical analysis of this sort should help the group see the spread of the issue, and even the national and international implications if appropriate. Rarely is a local issue as confined to one community as may appear on the surface, for a local issue often turns out to be just the local symptom of a much larger and broader-based reality. And, as usual, we try not to forget to ask the power question – who, in the last analysis, has control of the area? Who owns it and who can make decisions about the future of the community?

3. Gathering social information

The group will also need to discern more carefully the nature of the social relationships within the community or issue being studied. What types of household, family or group structures emerge from the study and how do the people concerned interrelate? The latest census figures from the internet[3] will help the group find out quite a lot about the population of an area, and the ready assistance of a planning department statistician can be a great asset. They get very excited about all their figures and can be very pleased to help us interpret them. It should be possible to find out in broad terms where people are employed, who employs them, what skills are registered, whether people are married, single, bringing up children alone, and so on. It will often be important to know how mobile local people are, and whether the youngsters leave the district as soon as they have the chance. Informal doorstep conversations around the area will give an insight into what local people do for their recreation and leisure, if they have any, and how they relate together in clubs and in families. It could be helpful to meet with any informal street gangs and interest groups, or there may even be another study group looking at the community with whom it's good to liaise. The local doctor, social worker and police officer may have altogether different perspectives to share, but the group will also try to find out who in the locality is considered by the community itself to be important. Street networks and communities are crucial factors in any locality and can lead the group into a much better understanding of how a community lives, plays and works.

   If the theological group is focusing upon an issue rather than a community, it will still be very important to find out who the people are that are involved in the issue. The group might ask itself who precisely is affected by the issue and in what numbers. Is it hurting them or helping them? Who wants to see change, and of what sort? Who is against change, and why? Who can change things and who can not? Interviews with representatives of the forces of law and order, communications media, education, and so on, will all help to chart the social forces and powers that are at work regarding the issue. And we must not forget to take photographs of the people and places that we meet along the way, since it all helps to keep the analysis concrete and vivid.

4. Gathering economic information

The group will need to gather as much information as it can about how money relates to the issue or locality it is exploring. It will be necessary to present as clearly as possible how wealth is produced and distributed in the community or in relation to the issue being studied. Where people work, whether local or at a distance, what they do and how much they earn, may best be displayed by means of maps and charts. The group must find out if the industries, shops or institutions relating to the area or issue are labour- or capital-intensive, what technologies are used, and who controls the production and the employment patterns. The group should try to describe how the wealth thus produced is distributed, what people do who are not in paid employment, and what taxes operate in the community. Money is always a factor in any situation and it will be necessary to know as much as possible about its power and influence over the issue or community being studied. It may be important to know if there are investments involved, and under what conditions those investments are made and what returns investors are expecting. What local people do with their money is also a key feature for a community study, and perhaps surprisingly, many people today seem quite happy to tell you. We have to remember, however, that in addition to the formal economy, there will usually also be a hidden or alternative economy at work, and the group will need to discern how favours, bartering or even scams are operating around their theme subject.

5. Discerning the culture

For those who want to look deeply into the matter of culture, how to discern it and understand it, I would recommend reading Robert Schreiter's *Constructing Local Theologies*,[4] and Gerald Arbuckle's *Earthing the Gospel*.[5] Although most groups will not have time to go into such minute detail, it is crucially important for us to address how culture affects us without us realizing it. It is said that whoever discovered water, it was not a fish. It is only when we are taken out of our normal environment that we begin to see that it is there at all. The language we speak, the clothes we wear, the way we interact with others are all taken for granted until we find ourselves in another culture and then it all stands out like a sore thumb.

There are certain key indicators that we can look to for pointers into the culture of a community. For example, the group may begin by looking to see where and between which groups conflict exists, and how that conflict is dealt with. It should not be too difficult either to ask how a community is seen by its residents or those who work in the area. Some residents might say that although the area has its problems, they would not want to leave because their family is there and because it affords easy access to their local place of work.

From that sort of response we can learn that family ties and employment are considered of importance to those residents. If they love living within easy reach of a large shopping mall, that may indicate how they value acquisition. Very often there will be all sorts of myths about the community, together with prejudices about residents in various streets. Inter-cultural rivalry may be rife, especially when there is ethnicity involved. There will be a variety of lifestyles apparent in most communities today, but friendship groups usually tend to focus around affinity groups, and listening to their stories will provide insights into those sub-cultures.

Symbolic stories will often carry the culture of a community. When vicars past and present are the focus of these stories, then they may very well indicate how the local residents feel about the Church. Symbols within the community may be understood in different ways by different groups, and if an issue is the focus of the group's theological work, that issue itself may turn out to be symbolic of something greater than itself. The church building, for example, may stand in the community consciousness as a symbol of continuity, sacred place, and perhaps community care, but it may for some be rather a symbol of privileged status. Near to my mother's house in the East End of London, a large Hindu Temple has been built. For me it is a symbolic reminder of happy times in India. For my elderly mother it represents her fear that her community has changed.

Another helpful and informal way of getting to the system of meaning and values carried in the community culture is through the use of pictures. A photographer or an artist may produce pictures that are typical of the locality or central to the issue being studied, and then interested groups are asked to talk about what they see going on in the pictures. Do they interpret a photograph of the boy running down the street as a picture of a vandal, a child having a game, or as a young man hailing a taxi? Is the policeman in the picture interpreted as a supportive friend, or as an enemy? Some social educators produce pictures and posters that beg similar social questions, and they can be used in this way too.

The Revd John Davies will show you a picture of the rubbish bins in the streets of his Liverpool housing estate. By reference to them he can describe many of the inner tensions of the community. I had not realized, for example, that they were coloured vivid purple because the usual green or orange would have sparked Irish rivalry in the community.[6]

In gathering cultural information, photographs, simple questionnaires and interviews with local leaders will come into their own. Local stories, folklore, graffiti and murals, and other lifestyle indicators can be drawn, sketched, photographed, or even presented in collages made up from newspaper or magazine cuttings – local schoolchildren are usually quite skilled in this art and can play a big part in supporting the group at this point. All the information that is thus gathered about lifestyle, class, self-consciousness and cultural identity will help to make clear the meanings and values with which a local culture has invested its experience.

6. Religious factors

Religions are extremely important carriers of culture. A woman in Madras shared with me that she saw her own Hinduism as not so much a religion, as itself a culture. Different religions will foster different family and economic structures, as well as a variety of attitudes and responses to issues. The place of children, money, women and men, food, work, music and leisure, will all be greatly influenced by religion and its attendant culture. Understanding religious cultures may, in some cases, be fundamental to the group's work. For example, one group who were focusing on the issue of evangelism discovered that a local Christian youth club had decided to give free copies of the Bible to all its members, not realizing that the Muslim members interpreted this act as symbolizing a renunciation of the Christian faith on the part of the youth club leaders because, in their culture, a Holy Book would not have been so cavalierly distributed by a true believer.

Even within seemingly non-religious communities we may be surprised to find religious images and theological concepts carrying the meanings and values of that culture. We have already referred to this as implicit or folk religion, and it is often most in evidence at times of death and bereavement. It may be far removed from anything that may be called explicit Christianity, but it may well contain vestiges of the Christian faith that have been reworked in the light of that culture's experience and temperament. It is important that we take popular religion seriously in the course of our theological work, for it can be where the majority of folk have to begin their theological thinking, and within it we may be surprised to find a great deal of theology going on already!

Hopefully, a theology group will follow my suggested six-fold framework of analysis by looking at historical, geographical, social, economic, cultural and religious factors in turn. This process of information gathering requires determination and discipline and cannot be rushed, but careful work now will pay dividends later. As a welcome spin-off, the group is also likely to become far more self-confident during this phase of the work as it begins to take all sorts of initiatives in seeking out data, interviewing local councillors, Members of Parliament and other responsible authorities. But before the group members try to make sense of all the data that have been amassed, it is important to check out what part the group participants themselves play in the issue or locality they have chosen to study.

The exploration of ourselves

By this stage in the theological process it may be that the group is beginning to recognize, as did the South African group we considered earlier, that they themselves are part of the problem and they never knew it! I therefore suggest that before moving on, the group now takes a little time to explore themselves more thoroughly.

By sharing with one another how they are feeling at each point in their work together, the group members will perhaps draw back the veil from where their angers, fears and biases originate. If, for example, a couple of members own up to having terrible fears about their own employment security, other group members will better understand that that is colouring some of the statements being made when employment issues are discussed in the group. But just as significant as recognizing the provenance of the feelings of individuals within the group, is the attainment of self-knowledge for the group as a whole. Now that the Exploration phase is well under way, do they still, for example, see themselves as an evangelistic group, a Christian action group, a simple friendship group, or what? It may be well worth talking that through.

Many Doing Theology groups meet under the auspices of a larger congregation or institutional Church, and if it is possible to describe it, then the style of faith of the parent congregation is well worth analysing. For example, has the parent church had a history of action or passivity with regard to the issue the group is discussing, and on whose side is the congregation perceived to be? It may be that the wider congregation is actually still operating at a folk religion level, so when the group shares its theological insights with them, there are surprises ahead if the group should ask the congregation to support its endeavours. If, for example, the group has taken the sensitive issue of the baptism policy of the church as its prime focus and intends to explain its findings to the wider congregation, the group needs to have some idea of where the congregation stands on the issue if it is to present its findings in a way that the congregation will be able to hear and understand.

There will probably be other church groups in the locality too, and the degree of ecumenical understanding and potential should be gauged, for if the group does not have a good ecumenical mix, this can prove very significant during the later phases of theological activity. For those theology groups that belong to institutions other than the Church, it will be just as important for them to analyse how their parent bodies tick and the relationship they themselves have with them.

Models of society

During the Experience and Exploration phases of the Doing Theology Spiral, I have known groups come alive and participants become expert analysts. They have worked with statistics and lists, surveys and questionnaires. They have conducted interviews and made investigative visits. They have written plays and stories, constructed dialogues and skits, used that 'word-association' method I spoke of earlier, repeated chants or made up choruses. They have made banners, painted murals, produced slide-shows, videos and tapestries, all as aids to describe and analyse the focus of their concern. But having done all this, the next step is to begin to make some sense of all the information being amassed and to see if there is meaning within it. It often happens that, as the group seek to present their findings to others, they begin to discern certain patterns and trends emerging, but in order to do this in a disciplined manner it will be helpful for them to be aware that there are at least three major ways of interpreting society – the traditional, the liberal and the radical.

The traditional understanding sees society as a natural, almost organic, phenomenon which gently renews itself in a cyclic fashion, like the seasons. It assumes that there can be nothing wrong with society in itself, so according to this understanding, power is best exercised through authoritarian benign control. Change will be viewed as somewhat deviant, since the prevailing social system itself is understood to be natural and right. Anyone who is in difficulty in society can themselves be blamed for their own ills since, if only they played their part in society more successfully, all would be well. All this may sound a little harsh but it is surprising how many people harbour more than a hint of this understanding of how society works.

The liberal model of society asks us to view things rather differently. Here, change is thought of as necessary, but only on an evolutionary and gradualist basis. Power in society will this time be viewed in managerial terms and there will be a seeking after what works and what is felt to be a proper balance in all things. 'Progress' and 'success' are the two key words, and 'reform' is considered to be the way to achieve both. People's difficulties are, according to this way of thinking, real and collective, but can be put right by allowing the social system to grow and develop naturally for the better. This understanding of society is often known as 'functionalism'.[7]

The third option available to us is to interpret our gathered data according to the radical model of society. The radical interpretation does not expect slow evolutionary progress, but looks for rapid transformational changes in society, brought about by creative conflicts within it. People's difficulties will be thought of as symptoms of the constant struggle that goes on between conflicting groups; and progress will result not so much from reform, as from restructuring society. This radical understanding is sometimes called the 'dialectical' model, since it sees society as a complex range of factors and groups constantly pushing and pulling at one another.

The reason I mention these three understandings of how society functions is because the Church, being generally a more conservative body, is likely to adopt a traditionalist view of society and interpret the collected data accordingly. In the group, however, the unearthing of so much information may prompt its members to see change slightly differently, so there may be tensions. Most of us probably utilize a mixture of all three models when we make our interpretations of society, but within the group there will be those who favour one model over another, probably quite unconsciously. This can lead to frustrations and misunderstandings within the group as they enter this process of making sense of the data. There is a temptation, as we look for meaning among the data, to try to make the facts fit too neatly into our own preferred model of change, so the group must take care to be sensitive to likely differences of opinion at this stage. How then should they go about the daunting task of making sense of the data they have gathered?

Making sense of the data

> # *Making sense of the data*
>
> 1 **Look for connections**
> 2 **Look for values**
> 3 **Look for causes**

Figure 4.3

1. Looking for connections

As all the information about our theme or issue comes together, meaning may emerge as different pieces of the jigsaw suddenly snap together. I once worked with a theological group at 'spaghetti junction' in Birmingham[8] where our historical analysis revealed that the Roman legions had seen our locality as an important intersection of military roads and waterways. This piece of the jigsaw connected with the recent building of the spaghetti junction motorway interchange which now dominates the area. The picture was emerging of a locality which had always been seen as a traffic routeway rather than a community in its own right – that it had never therefore been taken care of by the powerful forces that had driven their canals, railways and motorways through the heart of the area. One piece of historical information had become an important interpretative piece of the jigsaw, allowing us to see the whole social picture more clearly.

Another way to look for connections is to remember that most issues have repercussions at various levels – the personal level, where I feel the situation intimately; the local level, where the community together experiences the problem; the district level, where the wider society is involved; and beyond that, the national level and even the level of international affairs. So, for example, unemployment may affect me personally, but my employment will be related to events at levels far distant from my immediate experience. Similarly, if we are concerned about the local doctor's surgery always being crowded, the information that we have collected about economics, geography, culture and so on, will help us see how these all relate to what at first sight appeared to be only a local issue about our own local doctor's waiting-room. Sometimes our maps will help us to see the connections. If, for example, an older and inferior area of housing is also shown to be the area of immigrant population, this may help us interpret both factors. Fitting pieces of the jigsaw together helps us discern connections and sharpen the focus on our chosen theme.

2. Looking for the values

Having looked for what connects our data, we also need to search out the values which are at work in the situation. By this I mean that we want to find out what motivates the people involved. What are their hopes and concerns, and what ideologies are they working from? What systems of moral value do they appear to work with and what do they want from the situation? Different groups in the situation will probably harbour different values and have different dreams, but despite these differences it is usual that there will be one set of values which, by and large, is controlling the situation. We term these the 'dominant values'. What these values are will have been hidden deep in the data or within some of the answers that were given in questionnaires, interviews and conversations.

Here is an exercise that can help us discern the dominant values. Having drawn a number of lines to represent scales of value, we then mark onto those lines where we would place the people and agencies with whom we have engaged during our process of exploration. For example, we might write up at each end of a large piece of paper two opposing value words such as 'competition' and 'co-operation' . The group can then discuss where along the line between these two opposites they would place the various groups, characters and situations that they have met during their work together. Having done this a few times for different groups, the words 'competition' and 'co-operation' can be exchanged for any other value words that the group would like to try. Such value words might be 'unity' and 'diversity', 'material' and 'spiritual', 'peace' and 'violence', 'freedom' and 'control', 'equality' and 'hierarchy', 'money' and 'people', 'giving' and 'taking', and so on, just as the group thinks best. After some practice, the group may begin to discern which are the controlling or 'dominant values' at work in the situation, and those words can then be written up in big letters and some drawings or photographs attached for emphasis.

Once we have some of the basic value systems named, it may then prove possible to pinpoint the institutions and the main people who seem to us to be the holders and carriers of these values in the situation, together with those who have power to sustain them. Our investigations may even help us to see where it is that the people derive these values and what helps or hinders them in keeping true to them. Many situations will be complex, and different groups and interests within them will be operating from very different values. These value clashes are fascinating and really help our group discover what is going on. This helps us to discern what the real causes of the issue are.

3. Looking for causes

This is where we seek to look beyond the symptoms that are observable and dig down to the causes underlying what we can see. Much of the information which the group has amassed will describe only the obvious observable facts, but our task at this stage is to search behind those facts. We can ask ourselves, for example, in whose interests the present situation is structured, and who stands to benefit from any changes that may occur within it. If we constantly ask the question 'Why?' of all the factors that are emerging in our analysis, then eventually we will pinpoint those factors that we believe are not merely surface *symptoms*, but the underlying *causes*. The problem-posing, problematizing technique that I described earlier can be very helpful in checking the 'Why?' question hiding within factual statements. Eventually we will want to try to rank in order of priority what, in our estimation, the two or three most important causal factors are in relation to our issue. Although we can fine-tune them as we proceed, we might be able to make some useful provisional judgements about what the underlying causes are in the situation that we are investigating.

Throughout the process of looking for dominant values and underlying causes, it is imperative that we remain alert to what extent we ourselves may be a contributory factor in the issue being studied. I remember seeing a group quite recently that had decided to look at the question of racial discrimination in its local community. It was studying a picture which one of its members had found in a magazine. The picture portrayed a group of young, angry, white fascists eyeball-to-eyeball with a gang of incensed black youngsters. The startling discovery for the group occurred when they were asked simply to decide which group in the picture they felt most akin to and which group seemed to be most alien. While they had been dispassionately and clinically unearthing facts, they had been able to distance themselves from their own hidden feelings, but now they were shocked into realizing that they themselves were part of the equation that they had been exploring. They saw themselves in the picture. This is one of the reasons why it is so important for the group never to hide from acknowledging their own part in the situation, but instead to remain vigilant.

Celebrating the group

I have taken time to spell out in some detail the various avenues that may be explored during this whole Exploration phase of the spiral, but many groups will be aware that they will simply not have the time to work through this extensive agenda. I have belonged to groups that have spent as long as a year on this Exploration phase alone. They have done everything very thoroughly – and it has paid off in the end. But other groups only have three or four meetings to devote to this Exploration phase, so they must choose what methods and approaches seem most manageable. Each group must go about their theological work in the way they feel is most appropriate for them; however, the more precision they can muster for this phase of the cycle, the better will be their theology in the long run.

But now it is time for the group to move on. They have entered deeply into the issue by checking out their Experience of it and then they have carefully Explored and analysed data and a variety of facts about the issue. So much has been achieved. Therefore, before the next phase of the cycle comes into view, it will be a good time for the group to give thanks for the resources and insights they have already amassed. By now, all sorts of personal strengths and gifts will have come to light in the group. Maybe they have made all sorts of useful contacts during this Exploration phase, and these may help them in future when they come to plan their strategies. They may well have unearthed all sorts of positive aspects of the issue at hand and met people who have become good friends and allies. New spiritual resources may have come to light for them too. But most of all, they will now be in the very strong position of knowing the situation or the theme very well, and it will be out of this knowledge that their theological reflection can now be developed with clarity and power. Why not celebrate all that with a Eucharist and a party to follow?

Notes

1   The Revd Donald Reeves, while Rector of St James, Piccadilly, invited students to 'plunge' into the experience of the London homeless by living for a few nights on the Westminster streets with only a few coins in their pocket. After the plunge, the students would draw together to discuss their experiences and reflect theologically on what had happened to them.

2   Group members who want to be in a position to judge the material for themselves would do well to undertake an introductory course. In the UK, very useful Foundation Courses in both the Arts and the Sciences are available from the Open University, the Workers' Educational Association and the University of the Third Age.

3   To view information from the latest UK government census, type in the postcode at www.neighbourhood.statistics.gov.uk.

4   Schreiter, R. J. (1985), *Constructing Local Theologies*. London: SCM.

5   Arbuckle, G. A. (1990), *Earthing the Gospel: An Inculturation Handbook for Pastoral Workers*. London: Geoffrey Chapman.

6   See www.johndavies.org/jd-PIC-MONTH-05_06.html.

7   Functionalism has been associated mainly with the work of Radcliffe-Brown and Malinowski. See, for example, Manners, R. A. and Kaplan, D. (eds) (1969), *Theory in Anthropology: A Source Book*. London: Routledge & Kegan Paul.

8   See Green, L. (1987) *Power to the Powerless: Theology Brought to Life*. Basingstoke: Marshall Pickering.

5

Reflecting

Some theologians become so captivated by theological reflection that they become blind to the world around them. But we must likewise guard against the other extreme: of becoming so immersed in experience that we fail to reflect adequately upon it. We would be like Martha in the kitchen (Luke 10.38–42), so absorbed with the business and activity of our analysis that we cannot make the space with Mary for reflection and meditation upon God's presence with us. Some are clearly reluctant to move on to reflection because they have a growing sense of bewilderment at the overwhelming immensity and complexity of the situation they are confronting – the 'paralysis of analysis' we referred to earlier. However, the process of theological reflection upon the situation usually puts to rest any such fear of inadequacy and complexity. This is because it is during this Reflection phase of the spiral that so much light begins to dawn, and this gives the group a handle on the experience which once seemed overwhelming. It makes all the data and information much more manageable and understandable. The vision and the energy that is liberated during the Reflection phase is quite remarkable and should be looked forward to by the group, rather than evaded.

Challenge from the Christian tradition

The Reflection phase of the Doing Theology Spiral (see Figure 5.1, page 78) can be such a positive experience because it is here that we attempt to look afresh at the situation we have experienced and explored, and begin to see more clearly within it the very presence of God. This presence is made ever more clear and transparent when we bring the story of the Christian community's past experiences of God alongside the present experience that we have been exploring. I doubt, for example, whether any latter-day Jew or Christian who knows the story of Moses, would be able to walk past a burning bush today without stopping to ponder whether there was something of godly importance in the experience. The Bible, Church history, our experiences of

77

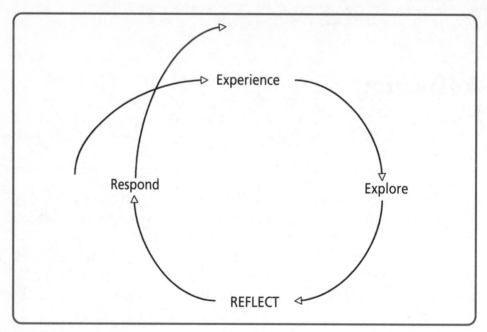

Figure 5.1

worship, baptism, sacred music, and so many other things that go to form our great Christian heritage, will all hold up pointers to where God has been experienced in the past and therefore help us to see how God may continue to be experienced in the issue we now have before us. As we bring biblical and liturgical insights to bear upon the particular issue, so we will see it in a fresh light and be prompted to redefine the meaning of what we are looking at. For now we will be looking more concertedly and self-consciously through the eyes of faith, and so what we perceive will thereby be transfigured through the new lens. We will find ourselves redefining, in the light of our Christian heritage, the problems we have enunciated and, on reflection, be prompted to ask what it is about that Christian heritage that has led us so to redefine matters. This is how the Christian heritage helps us to look at the world, but it is also possible that the world will in turn help us to look afresh at our Christian heritage.

I have described elsewhere[1] how, during my ministry in Birmingham, I worked with a group of Christians who began a biblical study of the parables of Jesus, asking what made them such striking stories. They soon noticed that each parable story begins with a short account of a situation in life that seems to present no great challenge, but then, usually towards the end of the story, there is a sudden change of gear, and the story whips round and challenges the hearers. In one parable, for example, the hero is happily building bigger barns to store all his wealth, when suddenly the story surprises us. He finds that his life is at an end and he cannot enjoy the fruit of his labour (Luke 12.16–21). In another parable, we are introduced to a villain who has cheated his boss and proved himself an unjust steward. Suddenly the story swings around and the villain is applauded for at least having the sense to realize how critical his predicament had been (Luke 16.1–8). So we find in every parable that we will be looking at an everyday situation when, suddenly, there is an unexpected twist in the tale – what the Birmingham group began to call 'God's Unexpected' – and we look again with a different understanding. When that group then looked back at their locality with 'God's Unexpected' in mind, they saw with fresh eyes certain features of the social landscape which would have been totally hidden from them before. Experiencing the Bible made their experience of their issue very different. They began to notice, for example, the hidden poverty that they had not truly appreciated before, the generosity of those in need, and the now obvious injustices of the community. They saw that the people who were paid to help the community were, contrary to expectation, not helping as much as those who were not paid to do it, and the more they looked, the more examples of 'God's Unexpected' came to light. When they then looked back at the Bible they saw more and more evidence of 'God's Unexpected' – in the birth of Jesus in a stable, in the death of God's Son as a criminal on a cross, the choice of lowly fishermen and the fact that Jesus took prostitutes as close friends. As the group looked back at the contradictions in their locality in the light of these seeming Gospel contradictions, new light dawned on their own society and, as they then looked back to the Bible, they could see things they had not noticed before. How subversive the Bible suddenly seemed too as the group now began to feel the urge and the mandate upon them from the Bible to do something about the injustices they were beginning to see in their own situation. So theological reflection on a situation can be a subversive activity when it begins to point up the contradictions and then spur a group to responsive action.

But it is not only the Bible that can do this. The same sort of challenge to our situation can also come from elsewhere in our Christian heritage. Some people have found, on entering a beautiful church building, that they have had to start asking questions about the ugliness of their own lives or the society that surrounds them. Others have looked at Christian symbols like the crucifix and have been brought up sharp. Some have received Communion and been shocked to think how different the equal sharing of Christ's body in that action is from the unequal distribution of gifts in our own society. If we receive God's wine at the Eucharist and then refuse to give to others of our own luxury, it takes only a short time of reflection before we sense how contradictory our actions are. There will be many symbols, actions and stories from the Christian traditions of faith, both within the Bible, in worship and elsewhere, which will serve to challenge our contemporary experience, and this Reflection phase of the theology cycle gives us opportunity to discern these challenges and focus them carefully.

During this Reflection phase we will be endeavouring to tease out the connections between, on the one hand, our contemporary situation as we have Experienced and Explored it and, on the other hand, the great wealth of Christian history, teaching and faith – what I will refer to in this book as our 'Christian heritage' or the 'Christian faith traditions'. As we make these connections so we will be helped to see our situation from God's perspective rather than merely from our own. For example, when we think of the Christian tradition of the incarnation we see there God choosing to experience things from the point of view of the suffering Jesus – from the perspective of those most in need in society. This should then prompt us to take that same perspective for ourselves and, as we do, so we begin to see the world very differently. We begin to see things which we were altogether blind to before we adopted the perspective which came to us from our reflection upon the incarnation. This opening of ourselves to God's perspective is referred to by St Paul when he prayed that we might take on 'the mind of Christ' (1 Corinthians 2.16) – that we too may see the world from the point of view of the servant, as did Jesus. So we learn, during this Reflection phase, to see the world through the lens of the great truths of our Christian faith – and that makes everything look different.

As we move into this Reflection phase of the Doing Theology Spiral we will be immersing ourselves in all that the faith has taught us about our experience of God through the ages. There are some, however, who argue that theological reflection does not necessitate this use of 'God-talk' at all, because in today's world Christians already have appropriate secular disciplines ready to hand which will offer all the insight we need. I want to argue that, in bringing our Christian heritage to bear upon our contemporary experience, we guard against a blinkered acceptance of the world that comes from an interpretation of the world using only the world's tools. For while acknowledging that theology of itself does not contain the necessary tools to analyse the internal structures and causal relationships within society, we do maintain with all seriousness that it is only 'God-talk' that can take the raw material which the social sciences have unearthed during the Exploration phase of the cycle, and work with that material to look for its deepest meanings and sense the relationship that the transcendent God has with it all. This looking for the Divine within all our experience is, to my mind, the prime motive of the whole exercise. Even though we save theological reflection until this third stage of the cycle, we are not allowing the world to lead us by the nose. We certainly do not come at experience merely to lay upon it the prejudiced dogma of a bygone age, but we do bring our faith traditions and our analysed experience of the world together into a creative mix that each may help interpret the other and that we may find God in both. This is what theological reflection is all about.

The connections we discover between our traditions and our present experience will be of various kinds. First, we will often sense similarities between the faith traditions and the issue at hand. Alternatively, we may perceive a startling opposition between certain elements of the Christian tradition and the situation. But third, the connections between the traditions and our situation may initially come to us as quite unclear intuitive hunches or suspicions. We sense that something is 'on' between elements from each side of the encounter and we feel that they must connect somehow, although we will need to take time to discover how.

In making these connections we do, however, have a problem. It has long been recognized that we live in a world that is very different from the world in which the great traditional treasures of the faith were born. The Bible, the early Christian creeds, the sacramental and early liturgical life of the Church, were all formed and developed in contexts vastly different from our own. Our modern world-view has moved on so far that making sense of what was in the minds of those who lived during those early Christian centuries is not always easy. God is the same yesterday and today and for ever, but the more we investigate the gap between biblical culture and our own, the more we realize the extent of the difference. There is a gap of language, of culture, of expectation and perception. If I try to straddle the gap I get myself into complex problems of integrity, for when I properly acknowledge myself to be a person from a scientific twenty-first-century culture, then biblical talk about illness being the outcome of demonic possession, for example, seems to be a violation of what I know about viruses, genes and so on. If, on the other hand, I take models from the Bible to look at contemporary political issues, that would seem to do violence to the specificity of the biblical history. If, for example, I want to talk about the contemporary city, and use passages about the city from the Bible, I may be forgetting at my peril that in biblical times many a 'city' would have had a population only the size of one of our contemporary urban parishes. I stand in danger of overlaying the biblical material with all sorts of modern psychological and sociological paraphernalia that have no place in the original culture, and of laying biblical cultural categories upon the modern world that have no right to be there. We are therefore presented with a problem: how can we make the leap, and interpret from one situation to another? This is what theology, in common with other disciplines, calls the problem of 'hermeneutics', the word hermeneutics meaning 'interpretation'. We will return to this knotty question of the hermeneutic gap in Chapter 7, but suffice it here to say that in the Reflection phase of our Doing Theology Spiral our task is to find some way of bridging this cultural gap and seeing connections between the Christian heritage on one side and our present experience on the other. And it can certainly be done! From one side of this gap to the other, we will hear resonances, sense similarities and challenges, eventually building up a whole range of sensitivities to the Christian treasure store of tradition so that they can be brought to bear upon our present actions and understandings, and see if our own story is part of the Jesus story, or if our actions are wide of God's hopes for us. Let us see how this may be achieved.

The liberation of the imagination

Our imagination has the facility to make leaps quite naturally, almost in a playful way,[2] and this faculty can be nurtured in the Church in order to help us across the hermeneutical gap. There will be a variety of ways of doing this, but the underlying process of making connections will, essentially, be the same. We do it by drawing elements from one side of the gap, say we start from our own situation, and then we draw something from the Church's heritage on the other side which seems to have a significant connection with that first element. The two things seem to fit together in our minds in some imaginative way. Groups can be helped to appreciate what happens here by referring to a further diagram. First of all we remind ourselves that during the phases of Experience and Exploration we have been seeking to face up to the situation or issue that we have decided to study (see Figure 5.2, opposite).

We have been looking intently at the situation before us, carefully noting our feelings and emotions about it and then moving on to explore analytically all the data and information we can discover. From all this, we have tried to perceive the important issues and the dominant values operating within it. We have been facing the situation.

It is only now, in this new Reflection phase of the cycle, that we look specifically at the Christian faith traditions of Bible, sacraments, Church and so on. Over more than two thousand years of history this great tradition has grown, offering us a vast reservoir of Christian texts and understandings. We now have two perspectives running in parallel. We have faced our situation using all the

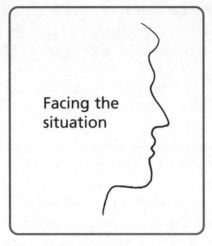

Figure 5.2

disciplines available to us and we now face up to our own Christian heritage of Bible, hymns, worship and beliefs.

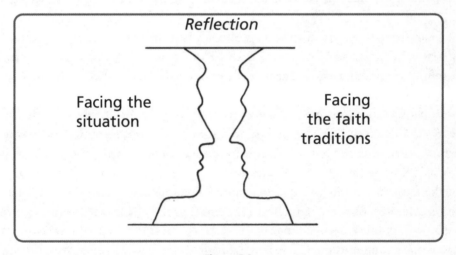

Figure 5.3

The situation now looks across at the Christian tradition and perceives new things there. Likewise, the tradition looks across at the situation and brings a critical eye to it. But as we watch the situation and the tradition confront one another, so we notice fascinating things begin to happen.

It does not take us long to discover that the two faces we have drawn, when brought together, create a whole new factor – and the shape of a candlestick emerges from between the two faces as if to shed new light on the old faces. The intuitive leap is made. The mind has been allowed to move into a new dimension and to look at the meeting of experience and tradition from a whole new vantage point. It is not simply the face of experience, nor simply the face of tradition but, as they meet, we have a new light shining upon both, and this encounter has allowed for the illumination of whole new spheres of under-standing. There is created here a new consciousness and a new-mindedness – reminiscent of what is now spoken of by liberation theologians as 'conscien-tization'[3] and by some philosophers of religion as a 'disclosure situation'.[4]

As the face of the gospel looks upon our experiences, so there is for the Christian disciple a new mind, a new way of looking, which is felt in the heart as well as the intellect, and demands change and response. So the encounter between the experience and the Christian heritage in our theological reflection is a moment of new-mindedness when the disciple is brought to a whole new awareness and very often a challenge to repentance. The penny drops! Indeed, the New Testament word usually translated as 'repentance' is *metanoia*, literally 'new-mindedness' – it is what Jesus demands of us when our present situation is brought up sharp by a realization of the Gospel expectations.

As we study the two faces in the diagram, we may experience the fact that the brain makes the transition from seeing the two faces to seeing the image of a candlestick in a fraction of a second, and clicks instantaneously from one interpretation to the other. If we wish to study one of the perceptions more carefully, then we have to make a decision to hold one or other of the two per-ceived pictures in our mind's eye for longer than just the few seconds that the brain would spontaneously allow were it left to play intuitively with the two images. This disciplining of our mind allows us to 'freeze-frame' in order for a more careful investigation of the alternative image of the candlestick to be made, before we hand control back to our imagination so that the first image of the faces may suddenly appear again. This same disciplining will also have to be a feature of our theological reflection, for we will often find ourselves intuitively coming upon all manner of snap connections between the contem-porary situation and the Christian tradition, but we will need to freeze-frame to allow for time to check out those imaginative leaps to discover what they have to teach us and to discern which connections are appropriate and accept-able, and which are not. Later in this chapter, I will discuss exactly how that happens.

Another way of picturing how the imaginative leap can be made across the hermeneutical gap is to be found in the well-known story of the fall of the apple upon Newton's head. He had for long periods immersed himself in the complexities of mathematical physics, but only when the apple fell, did his mind make the leap of discovery – he had grasped something of the mystery of gravity. There are many similar stories throughout history that record how these imaginative leaps of discovery have been made, when someone finds themself comparing seemingly dissimilar factors which serve to prompt a new disclosure. And this new disclosure is often experienced and spoken of as a moment of revelation[5] or even a *Kairos* moment.

Gutenberg saw an apple press and invented his printing press, Watson dreamt of the double helix and discovered the principle of DNA.[6] How then are we to develop methods of allowing this same imaginative flair to operate in the theological arena? First we must acknowledge that to try to make intuitive connections between huge and rather unmanageable abstract ideas from each side of the hermeneutical gap would require extraordinary perception and erudition. The process is made easier by the fact that, during the Experience and Exploration phases of our Doing Theology Spiral, we have already segmented our chosen study theme into its much more manageable constituent parts so we can make our theological connections at this more manageable level. This is precisely how Newton seems to have arrived at his moment of discovery, for he too had already analysed in his mind the various elements of the problem of gravity, so that the fall of the apple related directly to what was already becoming clear in his mind. When we go through the painstaking process of analysis in the Exploration phase of the theological cycle, we are doing the same thing – subdividing not only the data, but making preliminary sense of them so that the imaginative connection can more readily be made with elements from the traditions of faith.

But actually making the leap from our Explored data across the gap to the traditions of the Christian faith may not prove to be spontaneous and easy even then. We may need help to do it. For example, we could utilize once again our simple word-association technique with which we are already acquainted. The group can take a word that has surfaced during the Exploration phase, and allow itself space to let its collective imagination come up with as many stories from the Bible as possible that seem to relate to that key word in some way. Maybe other elements from the Christian tradition will be triggered too, such as passages from hymns or symbols from worship. Likewise, if we wish to start from the other side of the gap, say from the tradition of the Gospels, we might subdivide a particular Gospel into its stories, themes or characters, and then check across the gap to see if any connections come spontaneously to mind from within the situation that has been the object of our study. Using this word-association technique, we can allow ourselves to note down without question the first things that come into our minds, and give our imagination full rein, knowing that we will have time later to check more carefully to see

which of the spontaneous connections that have sprung to mind may be acceptable as authentic and valid connections to make. But our word-association game
can be supplemented by a whole range of other techniques and tools to help us
across the hermeneutical gap.

A selection of resources

Over many years I have been building up a compendium of further resources
or 'ways in' that help groups work with the Christian traditions, and I want to
share some of them here in the hope that groups will take them, modify them
as they choose, and add them to their own compendium for future use. Once
they become second nature, we can use them whenever they might prove
helpful to the group. First, let us look at some resources that help groups work
with the biblical text.

Biblical approaches

The Simple List

Some groups will find themselves impaired by thinking that they do not know
enough about the Bible, let alone able to make connections between Bible stories
and the contemporary scene. If this is the case, a simple list approach can help
them gain confidence. We ask the group to think, for example, of all the stories
that they can remember about the life of Jesus, or perhaps make a list of the
stories that he told. As people name a story, it is written or, even better, drawn
up, so that the memory is affirmed and reinforced. Most groups will be amazed
to discover how much of the Gospel story they do already know. They may then
wish to group the stories into the ones that the members think relate in any
way to the subject in hand – the issue that is the focus of their theological work.
Grouping stories or snippets from both the Old and New Testaments can help
members of the group develop a knowledge of the stories for themselves and it
can be a great affirmer of the group life. They may wish to see if they can make
a list of particular stories, perhaps those that relate to certain actions or events
in the life of Jesus, or they may try grouping stories as they feel they relate especially to certain people, places, actions, towns, the countryside, or some other
headings that the group choose as appropriate to their issue.

  If the group is still anxious about its lack of biblical knowledge, then it may
be helped by the use of a concordance. Within most groups there will be
someone who is quite good at 'looking up'. The large concordances are so

ridiculously big but work very much like telephone directories so that most groups are not intimidated by them at all. The concordance is simply a directory of biblical references listed in order, so that given a key word any number of references can be found in the Bible, both from the Old and New Testaments. There are many good concordances on the market, many now produced for the home computer, but using the big book in the group is more fun than huddling around a screen.

The Check List

Second, there are the well-known checklist approaches which are designed to help groups make biblical passages their own and make connections between a passage and their own situation. One example is the 'Swedish Method' of Bible study, in which the group is presented with a list of pictures to place alongside a Bible passage. The first might be a question mark, which indicates that the group should at that point look for questions to ask of the text; then an arrow to prompt the group to look for interesting new thoughts; and finally a torch, which represents any light that the group feels the text is able to throw upon the issue at hand. Groups can create their own variations on this, and I share here one which was created by a Birmingham Bible study group – so we called it the 'Spaghetti Junction' checklist (see figure 5.4, page 88). Each group member had their own copy and we used it often in our group work.

Bibliodrama

We may often have seen biblical stories dramatized by children in school or church, but adults can find that doing this themselves can bring a text alive in vivid ways.

First of all there is *dramatic reading*. This is drama at its simplest. On Palm Sunday and Good Friday it is becoming customary in our churches to have a group read the Gospel aloud, each reader taking a character in the story and all joining in for the words said by the crowd. Many groups will therefore be familiar with this style, and it can easily be adapted for other biblical passages for use in the group. We need to be careful not to embarrass people who find reading aloud difficult, but many groups really warm to this simple approach to the text and gain much from it.

Mime is a little more adventurous. One or more voices read the chosen story or text – or if we prefer, we can use a pre-recording of the passage – then other group members simply act it out. Others act as audience and give feedback

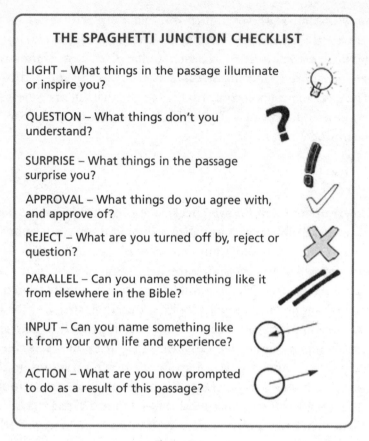

THE SPAGHETTI JUNCTION CHECKLIST

LIGHT – What things in the passage illuminate or inspire you?

QUESTION – What things don't you understand?

SURPRISE – What things in the passage surprise you?

APPROVAL – What things do you agree with, and approve of?

REJECT – What are you turned off by, reject or question?

PARALLEL – Can you name something like it from elsewhere in the Bible?

INPUT – Can you name something like it from your own life and experience?

ACTION – What are you now prompted to do as a result of this passage?

Figure 5.4

later. This can work very well if readers are carefully chosen beforehand. After the mime, everyone discusses the experience of how it was to read, to pretend to be a character, or to be an observer.

Role-play is even more imaginative. The group work out who the main characters or participants in the action of the Bible story are, then the roles are distributed. Some may act as the onlookers, others may group together as 'the Sadducees' , 'Herod and his followers', or whatever else the story may require. Where the group has more members than there are characters in the story, a small number may choose one character to play together. As well as lending support to shy members, this sharing of characters can be very beneficial in getting people to understand the role they have chosen, for some time together is always taken for getting into role before playing through the story. The story is acted through as many times as seems helpful. I have heard of role-plays like this going on late into the evening in one housing estate parish where non-churchgoers also turn up to act out the Bible passages. The role-play takes place in a house, using all the rooms and even the stairs. When the play is finished, everyone says their own name aloud to make sure all are out of the role they have just played and everyone then gets a chance to say what happened for them and what they feel they have learnt from the experience.

The *role interview* can be very creative. This is where one or more of the group opts to play a character from the Bible and is then 'interviewed' in role by another group member. Others look on, and then, after getting out of role, everyone discusses the experience. My most exciting experience of this method occurred when a man acted the part of Mary Magdalene. The group really pressed him about his feelings in that role and especially what, in the light of that, he now thought Jesus had to say about women. He could not believe what he found himself saying. It may not always be a biblical episode that is dramatized in this way of course, for I have seen this method used by a group to act out a period from church history, in which one member who had seen a film about Martin Luther was interviewed in that role by the whole group. The Reformation period of our Christian heritage was really put under the spotlight.

Character identification is another approach. Each group member chooses a character in the biblical story with whom they feel an affinity and then explains why. We can even do this without actually acting the story through, and this can be particularly beneficial for those who like to talk but are too embarrassed or frail to act.

In *Body sculpture* the story is performed by the group in one or a series of tableaux. Either the whole group act the story together, or else just a few act while the others look on. When the group feels it has captured the essence of a scene, it 'freezes' the motion for a few moments to feel the sculpture. Remaining as still as they can, they themselves look round to see how their own body positions relate to the position of the others in the sculpted picture they have created. As always, discussion follows. Remember to allow plenty of time for these discussions so that the insights can be unpacked from the experience.

Public enactment. While speaking of drama, it is worth mentioning street theatre, for bibliodrama can be enacted on a very grand scale too. Some groups construct a mini Oberammergau in their local high street during Holy Week and call it 'The Way of the Cross'. It clearly has an evangelistic emphasis, but much is also learnt by the players themselves. I once took part in one of these events which was acted out on a reasonably small scale on the streets of a council estate with very few church members to speak of, but local people actually stepped out of their front doors to take up roles when they saw that we didn't have enough Roman soldiers or crowd members. They soon got into the action. It really is important, if we are to get the most out of these experiences, to gather the actors together for discussion after the event, to discover together what has been learnt.

It takes a little more background information, but it is also worthwhile role-playing the part the first receiving community played, on hearing the biblical text. For example, if the passage in question is taken from St Mark's Gospel, which was probably written for the Christian community in Rome, the group imagines itself as part of that first-century Roman Church. It might ask itself, 'What can we, in our Roman situation, learn from this passage?' or 'How will we use this passage in our Roman context of persecution, and within our non-Jewish surroundings?', and so on. Role-playing in this way can help the group appreciate how the evangelist has used each story in his Gospel.[7]

Biblical theme charts

Many groups, as we have already admitted, may not know individual Bible stories well, but most seem able to name the major themes of the Bible. We have therefore developed another method that starts from those themes. If we are working with the Old Testament, the themes named may include Exodus, Creation, Babylon, and so on. In the New Testament, the themes may include Incarnation, Parables, the Call of the Disciples, and so forth. The group writes up these themes on a wall chart and perhaps names a few example stories for each of the themes just to make sure everyone knows what they represent. In the next column on their chart, the group writes up words that express for them the meaning of each biblical theme. So the technical theme-word 'incarnation' will elicit more normal-sounding words like 'giving birth', 'getting down to earth', and so on. From those two columns it is then possible for the group to think of examples from their Exploration work where they have seen this same theme occurring. They may think, for example, that their Sunday school classes could do with being a lot more 'down to earth' if Jesus is going to be experienced there. They have thus connected between the major biblical theme of incarnation and their own experience of Sunday school work. The biblical theme has rung bells in their experience and they are making the connection that may, in time, help them see the sacred in their ordinary experience. The chart may then be extended with more theme words and columns as the group requires. I have often used this method, which is developed from Dr John Vincent's work in Rochdale and Sheffield, and I have included on page 91 a few columns of just such a chart which was produced by a group of Christian educators who were looking for theological connections between their education work and the Bible.

Gospel theme	Our own words	Other examples	Educational implications	Practical responses
Incarnation	Living alongside. Hands on.	St Francis. Our own contexts.	Not just theory. Participation.	Start from experience. Commitment.
Disciples	Group and friends. Very mixed.	Our own team. Local congregation.	Not solitary. All abilities.	Questions and answers. Conflict allowed.
Miracles	Practical caring. Signs of the Kingdom. Help the marginalized.	Oxfam. Shelter. Prayer group.	Practice involved. Meaning within. Learner-centred.	Practical needs met. Empowers the weak. Non-significant are valued.
Parables	Everyday story but with new meanings.	Good films. Poster captions.	Ordinary happenings but Kingdom surprises.	Create experiences which point to God's action.
Sending	Try it yourself.	On placement. Apprenticeship.	Allow learners active engagement.	Not all talk but groups try it.
Table Fellowship	Feedback, support and prayer.	Annual assessment. Team debrief.	Support after experiences. Team-building.	Debrief experiences. Clarify aims. Affirm group.
Sacraments	Material signs. Interpretive pointers.	Beauty of nature. Commercial logos. Traidcraft.	Find symbol of the experience as a living resource.	Not just words but signposts in action.
Crucifixion	Total risk. Identify with oppressed.	Nelson Mandela. Oscar Romero.	Risk of injury and pain. Risk our life and image.	Expect trouble. Engagement is risk. Be aware.
Resurrection	Unexpected new life.	Wisdom of the elderly. Locals know.	Look where you don't expect it. Who moved the stone?	Don't give up! Be confident but don't take credit.
Ascension	'Unless I go . . .' Leader leaves.	Childhood heroes fade away.	Leader dispensable yet affirms.	No dependency, learner takes responsibility.

A similar exercise can be done by referring to biblical characters rather than biblical themes. Here, particular biblical characters are chosen as the point of entry, and their life stories, or whatever we know about the characters' activities, are written up into the second column of our wall chart. In the light of this, the group then considers its Exploration work, and whatever imaginative leaps can be made when the particular character is explored are charted up for all to share and discuss.

Charting biblical processes

John Vincent also uses this same cross-referencing exercise for biblical processes. He demonstrates for the group, that the order of certain biblical events follows certain patterns and can even be repeated many times in the Bible. He then helps the group to see how those very same patterns can be repeated in our own experience. Students in training for ordination are interested, for example, to note the order of events after Jesus' baptism. It becomes clear, on looking at the Bible, that immediately after his baptism and before he moves into public ministry, Jesus is taken off into the wilderness by the Spirit to think and pray about the shape of the ministry into which he is venturing. All sorts of temptations cross his path in the wilderness as he seeks to prepare himself. The Old Testament seems to follow a similar order, for as soon as the People of Israel pass through the waters of the Red Sea they too are thrust out into the wilderness to be tested and tempted before entering into their promised land and the ministry for which God has called them. The connection can then be made by those who are at present undergoing ordination training, for although they have heard the call and made the commitment, before they can go into their professional ministries they too have to be tested and trained in preparation for the task and role that lies ahead. It can even sometimes feel like a wilderness experience for them. They find that the pattern made by the order of events in the biblical record rings bells with their own experience, and this helps them to see where God is active in their training experience.

Narrating the Bible

Behind the printed text of Scripture there lies the spoken story, the early preaching and the worship from which the text originated. One method by which a group can experience the richness of the story is by moving themselves back into that oral tradition. The method essentially offers opportunity to learn the story or text off by heart as a group. This is done by first of all deciding as a group what the turning points of the chosen story are. Next, key words are selected that symbolize those turning points. The group then gets used to telling the full story with only those key words as a prompt. When that is accomplished, even the key words are removed from view and the spoken story comes alive in the group once again, even after so many generations of being only words on a printed page. Then the group works towards discovering how to bring life to their telling of the story, in the same way that actors would learn their parts and together would discuss which intonations and gestures best go with each moment of the story as they understand it. This experience can be a real eye-opener.

Prepared questions

Another method of Bible study is for an enabler to come to the group with prepared questions. In his book, *Transforming Bible Study*, Walter Wink offers a way of preparing questions that encourages groups to dig beneath the more obvious elements of the Bible story.[8] In response to the prepared questions, members are encouraged to use dance, clay modelling, pictures, song and so on, to express felt responses. Wink first of all requires the participants simply to read the text carefully. Then he might ask, for example, 'What does Jesus say to the woman?' Then later questions will ask for some creative and imaginative responses, for example, 'Who is the paralysed person in you?' or 'What does Jesus say to this situation?'

Using art materials

The Reflection phase of the theology cycle offers ideal opportunity for the use of the expressive arts. Painting or chalking pictures, working from television and video, computer graphics, photographs, dance, cartoons, clay modelling, murals, music and so on, may all have their part to play. I once had a fascinating experience in Germany where we were each given a lump of clay and asked to play with it as we heard an account of the creation story being read. Then we were asked to take the clay as God had in the story and, accompanied by live music, mould something that represented what each of us treasured. I was really surprised by the depth of expression and discovery that was engendered. I have also seen pictures, tapestries and dance sequences that open up Bible themes in remarkable ways. And of course our church buildings are absolutely full of symbols and artistic representations of our faith which can be used to spark connections with the situation that we have been exploring. Sometimes the group can work from artistic expressions of the faith that have already been produced by others, or use these various media to express what they themselves need to say.

We are lucky to be living at a time when Bible study packs are being published which utilize a participatory and committed group style. Many of these packs are ideally suited to our approach but some words of caution might be warranted, for any 'off the peg' study pack must carry the disadvantage that it cannot really begin from where the group itself is.[9] Nevertheless, some of these packs are very fine pieces of work and can usefully be built into a programme of theological discovery by the group. Examples are to be found in the Bibliography at the end of this book.

Connections with other Christian treasures

We have been concentrating on various ways of making connections between our own situation and the biblical material. These same methods can equally be used to make connections with other areas of the Christian heritage of faith. The great reservoir of Christian treasures includes our *worship experiences*, the sacraments, the creeds, the hymns and canticles – all of which can be brought alongside the situation that we are studying, and theological connections can be made. Similarly, we can use these same methods to connect with the *lives of the saints and theologians* of the past and present. To help us in this, magazines, television or DVDs will often give the group a sufficient amount of information about the character from which to work.

When the group becomes really adept at connection-making, and feels confident, then it is possible to use similar 'ways in' for making connections with some of the major *doctrines of the Church*. These are the great themes of belief such as the Trinity, Creation, the Fall, Jesus, Church, Spirit, Kingdom, and so on. In each case we utilize all the techniques we have used for the biblical material – analysing, listing, acting, painting and so forth – in order to reflect from this great heritage of the faith to see what these doctrines may tell us about the situation we are trying to face in our experience. The problem here can often be that, for many church people, well-known theological words such as 'redeemer', 'reconciliation', 'grace' or 'salvation' are not everyday words at all and may be felt to be somewhat obscure.[10]

One way to open up these specialized words is to use our old favourite, the word-association tool. So, for example, from the specialist theological word 'creation', the group might brainstorm such words and phrases as 'making things', 'power', 'image of God', 'factory', 'clay', 'gardening', and so on. These words begin to break open the many-faceted meaning of the theological word into manageable and understandable nuggets which can then individually be used to make connections in the usual manner with our theme. My rule of thumb in theological workshops is that whenever we find ourselves really stuck, the word-association technique should be considered, for it so very often removes the log-jam.

An altogether different way into this reflection is to ask the group to consider the *indigenous theologies* that they are already living by and working with. They might, for example, be asked to reflect at greater depth upon the life-lines that they were asked to draw when they first joined the group. Drawing a simple representation of their 'Life so Far', and then considering where in that life they have felt God to have been present, can be a stimulating way to unearth the theologies that people are already operating by. It is then possible to investigate the extent to which these indigenous theologies connect with the study in which the group is engaged.

In all this we must not underestimate the place of *prayer and meditation*. Quiet meditation together in the group, while surrounded by all the explored information about the subject in hand, can often bring to mind elements of the Christian tradition and heritage that resonate strongly with the situation. Periods of free worship in the group may also be opportunities for connections to be made between the situation under discussion and elements of the faith traditions. A member may catch herself or himself thinking about a Christian symbol, a line from a hymn or a service, a sermon they once heard, and so on. The key is to let the imagination have free range in God's presence. This allows for even tenuous connections to be made that later can be looked at more carefully and critically in order to see what it is that can legitimately be learnt from them. Books by Charles Elliott, Gerard Hughes, James Cone and others[11] may inspire groups to make up their own meditations and facilitate this exciting experience of connection-making. Others will find that listening to music, or meditation through the five senses, can all be mind-expanding ways into the experience of prayer. On the other hand, there are those who will find physical intimacy very alien, and so opportunity for individual, un-fussy meditations may help them make the imaginative connections in their own way. Some find that keeping a spiritual journal (written or recorded) or having an internal dialogue with an imagined figure can also allow theological insights to surface. Others have found the *reading of philosophy* or metaphysics a ready stimulus to more insight. Different group members come with different temperaments and learning styles, and variety of method will encourage all to offer their gifts and to benefit.

Making the connections

As the group works with the resource ideas I have offered and devises their own, a number of things begin to happen. First, participants find that they are getting to know the full range of the heritage of our Christian faith and becoming more confident in delving into the Bible, the words of hymns and worship liturgies, the stories of the saints and the big themes of Christian theology. They will often sense the need for more basic information and training, in which case they should avail themselves of courses and learning resources which introduce them to a deeper knowledge of the stories and themes of our heritage. For those who really do lack basic knowledge of the Bible stories, I would recommend adult 'Godly Play' which has proved an invaluable method with children and is now offering adults imaginative ways of learning the stories afresh.[12] Many other courses are available – but nothing is better than simply reading the Bible itself.

For those who want to know more about the basic theological themes of the Christian heritage, the Emmaus Course and others like it can be very helpful.[13] Publishers are keen to produce introductory books to assist, and for those who are just getting started, the minister or local theological college or course can help a group or individual find appropriate material.

I hope that the exercises I have offered will have helped the group to move with more confidence around the heritage of the faith tradition in order to be reminded of its breadth and vitality. We will have touched on the treasures of Bible, Church, worship, prayer, doctrine and so on. But we will not have been doing this for its own sake, but in order to make imaginative connections between these treasures and the issue that has been the focus of the group's work thus far. But we still have to recognize the enormous cultural gap that exists between our own everyday experience of a twenty-first-century world and the cultures out of which the Bible and the other Christian treasures have come. We will have been using these group sessions to make imaginative leaps and allowing intuitive connections to be made, but we will now need to make sure that our imagination has been leading us to connections that have integrity and that they are not simply illusory fancies.

Thus far in our theological Reflection work we have allowed our spirit-filled imagination to make a leap to an Intuition that we have thought a worthy connection between the situation or issue and the themes of our Christian heritage. We can picture it like this –

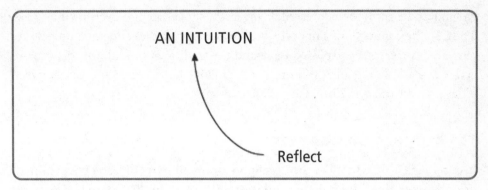

Figure 5.6

You will remember, for example, that towards the end of our analysis in the Exploration phase, we teased out those 'dominant values' that seemed to us to be operating in the situation. We may have decided, for example, that in our specific situation the values that were dominant and were driving those in control were money, growth and success. In this case, we can now take each of those values in turn and, using all the methods we now have at our disposal, hold the value up and let it trigger in our imagination any elements from the traditions of our Christian faith that come to mind. If we are holding money up for scrutiny as the dominant value undergirding those who are in control of our issue, we may make connections with the story of the Widow's Mite (Mark 12.41–44) and the passage where Jesus says how hard it is for the rich man to enter the Kingdom of God (Matthew 19.23). The hymn 'All for Jesus' may come to mind. We may be reminded that monks and nuns take a vow of poverty and that the 'rich young ruler' asked Jesus a question (Matthew 19.16–22). After we have done this with the key value, 'money', we could then move on to scrutinize the next value, and so on. We could do the same not only with the dominant values, but for each element from our Exploration, until a whole range of connections has been made. Each time a Christian faith tradition is thus focused, we can utilize all the participative study methods to get right inside that Gospel story, Church doctrine, hymn or whatever, to tease out even further any other connections that might intuitively come to mind.

As we have suggested, sometimes the connection occurs to us as an obvious contradiction – perhaps if our theme has been debt in the community, we have analysed the dominant values of the loan-shark as 'money' and 'power', whereas in the action of the woman in the story of the Widow's Mite there is a palpable absence of money and power. As well as such contradictions however, connections are just as likely to be in the form of positive similarities – Jesus said that riches *will* indeed be given to us, 'pressed down, shaken together and overflowing' (Luke 6.38). So the connections can occur both where similarities and antagonisms are perceived between the explored issue and the traditions of faith. In this way we arrive at a whole raft of Intuitions – imaginative leaps across the gap between today's world and our Christian heritage of faith.

The baby and the bathwater

It is very exciting when the group alights upon all sorts of perceived connections between their study theme and the treasures of our Christian heritage and arrives at an Intuition. But in our excitement we may forget that through the generations a great deal of painstaking research has been done regarding our Christian heritage which may prove to be of significant help to us at this exciting stage of discovery. We have determined that theology at its best is an active and communal process and that it must take place around the concerns of God's real world. But let us not throw out the baby with the bathwater by forgetting the wonderful contribution that some of our academic theological researchers can make when their work is brought to the service of the Doing Theology Spiral.

Thus far the group has been intent on making intuitive leaps across the hermeneutical gap between our own culture and that of the Bible and other treasures from our Christian heritage. These connections are important to us for a number of reasons. First, we want to see what our faith traditions have to say to our situation. Second, we want to see what light our present concerns and issues will throw upon our understanding of the Christian traditions themselves. And third, as Christians, it is important for us to know that we are being true to the values and traditions that have been important to our Christian brothers and sisters through the ages. We want to know that we are not going on our own sweet way, but that we are seeking with integrity to write the next chapter of the Christian story, the Jesus story, for our generation.

The danger is that, in our enthusiasm, we may fall into the trap that others have fallen into in the past. It is all too easy to make a verse of the Bible mean just what we want it to mean, but we all know that what on the surface we think it means may not in fact be quite right. Our new interpretation may be very valuable, or it may be completely off track. I once experienced an extreme example of this. I was out late at night as a 'street pastor' in Manchester, talking with a murderer at the back of a pub. He told me that he wanted to kill again because someone had given him grief, and he asked me if God would mind. He remembered the Bible text, 'vengeance is mine', and believed that that text allowed him to inflict vengeance on another person. I hurriedly explained that the text continues, 'vengeance is mine . . . *says the Lord*' – it means that only God is allowed vengeance, not us. The murderer was flabbergasted. 'Do you mean that all these years I've been getting it wrong?' I hope that we will not get it as extravagantly wrong as he did, but we too can make important mistakes if we do not possess the correct information.

Thus far we have been allowing our imaginations the freedom to make connections between the Christian traditions and our life's issues, but without those intuitions being critiqued in any way. We have simply surrounded them with prayer, worship and a meditative attitude, in the hope that our imaginations will have been Spirit-filled. We must now therefore enter into a period of double-checking our work to make sure that we are not making any simple errors for lack of information. And that's where the research theologians can help us.

Intuitions at the check-out

By using all the methods available to prompt us, the group thus far has had an Intuition that a particular element in the tradition – an element from the Bible, from a hymn, Church history or elsewhere – is somehow resonating with the issue we are exploring, and that it has something to teach us for today.

Our next task will therefore be to check out that this intuition is not an illusion or a misinformed mistake – have we read the text correctly or does the hymn really say that, or did that saint actually do that? This checking-out is very similar to what conventional theologians have been doing for centuries. They have been involved in a living process that, over the years, has added meanings and interpretations to the tradition, in relation to each challenge and age through which the faith has journeyed. The true research theologian has the task of checking at each turn of experience, to see if each part of the tradition relates as it should to what others have learnt along the way. They must know the biblical text intimately in its original language and be well acquainted with its historical background and the many cultural contexts from which it grew. They should know how the text came to be as it is and what people have said about it down the ages. They will know their Church history too and understand what has been learnt about worship and prayer over the generations. The group will be able to use this corpus of knowledge to check that their intuitions are being true to what we know of the facts so far and, if it is a thoroughly new interpretation, the research theologian can point out that that is the case and see how it might resonate with new things being learnt elsewhere. So it is that the Intuition comes to the check-out where we make sure that it is not flying in the face of all that we know about the Christian heritage. We can picture it like this:

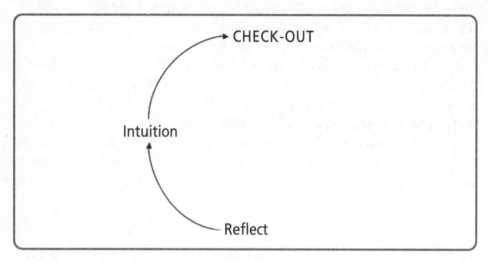

CHECK-OUT

Intuition

Reflect

Figure 5.7

It may be that we don't have a research theologian at our disposal in the group, so a couple of members can be given the task of making a phone call or asking a contact to do some of this checking out, or they may be able to look the question up themselves. All the academic theologians I know would be thrilled to be asked to be involved in this way, so don't be fearful of making contact. But don't forget the golden rule – it is for the group to set the agenda and to make its own decisions; the research theologians are only there as a resource.

Once these checks are made, the group can feel secure that their imaginative leaps are coherent with a proper use of the Bible and the Christian traditions. The group now knows that what they once called their Intuition, having been carefully checked, has now emerged as something of real substance. We might call it, therefore, a New Witness. We can express all this in a diagram (Figure 5.8 opposite).

Our intuitive imaginative leap always had the authority of the group itself, but it will now also be known to have integrity in relation to the whole Christian tradition. It has originated from a connection with the treasure store of Christian tradition, brought through the critical 'check-out' of reason and the wider Christian heritage of scholarship, and has now been brought back into the reflective encounter with the issue. I hope that the following diagram helps us see how the Reflection phase takes place, but let me offer an example so that it may be all the more clear.

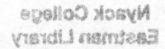

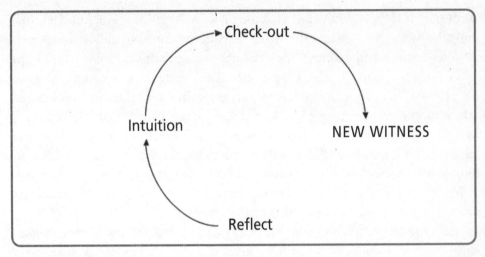

Figure 5.8

I was once working with a group of inner-city people who decided to take as their concern the issue of unemployment. It was a felt experience for the group but they also wanted to explore unemployment theologically. They therefore set about the Experience phase of the cycle by getting in touch with the feelings they had which associated with the issue. Then, during their Exploration phase, they amassed a great deal of information and evidence about the problem. When they felt ready, they moved into the Reflection phase with the word-association game in order to brainstorm all sorts of Bible stories that they felt related to the issue. Of the many that were suggested, one stood out for them as being particularly significant, and this was the story of Jesus healing the lame man at the Sheep Pool, which they found recorded in John's Gospel (John 5.1–18). The group had an Intuition that in this story Jesus was relating to a person who was sharing their own experience of being powerless amid the structures of life, and they felt that this Gospel story could hold insights into their predicament. The group felt that there was a resonance here between their unemployment experience and this story from the tradition, but as yet this was only an Intuition, an imaginative leap, as yet to be checked out.

They therefore began to explore the tradition much more thoroughly. They discovered that the Gospel story details how those who wished to be healed had to be raced into the Pool while the water was still bubbling, in order that the curative properties of the water could do their work. The man Jesus met, however, had not managed in all of 38 years to get into the water, and so he had remained lame. The group saw in this man's predicament an exact parallel with how it feels to be the last in a long line waiting for a job, knowing that only the first in the queue really stands a chance of employment. After a period of long-term unemployment, they knew also that their enthusiasm and hope would begin to wane, just as it appeared to have done for the man by the pool. Jesus asked the man a question that was so reminiscent of the question asked of the long-term unemployed – 'Do you really want to be healed? Do you really want a job?' And they knew that the answer is not always so obvious. They had experienced how self-confidence can drop away after a long period of unemployment. Jesus, however, ignored the rehearsed answer that the man had learnt to give, and cured him anyway, thus giving power and self-confidence back to an unnoticed man waiting in the queue.

The group then called in their minister to help check out the biblical passage and noted that the position St John gives this particular story in his Gospel does indeed point towards the possibility that their understanding of the passage was true to the original text. He suggested that if they looked ahead to the subsequent events in the story they would see how Jesus' words to the cured man in private about his sin (v. 14) all pointed to the fact that Jesus appreciated that the man was held captive not just to a personal illness but to societal structures and prejudices. So the group felt more convinced that their interpretation of the passage was at least strong enough to warrant careful consideration. They therefore took their investigations further and learnt how the causes of illness were at that time generally understood. What they gleaned made them feel they'd struck gold. They checked to see that their reading of the story was not contradicted by all that they could find out from the Bible commentaries about the narrative and its original context – always being careful not to invest the earlier interpretations with too much authority. It was then possible for the group to see their leap of imagination not only as authoritative for their own experience, but also as an authoritative witness from the tradition. This New Witness was that Jesus does seek to give power to unnoticed people waiting in the queue. He helps them stand up against structural oppression and cultural prejudices about marginal people, and gives them the courage to play their part in society again. It was from this discovery that there followed some fascinating responsive and faithful action on their part.

So within the Reflection phase of the Doing Theology Spiral we now discern a secondary cycle – a 'reflection' of the major cycle – which takes the intuitive leap and checks it out carefully until it can be decided whether we have here an authoritative word from the tradition which can stand as a New Witness to the situation we have been exploring. This secondary cycle is simply what goes on within the Reflection phase of our work. We can build this secondary cycle into the major diagram so that we can see more accurately what the total process of doing theology looks like. To see the whole expanded diagram is, I think, quite helpful at this point.

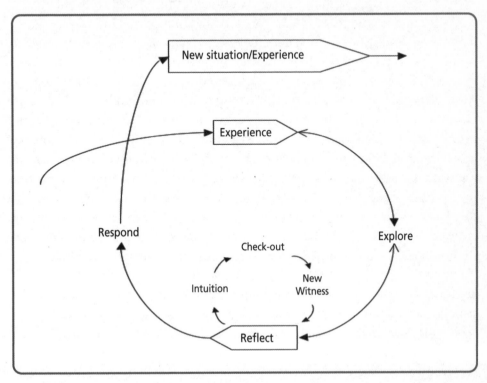

Figure 5.9

What the diagram cannot fully convey, however, is the way the two circles really must work together – almost as one. There is a danger that those who become enticed by the library may spend all their life moving around the secondary cycle of theological reflection, never engaging with the questions raised by the overall process of theology – the theological spiral which it is actually there to serve. Those who specialize in this more academic endeavour should therefore be brought more into the service of the active mission of the Church, so that their labours may be more readily utilized and integrated into the praxis cycle of theological action–reflection. If the Church ignores their endeavours and pushes them to one side then the present activity of the Christian community may not be sufficiently well informed, and it could find itself repeating the mistakes of the past. We must therefore remember that this secondary circle of the diagram refers to an activity which is an integral part of the main cycle – it is all one endeavour.

Focusing the vision

We can now bring the New Witness from the tradition of our faith to address and confront the issue that we have explored and analysed so thoughtfully. And we can do so with confidence since we have taken our Intuition so carefully through the 'check-out'. There may be, in fact, a whole range of elements in the tradition – from the Bible, the sacraments, the Church, Christian hymns and so forth – which have all been checked and which have been found to have something to say to the situation. There will be photographs, statistics and stories that show that elements in the situation accord with the values and promises we have discovered in the Christian traditions, but there will probably be other information and experience that is so far out of kilter with our Christian values that it causes the group to weep. The group should therefore draw up for itself a wall-chart list of ten elements in the situation which are, for them, causes for real joy about the issue as the light of the Christian tradition is made to shine on it. These will be signs of God's grace and causes for celebration. When this is complete, another list can be created alongside it of ten elements that are causes for sorrow in the situation. If the values in the Bible are totally at odds with what has been perceived during the Exploration of the situation or theme then these will be signs of humanity's sin, and causes for repentance and change. When the group has its lists completed, let there be a time of meditation, and if one of the members has a gift for it, they can help the group pray through each of the Ten Sorrows and Ten Joys. Some groups may find that the rosary forms an ideal meditative framework for prayer at this critical point, but use whatever style of prayer is most appropriate.

After such an experience, the group should be in the right frame of mind and heart to dream a few dreams together of how things might be if God's will were truly done for all the people involved in the situation. That vision or dream of how things could be, can be given expression in words or, even better, in a big group poster or banner. In whatever way the group finds most helpful, they spell out that vision so that it can be referred to from time to time as they move into the struggle to respond faithfully in the situation. It becomes their Vision Statement. It may not of course be the result of just one attempt – indeed, I have known groups add sections to their Vision Statement over a period of months as they have gained more experience and noticed omissions. This group vision focuses what the group would hope to see were God's will truly brought to fruition in the situation. This Vision Statement has a function similar to that of the parables of the Kingdom, in that it helps the group keep their eyes on their ultimate aim. The vision banner will always be ahead of them, like the pillar of cloud and fire in the Exodus wilderness, standing for their ultimate goal, spurring them on to see God's will be done.

Having a vision of the Kingdom so clearly expressed in a short Vision Statement will help the group in other ways too. First, it will prevent them from limiting their responses to the merely personal concerns that individual members may have, however important they may be. Second, having the vision writ large like this reminds the group that the final goal is bigger than anything we can achieve by ourselves. We must guard against seeing ourselves as the saviours of the situation in which we are working, but remember always that the victory has already been won by another, through his passion and resurrection. Third, the Vision Statement prevents us from forgetting that our little endeavours are intended to play their part in a much bigger movement, and that we may have many unknown friends in the situation who are also working to see righteousness prevail. They may share our vision without us knowing it. Having the vision written up rather than hidden away inside our minds, makes it into something that anyone can share if they so choose, for it makes it a shared and public cause. The Vision Statement almost serves as a policy document for the group, upon which they now base responses to their situation which are truly inspired by deep theological reflection.

Notes

1 Green, L. (1987), *Power to the Powerless: Theology Brought to Life*. Basingstoke: Marshall Pickering.
2 Dr John J. Vincent uses the children's game of Snap as a model of this playfulness. See, for example, Davies, J. D. and Vincent, J. J. (1986), *Mark at Work*. London: Bible Reading Fellowship, p. 15.
3 See, for example, Wren, Brian (1977), *Education for Justice*. London: SCM, pp. 80–9.
4 Ramsay, I. T. (1957), *Religious Language*. London: SCM.
5 See Kuhn, Thomas (1962), *The Structure of Scientific Revolutions*. Chicago: University of Chicago Press, especially pp. 110ff.; also Koestler, Arthur (1964 & 1969), *The Act of Creation*. London: Hutchinson (and Pan Books, 1970).
6 Watson, J. D. (1970), *The Double Helix: Personal Account of the Discovery of the Structure of DNA*. Harmondsworth: Penguin.
7 Bishop John Davies has developed a number of such methods designed to reach back to the experience of the receiving communities. See especially the account in Ian M. Fraser's *Reinventing Theology as the People's Work*. London: USPG, n.d., pp. 56f.
8 Wink, Walter (1981, new edn 1990), *Transforming Bible Study*. London: Mowbray. Wink utilizes his pre-set questions in a rather authoritarian manner, but it is possible for the group to formulate its own questions and then work from there in a similar way to that proposed by Wink.
9 See especially Peck, Chris (June 1988), *Participatory Methods of Bible Study*. London:

University of London, Department of Extra-Mural Studies. A number of points made in this chapter are dependent upon Peck's admirable study.

10 Cf. Ahern, Geoffrey and Davie, Grace (1987), *Inner City God*. London: Hodder & Stoughton; also see *Views from the Pews*, a report of the Inter-Church Process of the BCC (BCC and CTS, 1986).

11 Elliott, Charles (1985), *Praying the Kingdom: Towards a Political Spirituality*. London: Darton, Longman and Todd. Also see, Hughes, Gerard (1996), *God of Surprises*. London: Darton, Longman and Todd; Cone, James (1975), *The Spirituals and the Blues: An Interpretation*. New York: Seabury; and Green, Laurie, *Power to the Powerless: Bringing Theology to Life*. Basingstoke: Marshall Pickering, pp. 87ff.

12 Strong, D. (2003), *Complete Guide to Godly Play* (Vol. 5). Denver, CO: Living the Good News (Vols 1–4 by Berryman are available from the same publisher).

13 See www.e-mmaus.org.uk.

6

Responding

Fulfilling the dream

When, in the summer of 1963, Dr Martin Luther King preached his famous 'I have a dream' sermon at the Washington civil rights rally, he described, to the quarter of a million who attended, his vision of a new America. It was an inspiring vision that was at once all-embracing and yet specific in its focus. King spoke both of a general well-being for a land where all were believed to be created equal, and he also spelt out in concrete terms exactly what that might mean. He gave vivid examples of his dream – 'that one day on the red hills of Georgia, sons of former slaves and the sons of former slave-owners, will be able to sit down together at the table of brotherhood . . . I have a dream that my four little children will one day live in a nation where they will not be judged by the color of their skin but by the content of their character; I have a dream!' It was this dream and vision that had carried him through the harsh struggle of his campaigning for human rights in the United States, and it was a vision that, once shared, has proved an inspiration to countless men and women ever since, not least to the people of the USA as they voted in the first African-American President, Barack Obama.

We have suggested that the theological group gives expression to its dream in a Vision Statement, so that it too can capture something of the drive and inspiration that comes from sharing a commitment. The group by now will have struggled with the complexities of Exploration and they will have brought to that analysis the visionary insights of the Christian heritage during the Response phase of the spiral. As these elements have been focused together, a clearer vision has emerged of how God's Kingdom might be expressed in concrete terms within the issue that has been their object of study. They have placarded their Vision Statement on their banner and have spelt out their dream, but where should that now lead them?

The Doing Theology Spiral urges the group to move now from Reflection, into the Response phase, and to make the action–reflection relationship complete by commitment to informed action. Let us remind ourselves of how the cycle impels us now into Response, by referring once again to the diagram.

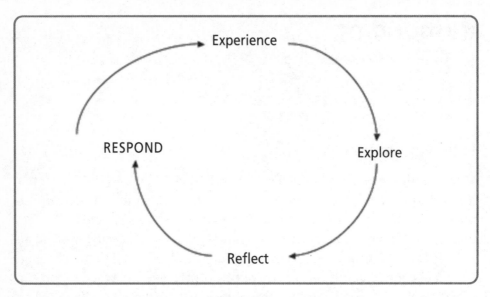

Figure 6.1

The style of theology we are espousing has a dynamic quality about it, and that dynamism is pictured for us in a spiral process that drives us forward, like Martin Luther King's dream, into faithful response. Christian faith has this dynamic quality, for a person of faith will reflect on God's presence with them, but at the same time their faith will give them courage and determination to act faith-fully. The life of Jesus stands out as the ultimate example of this same unity of meditative reflection and committed action. As we have journeyed around the theological cycle of Experience, Exploration and Reflection, it has always been with faithful Response in mind, and at every stage we have integrated action and reflection by making an 'experiential' style the prime way of operating within each phase of the cycle. But now, as we move into the Response phase of our cycle, action comes very much to the fore. This is so important that some theologians have argued that we should substitute the new word 'ortho-praxis' for the old word 'ortho-doxy', to do justice to the fact that it is not by the quality of our propositional beliefs that we are judged, but by the quality of our faithful action. During this Response stage, therefore, we must seek action which faithfully fulfils the particular Vision which has been so carefully worked out through the process of the Doing Theology Spiral.

Moving from our dreams into faithful response in this phase of the cycle will present us with some important challenges. We will have to take into consideration a twofold tension. First, there will be the tension between being active agents in God's world and continuing to be reflective thinkers and meditators. We will need to find ways of continuing our critical reflection, even as we move into active response. Second, we will have to juggle with the tension between the optimism of our Kingdom Vision Statement and the limitations and constraints of the real situation we are seeking to confront.[1] 'You can't always get what you want.'

Tensions will also arise from opposition, and this can be especially dispiriting if it is the local church congregation that does not altogether welcome the group's commitment to a particular faithful response. Those who have not engaged in the process of the theology group may not be as advanced in their commitment as they could otherwise be. When even our Christian friends are resistant, the group does well to find support and encouragement in prayer and worship. The Eucharist, enacted together by the group as it moves into this Response phase of the cycle, reminds them of the supportive and redemptive action of Jesus with them in a world beset with challenges. In the Eucharist, Christ comes alongside us in our common task of sharing God's dream and participating in the Kingdom vision. As we eat the bread and drink the wine we find our solidarity and strength in him who constantly bids us engage the world passionately and do it 'in remembrance of him'.

Knowing what is to be done

Being assured that God calls us to action, and having the Vision Statement clear, how is the group going to determine precisely what action should follow? Certain ideas may already have been suggested during various phases of the cycle, or maybe the group has already come to know what is to be done because the process of arriving at their Vision Statement has moved them instinctively towards one obvious outcome. I remember once being in a group that was upset by the use of exclusively male language in their meetings and Sunday worship. They were reluctantly allowed one church council meeting to consider the situation. The experience was addressed, explored and reflected upon, but there was not enough time in the session to make any decisions about what should happen. It was noticeable, however, that once the subject had been so carefully talked through, all the participants spontaneously made efforts thereafter to be more caring in their speech. Whatever the topic of concern, it is to be hoped that as we engage in the Doing Theology Spiral, so our lives will be changed and our instinctive behaviour transformed, simply through the heightening of awareness that the process affords.

It may not always be so easy to discern the appropriate response, and the group may find itself somewhat at a loss to know what to do. If this is the case, then the careful analytical Exploration work that was undertaken earlier will now be very helpful, because it will be there that a number of clues will be found. For example, if during that earlier phase the group had been able to specify what the dominant values were that were operating in the situation, then in the light of the later theological reflection, it should be possible to decide whether those values are the ones that a Christian group should reinforce or, on the other hand, seek to counter. The individuals and groups actively involved in the issue will also have been located during the Exploration phase and again, in the light of the vision they have arrived at, the group may find it reasonably easy to decide who they wish to support and which groups to challenge.

During the course of their work together the group will have become clearer in their own minds too about what Christian principles they need to act upon, and where they see forces ranged against those principles. With these values and principles in mind, the group places into the crucible the understandings of the issue they have come to during their Exploration. They will pour into the same crucible the deeper causes of the symptoms which they have discerned. They will pour in those dominant values which they observed operating. They will be aware of the patterns and inconsistencies they have detected as they have analysed the issue. And alongside all this will now be ranged all the fascinating connections that have been made from the reservoir of Christian tradition. As all the insights from their Exploration and Reflection are now brought together, a range of responses will begin to emerge. It is as if we were pouring all these things together into a crucible, while under the crucible, and energizing it, the inspiring flame of their Vision Statement burns bright. From this mix will bubble out a number of possible responses that the group feel they might make to the issue. Some groups are helped to understand the process by drawing a simple picture of the crucible (see Figure 6.2, opposite).[2]

The crucible picture reminds us that the responses we now make must arise not from outside the situation and then imposed upon it, but from deep within it. So often in our society, action is imposed from above by those who do not necessarily know the situation intimately and will not have to live with the consequences. But the process envisaged here, and which is pictured in the image of the crucible, reinforces the importance of our incarnational principle of engagement – that God works from within the situation itself and from those who are most intimately engaged within it. We are seeking God's presence incarnated within the situation, and the responses that emerge will be our

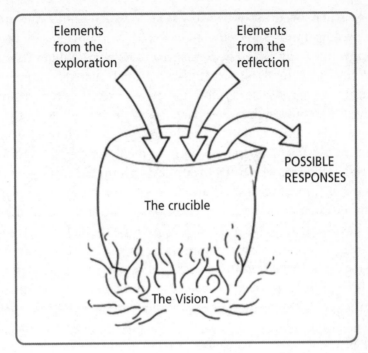

Elements from the exploration

Elements from the reflection

POSSIBLE RESPONSES

The crucible

The Vision

Figure 6.2

attempts to join in those suffering, or celebratory activities of the God who is already deep within the situation. From the crucible emerges a series of suggestions as to what the group might do as a consequence of all that they have learnt, and each of the suggestions that bubble up can be carefully considered in order to determine which might become the agreed group response.

Suggestions may initially look very obscure, but at this early stage none should be discarded without question. A few brainstorming sessions by the group may raise even more suggestions for action, so that before long there is a wide range of possibilities on the table. A group that has been studying racism may find that their awareness of racism has been so heightened as they have followed round the cycle, that that heightened awareness in itself becomes their response. Some may find that their theological work gives them a more positive sense of their own identity, and this enables them to have a better regard for themselves in future, and where self-esteem or confidence has been under attack because of social circumstances, such a response can be highly significant. Sometimes the whole group is so moved by new awareness that they feel led to make a more concerted response still by making a group resolve – to reduce their meat consumption perhaps, or to challenge racism or snobbery wherever they find it existing in groups, meetings or relationships.

Responses may occur at quite a personal level too within the group, one member perhaps finding herself able to make an important life decision, as Freda did in our early example. Some members begin taking new personal responsibility for themselves, perhaps seeking a job change, visiting an elderly relative again, or maybe taking more initiative in relationships at work or in the family, and so on. On the other hand, many groups will want to engage in more concerted group activity, such as the setting-up of a project. Maybe there is a need for a youth club, Sunday school, women's refuge, law centre or some other major initiative, which the group feels prompted to undertake. Some projects may be politically ambitious, or a community initiative may present itself from the crucible as the essential response to a local community problem that they have been addressing. Some groups organize high-profile projects in order to influence political or community decisions,[3] while others find themselves engaging in more traditional, pastoral support projects such as meals-on-wheels or playgroup work. On the other hand, rather than initiating new projects, the group may choose to respond by joining an extant organization. By active participation in a group such as Friends of the Earth, Shelter, a trade union, or a charity, the group may feel that it is adding its weight to an endeavour that already shares something of its vision and is already on its way to bringing their own dream to fruition in the locality. Sometimes the response takes on more of an educational flavour, and the group determines to share some of its learning and concern with the wider community or congregation. Part of the response that the Leprosy Mission knitting group made was to set up a small exhibition of their learning in the entrance hall of their church. Other groups may try to spread the word about their concern even wider and see awareness-raising in the local schools or street markets as their contribution to the issue that concerns them.

Some responses will have more to do with the restructuring of present activities than the introduction of new projects. It may be that it becomes clear during this phase of the theological cycle that the time has come for renewal in the worship at their church, or maybe the style of Church Council meeting that they have been used to requires remodelling in the light of their theological discoveries. New baptism or evangelism policies, the encouragement of more lay leadership in the local church, the revamping of the local playgroup programme or more emphasis on community care at the local residents' association, may each present themselves as viable restructuring-type responses. On the other hand, it may be that the theological group is so surprised and delighted by all that they unearth during the Exploration phase of the cycle, that their response is the celebration of all they have discovered by means of parties, banner-making, worship and praise, and the reinforcement and affir-mation of all the good qualities that they see emerging.

And so our list could continue. We could mention groups who might choose to set up residential communities; those who decide to move house to a location alongside the poor; those who decide to stay where they are in order to be a sign of the continuing presence of God in their challenging locality. Other groups have engaged in symbolic actions, some have responded in prayer, while others may even decide to stand in local council elections. But whatever the response may be, it will have derived from a determination to stay with their Vision Statement and yet remain open to the moving of the Spirit in the situation in which the group has immersed itself.

With so much to choose from, it is at this point that most groups will find themselves having to focus on just one response from among a number of alternatives that have bubbled up from their crucible. But before a choice can be made, there will need to be some clarity as to the criteria by which to judge between the possibilities on offer.

Theology is contemplative, instructive and transformative

Behind the decision as to which response to select, will be an assumption about the ultimate purpose of the theological group. I have tried to make plain from the very first that I see the purpose of theology not merely as study for study's sake, but let me now be more constructive by saying that I judge the purpose of the theological enterprise to be contemplative, instructive and transforma-tive, and our Response should encompass all three. First, theology's purpose is to offer a means by which we may draw nearer to finding that knowledge of God for which the soul longs. Theology gives us an opportunity for discerning more readily the presence and activity of God in the world and adoring God there. But this contemplative purpose could degenerate into self-indulgence if theology were not also instructive and transformative.

In the very act of discerning and contemplating God's presence, theology offers us opportunity to learn more about God's nature and action, and this knowledge in turn is edifying and builds us up into human beings who are even more aware of God's will and the world's destiny. This can be instructive in encouraging us to become better people, more sensitive to the complexities and pitfalls of our own human nature, and more attuned to God's hopes for us. As if to crown these contemplative and instructive purposes, theology also has, as its essential aim, the transformation of the present so that it may conform to God's hopes and yearnings for us, as expressed in the teaching of

Jesus about the Kingdom of God. Thus, theology helps us discern the presence of God, to learn wonderful things from that encounter, and to work with God in the transformation of ourselves and of society, as is God's desire.

It is essential therefore that the group Response should be transformative, for this is an essential ingredient of theology, but there is always the danger that the particular Response we choose to make, even after all our theological rigour and best-laid plans, may not lead us into transformation for the better, but transformation into something even worse. To counter this fear, Jesus gives us his parable story of the unjust steward who, when confronted with the moment of crisis, is applauded for having made a significant response to his situation, even though it turned out to be a rather questionable one (Luke 16.1–8). Jesus teaches us that we are called upon to take the risk of joining in Christ's trans-formation of ourselves and of society, even given that we may fail in the attempt. Martin Luther famously said, 'a person becomes a theologian by living, by dying, and by being damned, not by understanding, reading and speculat-ing'.[4] We cannot afford to let any risk of failure stop us from trying to Respond to the vision that God has given the group.

Criteria for selection

Having thus reminded ourselves of the ultimate transformative purpose of the whole exercise, it now becomes possible to formulate a number of critical questions which will enable the group to single out from the many possibilities for action which response to opt for.

1. Importance and viability

To begin with, the group must determine how important its members believe each of the proposed responses to be. They will have to be convinced that the response they select conforms to their vision in some worthwhile and impor-tant way. They will not want to waste a lot of energy on a project only to discover later that members never really felt that it was worthwhile. They must also choose something that is manageable for them. Therefore, in some cir-cumstances the group's response may have to be on a very small scale, but the group members should not allow themselves to feel downhearted about this. They may, for example, be a group of elderly patients in a nursing home who have begun a Doing Theology group and they may find themselves limited by a lack of resources and physical capacity, even though their vision is clear. There are two things in our Christian tradition that give considerable reassurance in this situation. First, Jesus teaches that the widow's mite is still a worthy contribution to the work of the Kingdom (Luke 21.1–4), for it is both a significant example to others and, in its own way, is a sign or glimpse of the greater presence of God's Kingdom. Second, it must be appreciated that a very small beginning can put a theological group into an altogether different situation from which new and perhaps even larger things in turn may come. That small group who decided that their response was to have a small knitting club for Leprosy Mission, ended up leading a service of worship on the theme of creation for the whole church congregation and, in addition, found ways of including the housebound in their membership. Great things can be expected from just a tiny mustard seed (Mark 4.30–32).

2. Who will benefit?

The group must next ask themselves for whose sake the project will take place and precisely what their own role might be within it. Will the group be operating over the heads of those who are actually experiencing the situation? Will they be acting with them, or are they themselves representative of those who are primarily affected by the issue? Our intention must always be to make sure that people are not being taken over by others, but that they increasingly take charge of their own lives.[5] They are the ones to make their own decisions in their own way about their own lives and situations. Any hint of paternalism on the group's part, however well intentioned, might serve to make the group feel better, but will not be serving Kingdom values.

3. Causes, not symptoms

The group must also be careful, when deciding which response to choose, to determine the levels at which each suggested project might operate. It is important, for example, that if at all possible the Response should affect the basic causes, rather than address only the symptoms of the problem. By mopping up the symptoms only, our project may serve to hide the real problem even further from public consciousness.

Of the suggestions that the group has before it, there will be some that aim more consciously at personal concerns, while others will relate more directly to group or community concerns. Others may highlight the issue at regional, national or even international level. If the group can settle upon a response in which the issue is focused at a whole number of levels, this will encourage a fuller appreciation of the wider implications of the issue, and help all to see the nature of the underlying problems more clearly than ever before. It is often said that in today's world we should think globally and act locally, and it is very good if any response we undertake likewise operates at a practical level in the locality, while at the same time points up to the greater truths. So a 'bring and buy' sale can be run in such a way as to draw attention to the wasteful squandering of the planet's resources if posters around the walls refer to how the sale recycles our possessions. Indeed, the very best Responses at this stage of the Doing Theology Spiral are those which could be called 'acted parables' or even 'sacramental actions' for they each point to a truth, and even participate in a truth, which is much greater than the local action itself might at first seem to encapsulate. This is why what may sometimes appear to be an insignificant Response can have deep meaning and wide-ranging repercussions if carefully chosen and well structured.

4. Who will be involved?

During the Exploration phase of the cycle, the group may have made contact with groups other than themselves who are also involved in the issue being addressed, and the chosen project should be a means by which these alliances can be fostered and developed. The response should therefore be ecumenical wherever feasible, should not duplicate work that is already being done by others, and should ensure that all who want to help have opportunity to be appropriately involved. Above all, the project should involve, or even be steered by, those who are affected by the issue and certainly should not be imposed upon them.

5. Will the response preach the gospel?

We fervently hope that any group Response will be a witness to the transcendent God in the midst and to the reality of salvation for all creation. In some small way, the chosen project should be the practical outworking of love that will point, as a living witness, to the potential reality of the Kingdom in that place. A good Christian project should itself be a Sign of the Kingdom.

Eventually, through this process of questioning, prioritizing and elimination, one or two manageable Responses are fixed upon by the group. This moment can be a very important one in the group's life, and it is worthwhile taking time aside for thankful celebration together.

Aims and strategies

Having decided upon a response, the next stage in the process is to determine what action actually has to be undertaken at ground level to see it achieved. If the response is to be in the nature of a major project, then it may be very helpful to interview those who already have experience in the field, although their advice will need to be checked against the particular Vision Statement and theological values to which the group itself is working.

Prayer and sensitive discussion should help the group get to the point where they can specify with some clarity what precisely it is that they wish to see happen. I usually find that groups work well if they make a simple list of their various practical aims; that is, what they hope their response is going to achieve. They can then append to each of these aims the phrase 'by means of . . .' and then complete the sentence with a few particular strategies which they hope will achieve each aim. This can all be made into chart form and put up in a prominent position in the group room so that all the participants have before them a mutually agreed framework for action. An example may prove helpful at this point.

I was once involved with a group that had taken as its concern the issue of homelessness on the streets of their city. After working round the Doing Theology Spiral, they decided upon what was, even for their rather profession- ally skilled group, a rather ambitious Response in relation to five homeless young people with whom they had become acquainted. Their chart of aims and strategies can be seen on page 118.

Having clarified their aims and strategies, a group now has to concentrate on each in turn and specify all the practical steps that must be taken to achieve each strategy. The first strategy for the Homelessness group required a whole range of practical steps – perhaps more than for any other of the strategies. It was necessary to find an appropriate house, acquire funding, find furniture and insurance, etc. People also had to be assigned to each task. If this process of deciding upon practical steps goes well, then there is every indication that the group has chosen a project which is manageable for them. If the project proves too complicated or large for them at this stage, then the group can easily move instead to a more manageable project – but don't give up too soon.

There are a number of techniques which may help groups through this process of strategic planning. The first is known as the Hopes and Fears diagram (see p. 119).[6] The group first draws a large chart similar in design to a rugby football goal or capital letter H. The left-hand upright represents where they are now, while the right-hand upright represents where they might be in

Issue: **Homelessness in the city**

Response: **To set up a home for five young people**

Aims and strategies

1. *Aim:* To get youngsters off the street.
    Strategy: By means of setting up a house in Woburn Road
    as a home for five young people.

2. *Aim:* To give security and attention to the youngsters.
    Strategy: By means of two of our adults living in and the rest
    taking constant interest in the home alongside the young people.

3. *Aim:* To get to know more about the problems of homelessness.
    Strategy: By means of listening to the youngsters and their friends.

4. *Aim:* To prompt the local authority to have more care for homeless
    youngsters.
    Strategy: By bringing what we learn to the attention of the local
    councillors and officers.

5. *Aim:* To be aware of God's presence with the youngsters.
    Strategy: By doing the whole thing sensitively as an
    intentionally Christian group.

Figure 6.3

one year's time. Above the horizontal cross-bar the group is asked to write all the good things or 'best hopes' they can imagine, and below the cross-bar, all the bad things or 'worst fears' that come to mind. At each of the four corners of the diagram the group writes up how it feels – at the top left will appear all those things that are presently the case and that feel good to the group, but below and to the left will be written all those things which are now present but that the group does not want to see remain. They can then move to the right-hand side of the goalpost and at the top write up how they hope things might be in one year's time if all were to go wonderfully well with their project. Below will be written all their worst nightmares about what could go wrong. So, for example, if a youth club project were being planned, then one of the many dreams that may be listed on the diagram might be the hope that the club should be full each evening, while below will be recorded the fear that no youngsters might come. A dotted line is now drawn to run from 'where we are now' up to join our best hopes for the future at the top right of the chart. Along this line are written up as many suggestions as possible, which, if followed up, may help to ensure that their dream is attained and the nightmare avoided. In the youth club example, in relation to concern about numbers, suggestions may include 'advertise well', 'go to the schools and inform youngsters there', 'have posters printed', 'ask youngsters what programme they would support', 'send out text messages', and so on. In this way the planning begins to take shape in the mind of the group, and members opt to take responsibility for each aspect of the strategy.

HOPES AND FEARS

Good things we want to keep

Practical steps

Our best hopes for the future

NOW

ONE YEAR'S TIME

Bad things we want to lose

Our worst fears for the future

Figure 6.4

A second well-known approach to planning practical steps in the group is to use a simple 'force field analysis'. Here, we look to each aim and strategy in turn and list first the factors that may prevent it being achieved, and then those factors that will encourage its achievement. We then work out together in the group ways of reinforcing the encouraging factors and discouraging the preventative factors.

A third and very simple method of working out the practical steps is by the use of a large wall calendar. The framework this offers enables the group to draft out what needs to be done, in what order, and by whom, so that each aim and strategy may be achieved efficiently. Each group will discover its own preferred way of planning aims, strategies and practical steps, but when all this is done it will then be time to take a deep breath, say our prayers and move to action!

Implementation

It is very exhilarating to be engaged in action that is the outcome of theological investigation, rather than merely to be an activist for its own sake. It is also exciting to be engaged in theology that has practical action at its heart, rather than be saddled with theological reflection that hangs back from practical engagement. The challenge can be daunting but the outcome is usually inspiring to observe. For, as they begin to engage in responsive action, the group learns to mobilize the resources of people and funding, to set up management structures, bombard the media about members' concerns, wage diplomatic offensives and encourage volunteers. So much is gained from this practical experience that can never be gained from theory, and so often ordinary members of the group prove to be far more adept at wise implementation than do the more learned members. If the group has never engaged in anything like this before, then things are never the same again! Even those responses which are much lower key and do not involve setting up grand projects, can be deeply fulfilling and intensely moving for the group participants. At whatever level the response, members have the profound exhilaration of undertaking the response with a new awareness and with the inspiration of knowing that their action is intimately related to their vision of the Kingdom.

Dealing with our fears

It has to be said, though, that many people are fearful of engaging in this phase of the Doing Theology Spiral, because they feel that certain activities may expect too much of them or else challenge them in other ways. However, there are ways of helping participants overcome these fears so that they may more adventurously confront the challenge of doing theology. For example, one simple rule of thumb for a group for whom this is a brand-new exercise, is to start with very small, manageable responses and only to develop bigger and more demanding projects as time goes on. In this way, the group slowly but surely gains confidence in itself and its abilities, and does so at a steady and manageable pace. One of my greatest personal delights is that so many people tell me that through their years in the groups, they have found themselves able to undertake all sorts of tasks very successfully, even though they would have been quite frightened by any new challenge when they first joined their group. But this is only achieved if participants are given the opportunity and time to gain confidence by small and incremental steps. The groups must not be rushed. Nor must any members feel they are undertaking a step which isolates them from their colleagues. During the life of the group they will have come to know one another well and established deep and dependable friendships, and this will prove to be a great support to each member when responsive action is required.

Another helpful way to build confidence is to have the group visit other projects together so that they can see what other groups have managed to achieve. Groups frequently return from such investigative visits full of ideas and much encouraged.

A third great asset, ideal for allaying fear of action in the group, is the great treasure store of parables that Jesus told to his disciples. So many of them seem to have been specially designed to allay similar fears among his first followers. For those who fear that the challenge will be too great, there are stories about faith the size of a mustard seed, and about mountains being flung into the sea. For those who prefer to hide their talents away, there is the story of the lamp on the lamp-stand; and for those who fear that their project may not succeed, there is the parable of the sower, who goes out to sow even though he knows that not all his efforts will yield a hundredfold. He tells them to be light, salt and leaven in the lump, rather than to opt for an inactive faith. And most important of all is Jesus' challenge to his followers that those who wish to gain everything must be prepared to risk it all (Matthew 10.39).

Continuing round the spiral

So often in church life we plan projects and undertake actions but do not make sure that they are properly evaluated thereafter. Our Doing Theology Spiral saves us from this danger because we are working to a model which is not a closed circle but an ongoing action–reflection process. As it continues round for yet another cycle, our response becomes the new Experience that the group will want to Explore and Reflect upon. So the group will automatically be monitoring itself thoroughly and deciding upon yet more faithful ongoing responses.

Operating in this way offers opportunity for the group to evaluate its work, but it also encourages a celebratory atmosphere for the whole enterprise. Fun, games and parties seem to come naturally, and celebration within the context of worship is an ideal way to mark turning points in the work. When a project is about to commence, it is very good if those who are going to have special responsibilities within it are commissioned during worship for the work that lies ahead of them, and are thus assured of the prayerful support and encouragement of others. Time and again I have heard it said in such groups that despite the difficult and painful issues that a group has tried to address, there has been so very much to celebrate and for which to give thanks.

*   *   *

The previous four chapters have presented a detailed description of each phase of the Doing Theology Spiral. But I have thereby run the risk of giving the impression that the whole exercise is exceptionally complex and too wide-ranging to be manageable. It has to be said that describing a process is usually a recipe for making even a straightforward task sound rather too complicated or boring. If I were to describe on paper how I would tie a shoelace, I could soon have the reader giving up in desperation and going out to buy a pair of slip-on sandals. In order to describe what is for many a relaxed and free-flowing process, I have taken it step by step, and in a rather more systematized fashion than would be natural. I hope that this has proved helpful in providing clarity, but when a group becomes well practised in the art of doing theology, it becomes a much more free and spontaneous activity, natural and enjoyable for all.

Notes

1   Boff, Clodovis (1987), *Theology and Praxis: Epistemological Foundations*. Maryknoll: Orbis, p. 172, adds the tension between social analysis and theological reflection and describes the resultant dynamic in diagrammatic form.

2   The crucible picture is developed from an idea once again originating from the Revd Dr John Vincent at the Urban Theology Unit, Sheffield.

3   Immediately after receiving the Nobel Peace Prize in Norway in 1964, Martin Luther King addressed a meeting in Harlem, explaining that he felt that he had had a trans-figuring experience – he had been on the mountain top – but he felt now that he had to return to the valleys to see his dream fulfilled. From that point on, King became more concerned about the institutionalized urban poverty of the northern black ghettos and his mind turned to more political and structural programmes. This forms a fascinating parallel with St Luke's Gospel where, immediately after the transfiguration, Jesus sets his eyes on Jerusalem, the centre of the political and religious structures of his contem-porary society, and he travels to his destiny. In each case, the Vision has been clarified and then comes the time for responsive committed action.

4   Luther 82. *Vivendo, immo moriendo et damnando fit theologus, non intelligendo, legendo aut speculando.* WA 5.162.28.

5   Human beings must become the agents or subjects of their own history. Paulo Freire argues this strongly in (1972), *Pedagogy of the Oppressed*. Harmondsworth: Penguin, Chapters 3 and 4. Wren, Brian (1977), *Education for Justice*. London: SCM, begins his whole argument from the issue of subject–object relationships (pp. 2–8).

6   This method was designed by John Vincent, and an example of its use can be found in Green, L. (1987), *Power to the Powerless: Theology Brought to Life*. Basingstoke: Marshall Pickering, pp. 62–4.

Part 3

Thinking it Through

In these final chapters we will address the critical questions which arise from this style of doing theology. We will also see how other practical styles have been developed since the first edition of this book was published, and we will make sure that what they teach us is integrated into our theological method.

Finally, we will gather together our concern throughout the book that theology is a spiritual exercise and is most successfully undertaken in the context of prayer and a commitment to put ourselves in the presence of God in the world.

7

Challenging Implications

At the beginning of this book I questioned whether our conventional under-standings of the nature of theology were adequate, and suggested that the time was ripe for the discovery of a new way of doing theology together that would no longer be solely dependent upon those who have academic gifts to share. I have therefore offered a style of doing theology that has been largely developed alongside those who have alternative gifts to offer, and I have taken time to describe some of the details of this more action-orientated theological method. Since the first edition of this book was published, others have since offered alternative methods and styles of doing theology and I want to introduce some of them in the next chapter but, before we move on to that, it is of signal importance that we address some of the pressing questions that surface as soon as any of us seek ways to do theology.

First, then, we turn our attention to a rather thorny issue – a concern that I touched upon in an earlier chapter – namely, how we might legitimately translate something across the gap from one culture into another without gross distortion. Scholars from many disciplines refer to it as the question of 'hermeneutics' – the word coming from the same stem as the name Hermes, the messenger and 'interpreter' of the gods.

The problem of hermeneutics

Perhaps the best way to express the problem which hermeneutics represents is to recount an experience I had many years ago when attending a conference on Practical Pastoral Theology in Manchester. I had put my name down for a workshop on 'bibliodrama' – that technique of Bible study which brings our dramatic gifts of self-expression to the study of the biblical text. After an intro-duction, we were asked to choose characters from the story of Jesus stilling the storm at sea (Mark 4.35–41), in order to act out the experience of those characters as the Bible story unfolded. Coming from a long line of merchant seamen, I thought I would try my hand as one of the fishermen. We talked through the roles carefully, in twos and threes, before acting out the episode and decided that, as the storm rose, we fishermen would offer all our skill, courage and seamanship in an attempt to keep our Lord from drowning. So we acted out our story – Jesus sleeping despite the gales, and us labouring hard in a valiant effort to save him. But then someone in the action woke him up. He stood and, with a mere gesture of the hand, stilled the raging sea. We fishermen had expected to feel overwhelmed with gratitude and admiration at what he had done, but instead we were amazed to find ourselves really upset. For, at a stroke, Jesus had made our sailing skills redundant and had, by implication, made us redundant too. The only thing we had to offer was our seamanship, and he did not seem to need it. In fact, he was better off without us. We felt that next time we'd let him walk, and we told him so! It was not at all the response we had expected of ourselves.

We were so nonplussed by the experience that we really did not know what on earth to make of it. A simple piece of bibliodrama had hit us sharply with feelings and actions that had no place in the original text. We had been asked to get ourselves into role, act it out and feel our responses, and we had done that faithfully. But our responses turned out to be altogether different from what we had anticipated and we were left feeling far from comfortable. However, that episode does help to pinpoint our current problem, for what we had done to the text through our bibliodrama was to 'psychologize' it in a very twentieth-century way. We had tried to begin from our personal feelings as fishermen and had worked from there into the text, only to find that those modern feelings were at odds with what originally appears to have been the intention of the text. So the problem presents itself: should our own context or should that of the original writer take precedence in our interpretation?

When first we approach a biblical text, for example as Sunday school children, we approach it quite naturally, and naively jump happily from our own culture into the culture of the text. We are quite unaware that the first-century Palestinian culture that surrounded the original text would have been quite different from our own. But, as children, if the two cultures are at odds one with another, that is of no consequence. We recognize the passage simply as a good story and we make of it whatever we fancy, in a wholeheartedly subjective fashion. And, as children, we do just the same with the texts of the Sunday service and the hymns. On this basis, I knew a child who had named her teddy bear Lee, as a result of singing the phrase 'Glad-ly, the Cross I'd bear'. We happily laugh at the child's mistaken interpretation of the hymn's true meaning, but as adults who have a sense of how contexts and cultures differ, we would be embarrassed to make a similar mistake. So it is that we become aware that there is an immense contextual difference between an original biblical text and that of our own contemporary situation. The more we learn, the more we might begin to feel that only the highly skilled, Aramaic-speaking, theological anthropologist can even begin to get over the cultural hurdles that stand between us and the original meaning of the text! Many scholars become so aware of the cultural and linguistic gap that exists between ourselves and the biblical writers that they are very wary indeed about assuming to know what the writer of any scriptural passage may have possibly meant when it was first written.[1] And if the theologically trained preacher has only a very slim chance of understanding what the original texts actually meant to their first hearers and readers, then where on earth does that leave a busy parish priest or a group of lay folk, who simply do not have the time for such an exhaustive scholarly exercise?

This, then, is the hermeneutical problem – the problem of interpreting a text from one context into another. Even a conversation between an adult and a young person today may suffer as a consequence of the 'generation gap', so a conversation across thousands of years of world history as we read the Bible is bound to present us with a similar problem – the 'hermeneutical problem'. The Church over the last century has therefore trained its ministers to face up to some of the intricacies of the complex science of scriptural analysis we call 'biblical criticism'.[2] But, when confronted by a congregation, many ministers have thrown their college notes into the waste-paper basket in desperation, closed their eyes, crossed their fingers, and got on with preaching from the heart. Not without a tinge of guilt, they have given up on the hermeneutical challenge, and adopted a pre-scientific approach to the text and to their theology. They have constructed what I might call a naive 'rainbow of faith' across the cultural gap. By this, I mean that they adopt a preparedness to take it all on trust, without recourse to reasonable verification, relying rather on a simple and emotional 'assent'. They speak as if God has provided Christians with the hermeneutical problem as a test of their faith, which demands of the truly faithful a blind and unreasoning submission. Many Christians are happy to go along with this approach, even though we might feel that such a submissive attitude to the text is probably more Islamic in style than Judaeo–Christian.

I am glad to say, however, that many scholars suggest[3] that there are certain life-lines across the hermeneutical gap that do allow us to make connections, in all reasonableness, between our contemporary culture and our Christian heritage of treasured traditions.

The first life-line across the gap is *language*. For all its complexity, the biblical text, or any other text for that matter, cannot mean just anything we want it to mean, and the science of language has helped us to get at what some of the original meanings might have been. Our tools for translation are getting better all the time. I have, in the Appendix to this book, outlined some of the tools that the scholars will bring to the interpretation of the text, and although those tools are always in need of further refinement, they do offer real insight.

A second life-line across the gap is the fact that many Christian texts, the Bible included, are also pieces of *literature*, and as such depend upon understood conventions which writers and readers have always taken for granted. There are certain styles of writing that are appropriate to certain circumstances; for example, there will be different styles for worship, cinema scripts, newspaper columns or medical reports. Within each 'genre' or writing style there will be conventional phrases, structures of writing, and repeated protocols, all of which will be perfectly well understood by the people who are conversant with that style. If, however, we take a text originally meant as a song and give it into the hands of a person expecting a medical report, then, when they read the words 'I'm forever blowing bubbles', they may be completely bemused until they become aware of the 'genre mistake' that they have made. So it is that scholars of literature can discern from the structures of a text what genre is in use, and from that, determine at least something of its original meaning and context.

Third, we also have the practice of *spirituality* to help us bridge the hermeneutical gap between our contemporary context and the original meaning of our Christian traditions. Sometimes we are surprised to find that some of the rather archaic language can mean quite a lot to our 'spiritual ears' if they have been trained in the school of prayer. We do share this very basic and profound Christian experience with those first-century writers, and worship and meditation can build some bridges into the past at a deep level. Jungian analysis is helping us to understand how this linking may function[4] and Benedictine spirituality has long practised the art of *Lectio Divina* (Holy Reading) – a fourfold discipline of reverential reading of a biblical passage, repeating key phrases from it and then resting back into God's arms allowing the spiritual presence of God to reach out to us from the passage.

Fourth, there is no doubt that the volume and scholarly integrity of our store of *historical information* about the ancient world has come on by leaps and bounds in recent years. The work of such scholars as Crossan, Meeks, Horsley and Reed[5] has opened our eyes to everyday life in the time of Jesus and the early Church. Similar research into the history of worship, empire and economics has opened new vistas of understanding about the historical and sociological background to much of the Old and New Testaments and the history of the Christian Church. It is that sort of hard information that can help to prevent us from getting our biblical role-plays into a frightful anachronistic mess.

Some scholars will maintain that *tradition itself* is a seamless robe which stretches across the hermeneutical chasm from one culture and on into the next. Original texts have been interpreted repeatedly through the ages and these accretions of meaning have gathered around the original texts so as to become part of the community's corpus of understanding. Thus, by immersing ourselves in the tradition as it presently stands, we are merely playing our part within a living and developing organism, which reveals God's truths today as vividly as it did in first-century Palestine. It is true that this approach can, if we are not careful, rely on a rather nostalgic understanding of tradition and it can forget how profoundly our cultures have shifted over recent decades; but to remember that we are kindred spirits with those who have explored the tradition before us through the ages provides us with a strong link across the divide.

The study of *Church history* has been known to provide a tentative line across the cultural gap that divides us from our earliest traditions. This is certainly so, but this scholarly approach to the history and politics of past Church life must again be distinguished from a nostalgic use of Church tradition as some kind of infallible and authoritative interpreter to us of the early texts. We have to realize that bringing one text from an alien culture to help us to interpret a text from an ancient culture is not the same as trying to understand the contexts from which both texts derive. Such a resort to the authority of tradition may provide a spider's thread, but never a sturdy bridge across the gap that divides us from our founding documents. Good and appropriate use of Church history can nevertheless be a very helpful support to us.

Some hermeneuticists approach the question from an altogether different viewpoint. Following in the steps of scholars like Ricoeur and Schweizer[6] they judge that *a text once inscribed* takes on a life of its own and that the writer knew full well that the reader would not have any way of knowing what was in his or her own mind at the time of writing. The writer was prepared to let it go at that, hoping that we would be inspired by it nonetheless. After it is released from its original context, a text accrues to itself 'surplus meaning', and so the interpretations through the ages become as fascinatingly a part of the meaning of the text as that which was originally intended. This approach allows the traditional stories to live for themselves, acknowledging that there can be no interpretation of a biblical text that is absolutely faithful to its original meaning while at the same time being totally relevant to our modern context.

In the face of that challenge, the approach opts for contemporary relevance rather than faithfulness to its original meaning, on the reasonable assumption that the person who originally released the text to be read knew that that was how it would have to be. However, many unwittingly adopt this approach without being aware of its inherent risks. The danger of this 'story telling' approach to the traditions of our faith is brought home to us in the admonition not to 'tell stories'. The reason that stories have not always been trusted is that a story can leave us with no way of verifying whether or not the story is true or simply based in fantasy. The problem therefore becomes one of authority, for if we allow our traditions of faith to be interpreted in this subjective fashion, we are simply deciding for ourselves what is true. We could, however, have come to that same subjective interpretation without any recourse whatsoever to the text in the first place – it is simply our own idea injected into the text. On this basis, even a fascist would have to be allowed to adopt a racist interpretation of the text, for as once was said, 'everyone would be their own Pope'.

In the light of our concern to bridge the hermeneutical gap with integrity and at the same time to recognize its inherent difficulty, the method of doing theology which I have espoused in these pages seeks to integrate the very best from each of the approaches I have here described. I have chosen a method which gives free rein to our imagination, allowing us to take elements from the Christian tradition and connect them spontaneously with our present explored experience. But I have also introduced into the theological spiral the conventional disciplines of theology so they can help to 'check out' what our inspired intuitions have generated. This methodology then places the reader (or role-player for that matter) at a crossroads, forced to make a decision now in the context of their own culture, so that their life may play its part in writing the next page in the text of the Good News. She thereby becomes a gospeller herself and a living carrier of the tradition rather than merely a recipient of it. And, after all, was this not the original purpose of the biblical writers? Surely the evangelists did not merely write in order to record an archive about Jesus, but to present to the readers and hearers a fresh moment, a contemporary challenge, and a new yearning.[7]

The question of authority

This debate about the hermeneutical problem therefore leads us back into the issue of authority, for the question still remains: How do we know whether we have read into the text what we prefer to see there, rather than what is in fact really there? For it may be that the experiential style of our theology has made us cavalier with the text, ignoring its internal integrity and its original meaning. In traditional biblical scholarship our usual intention is to be guided out from the text to an interpreted understanding, whereas the methods we are espousing run the risk of allowing us to read into the text from our own subjective ideas – ideas that were not originally there. However, in passing, it is fascinating to see that the New Testament evangelists delighted in just this sort of subjective use of the Hebrew scriptures. St Matthew, for example, knowingly takes certain Old Testament passages way beyond their original intention and is quite content to read his own meanings into the text (e.g. Matthew 1.23 and 2.15, 18 and 23).

We can begin to explore this question of authority by looking again at my experience of acting out the story of the Storm on the Lake. You will remember the unexpected responses of those who were acting as fishermen and how their responses seemed far from the intention of the original text. However, as the participants discussed the experience afterwards, it led them into an intensely helpful examination of the nature of miracle. The fishermen's discontent with Jesus' intervention prompted the question of whether miracles, if taken to be historically true, might be said to plunge us back into the chaos from which God at creation initially saved us. If the order of creation is suddenly upset by a miracle, does that negate the order which God first wrought, even if that upset is itself caused by the creator? That discussion was fascinating and extremely helpful to all who took part, but we could not legitimately have then taken the scriptural story of the Storm on the Lake as some sort of authorization for our findings. The actors' anger at Jesus was, in the context of our Manchester conference, perfectly authentic, but the actors' anger was nowhere to be found in the original text. A participative approach to theology does not make it legitimate to pretend that things are in the text that really are not, but it does allow the text to raise up for us very important questions of faith and prompts us to transformative actions. It has that relevance and authority (and much more, as we shall see).

We must presume from all that has gone before, that the biblical writers were, like us, engaged in a dynamic and creative exercise. They too were selecting from living stories that were carried within their community of faith and drawing ideas from them which seemed authentic for the situation and context in which they lived and in which they wrote. But they, like us, had certain safety nets under them to save them from straying too far into total subjectivity. They, like us, did not do their theology in isolation from the group, but were themselves members of the fellowship of faith, and no doubt that fellowship restrained them if they seemed to be straying too far from the community's shared understandings. It is exactly the same for us, as we too are 'checked out' by our membership of the fellowship of faith. But saying this is not to deny the importance of objectivity, but it is to take very seriously the fact that humanity only knows things through subjective experience of them, and therefore we have to accept that the subjective element must always be quite fundamental in any human knowing. The difficulty is compounded when we recall that it can, on occasion, be a prophetic minority group, going against the collective mind and interpretation, that can sometimes put the wider society back on course. I would argue therefore that it is the collective solidarity of the believing group (the *koinonia* fellowship) that can make all the difference. Add to that the fact that we have at our disposal all the modern tools of historical criticism and scientific scholarship, then we do have strong criteria against which to judge our subjective interpretations. That is why we have built these additional tools into our spiral method of doing theology.

Setting the agenda

The Doing Theology Spiral is sometimes accused of allowing the world primacy over Scripture by virtue of the fact that it requires the contextual situation to be Experienced and Explored prior to later theological Reflection, when those resultant findings are brought at last into confrontation with the Christian traditions. Surely, it is argued, the Christian should let the Bible set the agenda so that the world can be conformed to its mandates – not the other way around. In response to this concern, it is first of all necessary to remember that God is in the world as well as in the Bible. God is to be found there, setting our agenda in God's world, and God is to be discerned and obeyed within that world. This is how it was possible for Christians to live faithfully in Christ even before the New Testament texts were written. The Doing Theology Spiral allows us to look for God in God's world just as much as it allows us to seek God in the Bible.

Second, we need to recognize that Jesus was quite antagonistic to those of his contemporaries who chose to take their lead from the religious traditions and from Scripture rather than let the Scriptures interpret their contemporary situation. Jesus is recorded as having called the Pharisees 'hypocrites' (Matthew 15.7) precisely for this reason. According to the evangelist, the Pharisees and Sadducees had uncritically sought to superimpose the scriptural traditions upon Israel, rather than listen first for God's present response to the suffering needs of God's people in the world.[8]

Third, as the group proceeds around the Doing Theology Spiral my hope is that conventional, academic theology should stand back during the Exploration phase as much as possible so that the secular disciplines, such as sociology, history and urbanology, may be allowed to do what conventional theology cannot do – that is, analyse the data and name some of the causal relationships within the situation. After the secular disciplines have done their work, theological reflection is thereafter able to look for transcendent presence and meaning – a task that those secular disciplines simply cannot perform. We acknowledge that different disciplines are given to us by God to do different things – I would not attempt to use the discipline of psychology to mend a motorcycle, nor do I wish theology to describe the internal workings of a local government department. However, once a situation has been thus described by the appropriate discipline, I do then expect theology to understand it and interpret it – perhaps even to reinterpret it prophetically. So the Doing Theology Spiral diagram acknowledges the prior order of other disciplines over theology, but affirms the authority of theology as primary when it comes to the more important task of helping to discern God's presence with us in our experience.[9] So when we begin our theological work from experience rather than the Bible I am in no way seeking to imply that the Scriptures have no authority for us, but I do maintain that Christ died for the world, not the Bible – the Bible is there to help us understand God's action in the world but not to be our prime focus. Christ's prime focus was not a biblical text, but the presence and action of God in the world, and so it must remain ours too.

The model of doing theology that I have proposed does not foster the creation of a single theological corpus. My model encourages the development of many different groups operating at all sorts of levels, each working out its own local theology by bringing its own experience together with the faith traditions. A profusion of groups would inevitably lead to a proliferation of theological insights, and I would take that resultant diversity and plurality as an indicator of life and growth within the Church. Such an array would represent the great variety of gifts and functions that are there within the body of Christ (1 Corinthians 12) and would be a sign of the abundant diversity of the grace of God, active in Christ's Church. This diversity usually causes great anxiety among those who want to see the Church as an institution of control. This pressure to conform to a unity without diversity adds a political slant to the question of authority, for if many local theologies are spawned, who is to tell where truth ultimately resides? We are required as a consequence to frame afresh the question of biblical authority thus: 'Who is it in the Church who should have the power to decide what the Bible means for today?'

Who should do theology?

The people who are best placed to do theology, and to tell the Church what our Scriptures mean for us today, are those who know God best, and 'God is known in proportion as he is loved', not in proportion to our erudition, nor the validity of our ordination. So the academic and the ordained have no special claim to be our best theologians. It seems to me that theology, this privileged instrument of the Church, should be in the hands of the whole Christian community acting together and incorporating into its deliberations the special experiences of many different types of Christian people. This calls for an 'every member ministry' or 'lay apostolate'. Nor does this mean that the laity should share the vicar's ministry, but that every Christian has a vocation to discipleship – and a responsibility to be theological by virtue of their baptism. Vocation, ministry and theology belong together to all of the people of God. The question that the Church therefore has to struggle with through each generation is, in what way should the inevitable diversity of an incarnate Church be held together in unity? How do we 'discern the Body'? This is the perennial question.

I have argued that vocation, ministry and theology belong to all Christians by virtue of their baptism, but I would also affirm that in pursuance of each of these responsibilities – and also in order for us to hold together as a family – there will be specialists who help to promote and focus each of these aspects of Christian life. In the theological sphere there should be those who immerse themselves in the Christian faith traditions – some seeing themselves primarily as 'technicians' who encounter the complexities of the texts, the histories, languages and so on, using all the scientific and critical tools available to them to do their work. Their task is to excavate the traditions, that they may be put at the disposal of those who are seeking to 'do' theology. In addition to these theological technicians, there will be others who seek to act as bridge-builders, making the connections between these specialist researchers of the theological traditions and those doing theology in the field. These bridge builders will need to have a number of special skills and a great deal of sensitivity. I like to call these enablers, the 'People's Theologians',[10] and I suggest that their task is fourfold.

The People's Theologians

First, the People's Theologian works within and as a member of the group, and will have a role somewhat akin to the animator in community work, whose task is to provide appropriate learning exercises and opportunities for the group members to take up their responsibilities and to make their own decisions. This will call for all the skills of the adult educator. Bibliodrama, expressive arts, charting, brainstorming and so much more – all these will be elements of the repertoire which the People's Theologian can offer.

Second, in order to fulfil this role, the People's Theologians will need to be soaked in the tradition sufficiently to be able to draw upon it liberally and to know what the theological technicians are saying about it. If they have imbibed the fruits of theological scholarship, they will be better able to check out the imaginative leaps the group makes. But the People's Theologian will never have the final judgement in anything, for that authority must always remain with the group itself. They will have a responsibility to be servants of the Christian faith tradition and not controllers of it. There has been, it must be said, a tendency both in human relationships training and in participative Bible study for specialists to make great claims for themselves and their expertise, and the People's Theologians will be under the same pressure to forget that they are only there as servants. This will call for considerable spiritual depth.

Third, the People's Theologians must have integrity among the poor and be acceptable to them. We might say that such theologians need more street cred than restaurant presence, and the acquisition of this integrity will very often require an option for downward social mobility on their part, and a preparedness to learn the language of the downtrodden – if it is not already their mother tongue. Only then will the People's Theologians be able to help their group see society from the perspective of the marginalized, and to communicate with members of groups who find themselves in those situations.

Finally, the People's Theologians must affirm the theological responsibilities and abilities of the group and never allow a group or its members to give the theological task away to others. It is in the nature of oppression that the oppressed begin to think in the same categories as the oppressors, and so group members will themselves believe what they have been told for so long – that they are not academic enough to handle theology nor 'ordained enough' to be theologians. So the People's Theologian must be constantly vigilant lest he or she be considered by participants as the only theologian in the group. Each and every group member will be bringing specific gifts to the shared theological task – so they must own that they are all theologians together.

Very often the local ordained minister will in fact prove to be the People's Theologian for a group, for he or she will have spent many years studying the work of the specialist theological technicians, will know their own local context and be at home with the local people, trusted and welcomed by them. It is important, therefore, that all clergy have learnt how to put themselves at the disposal of those who wish to engage contextually in the Doing Theology Spiral.

Notes

1 The possibility of unearthing the original words of Jesus is hotly argued. See for example, Franklin, Eric (1982), *How the Critics Can Help*. London: SCM.

2 Reference to the first section of the Appendix will indicate something of the style and content of this scientifically orientated approach to biblical analysis.

3 In the argument that follows, I am indebted to Professor Frances Young's unpublished lecture on the subject, delivered at Birmingham University, on 10 November 1984.

4 See, for example, Christopher Bryant's (1983), *Jung and the Christian Way*. London: Darton, Longman and Todd.

5 There is so much new archaeological and historical research bearing fruit at present that it is difficult to point to only a few scholars, but note, for example: Crossan, J. and Reed, J. (2001), *Excavating Jesus: Beneath the Stones, Behind the Texts*. London: SPCK; Meeks, W. (1983), *The First Urban Christians*. Yale University Press; Horsley, R. and Silberman, N. (1977), *The Message and the Kingdom: How Jesus and Paul Ignited a Revolution and Transformed the Ancient World*. New York: Grosset/Putnam. See also, Gottwald, Norman (1979), *The Tribes of Yahweh*. Maryknoll: Orbis; Tidball, Derek (1983), *An Introduction to the Sociology of the New Testament*. Exeter: Paternoster Press; and Kee, Howard Clark (1980), *Christian Origins in Sociological Perspective*. London: SCM.

6 The opening chapters of *Jesus* by Schweizer, Edward (1971), London: SCM, give a simple and clear indication of this style of approach which respects the integrity of the text and at the same time allows the Spirit ready access to our interpretative process through our concerns for present issues. See also Ricoeur, Paul (1980), *Essays on Biblical Interpretation*. Philadelphia: Fortress Press.

7 See the introductory pages of Davies, John D. and Vincent, John J. (1986), *Mark at Work*. London: Bible Reading Fellowship.

8 The biblical account of Jesus' arguments with the Pharisees caricatures the Pharisees rather unfairly, but the point still stands and is carefully argued by Segundo, Juan Luis (1977) in *The Liberation of Theology*. Dublin: Gill & Macmillan.

9 'The ultimate reason why theology follows social analysis is that the understanding of the sense of a fact can be satisfactorily effectuated only on the basis of an explication of the fact in question from a point of departure in its internal, "profane" structure . . . It will take everything as a reading text to be deciphered in accord with the "syntax" of faith' (Boff, Clodovis (1987), *Theology and Praxis: Epistemological Foundations*. Maryknoll: Orbis, pp. 85–6). See also the often quoted words of Segundo, 'Any and every theological question begins with the human situation. Theology is "the second step".' Segundo, Juan Luis (1977), *The Liberation of Theology*. Dublin: Gill & Macmillan, p. 79.

10 Such enablers are sometimes referred to as 'pastoral theologians' in the literature and practice of Latin American Liberation Theology, but the word 'pastoral' is a specialist Roman Catholic word and may not be understood by others. Perhaps also, the meaning of the word is not very obvious to those from more heavily urbanized communities. See Michael Taylor's fine paper in *Putting Theology to Work*, ed. Derek Winter, British Council of Churches (1980), pp. 17ff.

8

Other Styles of Theologizing

I first studied theology at London University in the 1960s and vividly recall receiving back one of my essays from the professor, upon which he had written, 'Keep your own emotions out of your theology young man.' I'm sure we have all progressed significantly since then, but the incident does alert us to the fact that different people prefer different styles of theological method. It may be, for example, that the reader found my indulgence in methodological detail in Chapters 3 to 6 simply not for them, and decided to skip a chapter or two. Reading the detail made it difficult for them to see how the whole thing fits together smoothly and naturally. For another reader, if they were of my own temperament, the detail would have opened up the method and made it come alive for them. Someone else will have been excited to think that theology can include drama and group activities, while another will be fearful of any such tactile game-playing. It takes all sorts to make a world, and we can thank God for that, but that fact leaves us with a problem. Different people will be attracted to certain styles of theology because of their personal temperament, while others will be attracted to other styles of theology because of their own pre-ferred style of learning. I have mentioned already that when working in a group it is important to make sure that we use a great variety of styles and method-ologies so that all can feel there is something there which works well for them.

In this chapter I want to introduce a selection of other styles of doing theology, with the expectation that the reader will 'shop around' a little, not simply in order to find the style that suits them best, but even more hopefully, so that they can introduce into the Doing Theology Spiral any elements which they feel would benefit its operation. I offer the theological spiral as a skeleton upon which all sorts of preferred approaches can be hung, so do feel free to adapt it in whatever way helps you in the theological endeavour.

In an attempt to make the theological jungle a little more negotiable I will set out the various theological styles using three modes of categorization, although the reader will find on closer scrutiny that grouping theological approaches into categories always does less than justice to each. Nevertheless, it seems to me that the different styles of theology will largely derive from, first, the role that the theologian is asked to play in society; second, the particular temperament with which the theologian comes at the task; and third, how they see God impacting upon their experience. Let's look first at how theological style can so much depend upon the role that we are asking it to play.

1. Styles deriving from role

David Tracy, in his book *The Analogical Imagination*,[1] suggests that, just as a writer will use very different literary styles to suit different audiences, so too we can spot three very different audiences for the theologian – the Church, the college and the wider society – and each will influence the style of theology used. First, when theology is done for church members, we can expect a systematic kind of approach, using the traditions of the Church and especially Scripture, as an assumed authority. The theologian will be seeking to help other Christians to see ways of living out their responsibilities in the world in the light of the faith they already profess. It may be that new meanings will be suggested, but only about a faith that the hearers already hold dear. Next however, if the theology is being done in the context of the theological department of a university, then the style will have to be very different. The hearers there will assume nothing until the theologian explains it and demonstrates it in a logically coherent manner. It will not be possible to assume that the students accept the authority of Scripture or Church tradition or even that there is a God, and rather than trying to build up their Christian life, theology in that context will be seeking to argue by philosophical means the validity of the religious statements being made.

As well as the Church and the Academy, Tracy suggested that a third audience for the theologian is to be found in the wider society – the public domain. For public consumption, theology will need to be of a rather practical nature, pointing out the ethical dilemmas and challenges in today's world, offering some value-laden critique and suggested action for a better society. These three different audiences, Tracy argues, will demand three different theological styles. Given these three very different roles which have to be played by the theologian, we might not expect the resultant theology to be the same, although we would still hope for some underlying coherence across the board.

I would like to suggest, however, that the three 'audiences' which Tracy names are not the only ones to which theology is addressed. Indeed, I want to propose that there are at least four more, and in each case a different style of theological method will be appropriate.

i. The personal walk with God

Some theological methods clearly derive from an internal dialogue, where the audience is one's own soul. It is a style of theology which is concerned mainly with one's own religious experience. Here the theologian adopts the role of the seeker after personal spiritual wisdom, meditating and reflecting upon the inner burdens and challenges of the soul as it guides the life and decision-making of the Christian from within. Bernard Lonergan[2] uses the image of a pair of scissors, the upper blade (one's experience of one's self) cutting across the lower blade (one's experience of God), both blades acting together to cut their way through the business of life.

Patricia O'Connell Killen and John de Beer have offered a full theological methodology designed to help the individual gain religious insight in this personal way. In their book, *The Art of Theological Reflection*[3] published in 1994, they first entreat the reader to eschew self-assurance or dogmatism and open themselves up to an attitude of exploration. They invite us to select one of life's experiences and step back into it in our imagination. The chosen experience may be a particular life situation, a personal conviction or even a Bible text, and we explore that experience very personally and gently by slowing it down in our imagination and then concentrating on our feelings as we focus in. They suggest that first the encounter with the experience and then the encounter with our feelings about it will spontaneously issue in an 'image' which symbolizes the fullness of the experience – or as they term it, the 'heart of the matter'. The image can be a mind picture or an imaginary sound, flavour or sensation, and because an image is not precise, it encourages multiple reflections and moves us on to a new point of sensitivity drawn from the experience. In our imagination we ask if God is close to us as we explore the image, if there is healing necessary for it or if the image speaks to us of wholeness. Killen and de Beer now suggest that the image – symbolizing the heart of the matter – will also elicit themes, texts or other snippets from our Christian tradition and they encourage us to allow God into our reflections upon those Christian treasures in the same way. We then open up a conversation in our hearts, or within an intimate group, between the meaning of the images and the meaning of the themes or snippets from the Christian heritage. We look for similarities or differences between them so that a theme emanates from the juxtaposition of the two, and from this we find that a profound realization strikes us personally and deeply. We may wish to write down what the implications are for our lives – what changes we may make or what different beliefs or attitudes we may come away with from the exercise. In this way Killen and de Beer's book offers us a model for reflecting with our own soul upon the things of God and building an inner 'spiritual wisdom' as Christian believers. According to this style of doing theology the theologian meditates upon their own personal journey with God.

ii. The awareness of identity

Having grown up in a poor working-class environment within a class-ridden Britain at the end of the Second World War, I found myself very much a fish out of water when I entered the educational world of a British university. I was at a loss to understand the 'officer class' culture of effortless superiority that then surrounded me. I was angered and envious, deskilled and argumentative. After three years immersed in British academia I travelled to New York to continue my studies, and that gave me opportunity to step back from the fray and reflect upon what had happened to me. I arrived in the USA at the height of the Civil Rights Movement and, by listening to my black student colleagues tell their stories, I was given new tools with which to analyse and understand my own British class experience. Since then we have all been greatly assisted by feminist theologians as they too have looked at their own experience of being women in a male-dominated world, and then have spoken out theologically from that perspective. Whenever a group which has been exploited seeks to analyse the hidden implications of that exploitation, there arises for them a new understanding of identity, belonging and power, and this in turn opens up new insights into humanity and fresh insights about God.

At present the theological world is very excited by what have been called postcolonial studies[4] – 'post', not to mean that colonial attitudes are a thing of the past, but 'post' to indicate how we may hear the stories of those who were oppressed by empire and explore how that dynamic still operates in so many ways. Imperialism has impacted upon the Bible – from the enslavement of the Hebrew nation by the Egyptian Empire, to the brave epistles of St Paul as he awaited trial at the hands of the Roman hegemony. Imperialism has been an implicit force in the spread of Christianity across the world in the wake of the British and American imperial surges. And now those who were once colonized are finding a voice and asking penetrating questions of that brand of theology which has emanated from Europe and America and which has dominated the intellectual life of the Church around the world until now. These insights into more recent history alert us to the dynamics of earlier pivotal and foundational events in the history of our faith. We are, for example, prompted to ask if the texts of the Tanach (the Old Testament) have come down to us unscathed by the hand of elitist groups. They ask why it might be that the New Testament offers such a male voice when it is evident that Jesus surrounded himself with so many vocal female followers. These and other biblical issues are being newly addressed by the postcolonial scholars.[5] As well as bringing a postcolonial critique to biblical studies, they ask questions about Jesus' hybrid nature as both God and Human and they do so from the perspective of the hybrid experience of those who feel neither one thing nor another because of their colonized experience – be they an African-American, or a Filipino whose very country bears the name of a Spanish king. They ask questions about the nature of mission and the expectation that those colonized by mission should mimic the colonizer rather than find God from their own culture and context.

But while Postcolonial Theology is still in its infancy, thus far it is perhaps Feminist Theology which has affected theology more obviously of late. Women theologians have sought to become ever more conscious and discerning with regard to the place women have had in our societies, and have offered that perspective as an oppressed group to the wider theological endeavour. Women like Rosemary Radford Ruether, Kwok Pui-lan, Mary Daly and others, have shown us how sexism around the world has impacted the life and witness of the Church through the ages. Their method has been, first, to discover among themselves the commonality of their experiences of the distortions of life at the hands of sexism. Groups of women have listened with rapt attention to their sisters until they have empowered them by their positive regard – 'hearing one another to speech'.[6] Having been systematically silenced themselves, they now begin to search the faith traditions to see where in the formation of our foundational documents the voice of women (and other oppressed groups) may also have been systematically silenced. Ann Loades speaks of 'finding lost coins'[7] in the tradition – as feminist theologians have reconstructed from hidden fragments of the text clear indications of the early Church as a subversive egalitarian community in which women exercised a very full leadership.[8] They have adopted a phrase from Habermas – 'a hermeneutic of suspicion' – to indicate that it is no longer acceptable simply to take the traditional interpretations of the text, nor the texts themselves, as indicative of the original event. All sorts of power-dynamics were at play in the formation of our Christian tradition, and feminists have helped to design critical tools to excavate beneath the present interpretations and unearth the original revelation. Finally, from their new awareness, feminist theologians have offered the Church altogether new insights into the nature of God, God's ways with us, and a commitment to a distinctive way of doing theology. Feminist theologians offer us a style of theology which emanates from their experience of themselves as a particular oppressed group in the wider Church. Postcolonial theologians speak from experience of being oppressed or from knowing that they have themselves played their part in the oppression. They all offer a style of theologizing which derives from a clearer appreciation of their own identity within society.

iii. Training for ministry

We have considered theologians who focus on their role as an individual soul before God and those theologians who have spoken from among those who share common experiences one with another. Now we look to those who play a distinctive role within their faith community. Those who are educated for a leadership role in the Church are trained in specific pastoral skills, steeped in the traditions of the faith's heritage, and enter into a process of what the Church calls 'formation'. Edward Farley in his book *Theologia*[9] referred to the fact that the earliest theologians of the Church thought of theology not as a system of doctrines to be handed down, but as 'the wisdom proper to the life of the believer'. They saw religious knowledge as that deep learned sense of how to exist in the world as Christians before God.[10] This is a way of life, a breathing in and out of the faith day by day, which is learned by immersing oneself in the biblical, liturgical and devotional traditions of the faith. It is a training which develops a Christian 'character' born of attaining, God-willing, the 'mind of Christ' (1 Corinthians 2.2). Edward Farley referred to this deep theological education as 'Habitus' – attaining over time the 'habit' of devotion and grace which is God's gift to us. On visiting the English College in Rome it was clear that the routines and the communal life of the seminary – which extends for seven years of residential training – are designed to instil the 'habitus' required of the Roman Catholic priest. Lifestyle, daily rule and the constant presence of the institution, all played their part in 'forming' the character of the ordinands.

James and Evelyn Whitehead are consultants in ministry education, based in Indiana. Their book, *Methods in Ministry*,[11] presents a careful methodology for Church leaders which they believe to be 'portable, performable, and communal'. It is a dynamic model which considers very carefully Christian tradition, personal experience and cultural resources. Its method is to take each of these in turn and listen with great discipline, not seeking to bring God *into* the experience but letting God speak *from* it, and to give this 'attention' with an ascetic expectancy and patience. So, for example, as a passage of scripture is attended to, we learn of its place in history, in liturgy, its moment of composition and how it has been used by the Church through the ages. Likewise,

God's revelation is registered through attentive listening to a personal or communal experience of God. Third, the same attention is paid to the cultural infrastructure which brings our experiences to us. We reflect upon how the context in which we live affects the subject at issue – be the subject a passage of scripture, doctrine or a personal experience. As this theological process develops, the role of pastor or leader comes to the fore because we are now asked by the Whiteheads to 'assert', forthrightly but without violation, the faith insights that come to us from the juxtaposition of these three elements of Tradition, Experience and Culture. Because the faith tradition is normative for the Christian community, in this style of theology, Christian leaders-in-training learn to speak to it and from it – struggling with each experience from the standpoint of faith. The Whiteheads offer examples of how this method can be used to assist ministers in their work with congregations or with parish professionals and prompts them to acknowledge always their responsibility to let theology be a lively tool in the life of their local church. The Whiteheads thus offer an example of how theology may be tailored to suit the inculcation of a theological 'habitus' for leadership ministry in the Church.

iv. The Church in society

The theologian's role is in no way restricted to the part we play within our own group nor to our leadership role within our own faith community. We must also find our role within the society which is all around us and act out our response to that by belonging to it both thankfully and critically. The British theologian, Duncan Forrester,[12] draws our attention to the fact that as Christians we can look at the world in two ways; like Aristotle and Aquinas we can look with wonder at God's beautiful creation and, seeing that it is essentially good, adjust our human behaviour accordingly; or like Hegel or even Marx, we can come at the world from a sense of despair and dissatisfaction, determined to put the world right so that humankind can flourish. David Tracy[13] takes up this thought and refers to the two approaches as, first, the 'analogical imagination' – wondering at the perfections of the world around us and the graciousness of God in its creation – and second, the 'dialectical imagination' – the determination to help transform the world because of its distortion and sinfulness. Most Christians feel the truth of both claims[14] and paradoxically extol the perfection of nature while still acknowledging its imperfections. This being the case, we have to determine how we as Christians should relate to the world, and especially to the cultures and societies that surround us – are we to act as their affirming 'chaplain' or as their critical 'prophet'? To answer this pressing question we need the resource of an adequate method of theologizing about our relationship with the world – what has come to be known as 'Practical Theology'.[15]

We certainly have many tools to understand the world, for just as in ancient and biblical times the great myths were the template through which we viewed its great issues, so today we have the natural and social sciences to provide a framework from which to observe and understand society. Developing an idea from the British philosopher Gilbert Ryle,[16] Clifford Geertz[17] in 1973 developed ways to offer a 'thick description of culture', whereby all the scientific disciplines are brought to bear upon a particular culture so that we might describe it from every aspect. He particularly helped us to see culture as an array of signs which enable the human being to make sense of the world around, and showed us that by observing these cultural signs we can unearth the values and meanings by which a particular people live their cultural lives together. The theologian then has to create tools to evaluate those values and meanings in the light of the Christian faith and make decisions about how to enter into that cultural world and relate to it.

Using this style of theological method, the Christian will be assisted in answering significant critical questions. For example, in mission, 'are we to enter into a particular mission field assuming that God is antagonistic to that culture, or by expecting to find God already within it?' Again, 'How are we to speak out in the public square on questions of public ethics and moral well-being from a Christian perspective?' 'What will we have to say about abortion, ecology, nakedness or headscarves?' And again, some will ask what a 'Christian' perspective could possibly be once it has been denuded of its particular cultural overlays – are certain Christian values somehow independent of the culture which first defined them? As we shall see later in this chapter, how we decide to respond to these questions will have crucial consequences, but it is clear even now that this style of doing theology is very different from, for example, a theology which concentrates on our personal walk with God.

2. Styles informed by learning preferences

The theological cake can be sliced up in many different ways. We have so far looked at the way in which different theological styles have developed in accordance with the role we are asking theology to play. We have looked at how theology has been made to help us understand our own inner walk with God, our role as a member of a group in society, our role in the Church, and our role in society. We can, however, come at the various theological styles from a different perspective and investigate how different methodologies have arisen in relation to our own particular temperaments and preferred learning styles.

In 1980, Walter Wink[18] made popular, in Bible study circles, the realization that the human brain has allotted particular types of task to each of its hemispheres. The left side of the brain deals largely with the more pragmatic and logical tasks such as mathematics, whereas the right side is more artistic, allowing us to make music, write poetry and create emotional drama. Wink then explained that most of us will have a preference for working from just one side, so our preferred theological style will be strongly influenced by that.

Again, the psychiatrist Jung offered the insight that human beings can be largely motivated from within themselves as 'introverts', or energized by the company of others – those he labelled 'extroverts'. Yet again, we have already mentioned Kolb's realization that some people seemed more at home with one element of his learning cycle than others.[19] Educational psychologists build on such theories to explain why it might be that different human beings have a propensity to learn in very different ways. The most popular of these constructs remains undoubtedly that created by Myers and Briggs – based largely on Jung's work.[20] Any theological group would do well to undertake one of their workshop sessions to investigate the temperaments of each of their members using the Myers-Briggs Type Indicator. Understanding what sort of temperament others in the group have, helps the dynamics of the group and also indicates which members will flourish with which tasks. Some will be organizers, some imaginative thinkers, others will be very concerned for the group's well-being, while others will be maverick and ready to try anything. They all have their place in the working of a successful group and in the creation of a dynamic theology.

Different styles of theology, to some extent, emanate from different human temperaments and, without trying to be too prescriptive, I am going to sketch out how I think that might present itself. In doing so I am building on the categories suggested by Elaine Graham, Heather Walton and Frances Ward in their fine book, *Theological Reflection: Methods*.[21] They set out seven different theological styles and, although the writers do not make this connection, some of the styles they catalogue seem to me to follow from certain temperamental preferences. The first method on their list they call, Theology by Heart, or 'the living human document'.

i. The living human document

This style recognizes that God can be experienced as personal and intimate, speaking through the interiority of human experience. It therefore finds expression in very personal autobiographies, the greatest theological example being the *Confessions of St Augustine*,[22] in which Augustine spills out the story of his life before God, repenting of his failures and acknowledging that God is nearer to him than he is to himself. Other theologians offer their personal letters, John Wesley offers his journals, others verbatim accounts of therapy, and the Hebrew Psalms often spill out from the psalmist's ruminations on their own inner life with God. So we might expect this style to appeal especially to a theologian with the internal energy of the introvert. It is as if the writer's audience is largely intended to be only God and the writer, but the theology is then released to the world in the expectation that others may be served by reading what has been going on in the hidden life of one who has taken time to meditate upon their own journey with God. The writer seems to have become a living document of faith experience.

ii. Constructing stories

Here the imaginative flair of the right side of the brain is given leave to create narratives with purpose. Jesus grew up in a world where the telling of purposeful stories was a fundamental of his culture – a trait which continues to this day in Jewish communities. Through the ages, rabbis have read the words of the Tanach (the Old Testament) and, with a spirit of theological freedom, made up stories which open up the possibilities of the given sacred text.[23] The *aggadot* stories, some down to earth and some quite fanciful, were brought together around the original text to become the famous 'Midrash', now a fundamental element of the tradition of the Hebrew people. Jesus stands in this creative tradition, telling his Parables of the Kingdom, each tale constructed to open us to God's purposes.[24]

John Bunyan, imprisoned in 1660 amidst the religious turmoil that surrounded the restoration of the English monarchy, wrote a fantastic tale modelled on his own faith journey in which the pilgrim finds his way eventually to full salvation. His *Pilgrim's Progress* is a fine example of a theology created by one whose inspired imagination and creative temperament has been given full rein. In our own day, the Indian Jesuit, Father Anthony de Mello, has published many books of inspirational little stories which thrust us deep into the truths of the faith. As he says, 'the shortest distance between a human being and truth is a story.'[25]

iii. Acting out the Mind of Christ

For the person who is not energized by theory and abstraction, this method of theologizing offers the opportunity to act out radically in practice what the Christian tradition inspires and mandates us to do. For such a person, if they should seep themselves in the Scriptures and in prayer, there can come a moment when they feel they must shape and transform their life to conform with their reading of the Christian tradition. Famously, St Francis heard the Scriptures, threw off his privileged life and began to build the Church afresh. St Ignatius Loyola, the founder of the Jesuits, writing from his own experience, told us how to undertake 'spiritual exercises' that will allow us to follow in Francis' footsteps, meditatively reliving the story of Jesus so that we can imagine ourselves into the story and then seek ways to keep acting that out in our lives.[26] So theology of this sort is acted out in our life not only because we have become imbued with 'the mind of Christ' (1 Corinthians 2.16) but also have the temperament and adventurous self-discipline to make our lives an acted theology of God in the world.

iv. Living the Body of Christ

Those who gain inner energy from being with others are more temperamentally prone to act out the Mind of Christ in their lives in company with others. Often in Christian history those who acted out their faith in these graphic personal ways may well themselves have been 'loners', but they nevertheless attracted the attention of others who then gathered around them and formed a Christian community. St Benedict lived the life of the hermit until the community that gathered around him desired of him a Rule by which they could live life together – and so the western monastic tradition was begun. Bonhoeffer's little gem, *Life Together*,[27] offers a picture of how a small community can act out what it is to be the Body of Christ in a modern world, while the Base Ecclesial Communities of Latin America have been a source of encouragement to all who wish to learn from these radical and reflective communities of the poor.[28]

v. Speaking out about God

This style of theology seeks to speak about God using the thought forms of the present age, and will prove attractive to many temperaments. The analytical observer will enjoy describing society carefully, and will then be helped by the reflective and imaginative person to consider how the truths about God can best be discerned by those within that culture. Aquinas, says David Tracy, was a person of an 'analogical imagination' who saw no great contradiction between God's self-revelation and the natural order around him, and so was able to speak of the things of God using the philosophical categories of Aristotle. St Paul himself had similarly looked carefully around Athens so that when speaking in public at the Areopagus he could base his sermon on the Greek thought forms of his audience (Acts 17.22–31). As a young man, I attended a lecture by the great theologian Paul Tillich,[29] who was very enamoured of the existentialist philosophy which was then all the rage, and so he maintained that we could engage modern understanding by talking of God as 'the ground of our being'.

It is said by some that those who prefer this approach to theology are not sufficiently critical of the culture that surrounds them and that they should, instead, rail against society's ills and shortcomings rather than simply use the contemporary culture as a ready vehicle for the propagation of the gospel. Those who have that more prophetic temperament might prefer to engage with what Elaine Graham calls value-committed, theology-in-action.

vi. Value-committed action

This style of theology, which I have described in this book, is for those whose temperament inspires them to see their thinking cashing-out in practice, but who also have a deep need to reflect upon what they are doing. The nub of this style of theology is performance and, just as a theatre performance calls upon the skills of many, so this method calls upon the many temperaments of a group – although, as we have suggested, it can be attempted by a person acting alone if they are able to bring many aspects of themselves to the task.

This theological style is also committed to the transformation of society in favour of the marginalized and so appeals to the person who has a real heart for the poor. It is a reaching out to those who are told by society that they are not of concern to God,[30] and is an active critique of the society which demeans certain of God's children. This style is, therefore, for people who have a prophetic edge and a warm heart.

vii. Theology with a local accent

This style, says Elaine Graham, tries to 'understand the distinctiveness of each local context *from within* in order to offer theological responses that respect the integrity of that situation'.[31] This suits those who like getting alongside people in their local circumstances, listening to them and learning from them. It also attracts those who revel in making connections across the gaps, because learning the vernacular is done here with the clear intention of either finding God in the culture and naming God there, or planting the Christian faith into the culture where it has not been known before, but in terms that make local sense. If we do not learn the local accent, it is easy to make a cultural mistake – for example, when water is poured over the head of a Masai woman at baptism, her own culture has always understood that such an act will curse her to barrenness.[32] So this style of theology takes culture very seriously indeed, realizing that the gospel is always mediated within a cultural frame. It asks us to remember that western culture, for example, is not to be foisted upon other cultures as if it were the obvious or only carrier of the Christian faith. This issue and its ramifications have very great significance for the theology of mission.

This focus upon the importance of culture for theology leads us into a third approach to the categorization of the various styles of doing theology. We have thus far looked at theology from the perspective of the various roles we ask it to play in society, and latterly we have recognized that certain styles suit certain human temperaments and learning styles. The issue of culture, however, prompts the pivotal question – 'Is the Christian faith already to be found in any particular culture or must the Church plant the faith there?' So the way we see God in relation to culture proves to be yet a third perspective from which we may describe the different styles of doing theology. Let me do that now.

3. Where do I see God?

Stephen Bevans, in his book *Models of Contextual Theology*,[33] helps us look at the way Christian faith and cultures interrelate, and how any particular theological method can derive from how we believe God connects with culture. At one extreme there will be those who believe that God is so deeply incarnated within our experience that our task as people of faith is to hunt for signs of God's presence within each culture. At the other extreme are those who design their theological methodology on the basis that human cultures are so corrupted that they need a strong injection of the faith so that God's presence may be allowed in.

i. Treasure Hunt theology

Max Warren famously said that when we meet another culture we must 'take off our shoes' in veneration of the God who is already within it.[34] This style of theology assumes that from its beginnings a culture will have had within it the seed of God's word and so the theologian is there to listen, look and stand in awe of God's incarnation in all things. The method asks the theologian to immerse herself attentively in a culture, using all the tools of personal sensitivity, the social sciences and the disciplines of cultural analysis, and then, when she is totally steeped in the culture, to reach back into the past and bring from the Christian heritage of scripture and tradition any resonances which emerge. This theological approach sees God's love writ large in a world which is full of God's glory and acknowledges revelation as not so much a message to a culture, as an encounter with the ever-present God of love already there in the ordinary things of life. The theologian therefore digs down into the culture to find a series of local theologies hidden in ordinariness. So, for example, within the Filipino *sakop* culture a woman experiences herself not as an individual so much as a member of a group,[35] and, by meditating upon her deep communal sensitivity, all Christians will be helped to appreciate yet more of the mystery of what it is to belong to the Body of Christ.

ii. God on the attack

At the other extreme stands the counter-cultural model of theology which is anything but romantic about local cultures. When Bishop Lesslie Newbigin arrived back in the UK after years of work in India he experienced a profound cultural shock and felt very antagonistic towards a British culture which he believed to have lost all sense of God's presence. It was necessary, he proclaimed, that we should advance on the Western cultures, learn to understand their dynamics, and engage them with the authentic gospel message.[36] Culture is not, of itself, evil he affirmed, but it is in dire need of God. We might discern in Newbigin's approach that he had learnt something from Gandhi's even more radical Hindu stance. On looking at the British Raj, Gandhi had announced that it was a moral imperative not to co-operate with such an evil culture. This style of prophetic theology begins from the assumption that there is in some sense an alternative world – that which is described in the foundation documents of the faith – and with this in mind, there is then an inevitable confrontation with any human culture. Each culture must therefore be fully analysed and understood so that it can be transformed into the likeness of the alternative Christian culture. Careful analysis will allow us to reveal the hegemony which the culture has over the minds and lives of its people. Once having 'unmasked the powers',[37] the Church then has to point to the Christian alternative and demand a total change of heart and mind, so that they be made to conform to the Kingdom of God as pictured in the Beatitudes and other basic texts.

While proponents of this view are often charismatic and impressive leaders – Dorothy Day and the Anabaptists among them – this style of theology can lead to an exclusivism on the part of the Church which sees it as a moral duty to purify itself from the prevailing culture, and this can lead to a rather preachy Christian style. The sacred text is understood to place the believer as a 'resident alien' who must make no compromises with a fallen culture.

iii. Planting the gospel

Those who are not altogether convinced of the totally counter-cultural style, may nevertheless feel happy to see the prevailing culture as a seed bed into which the Christian gospel must be planted or translated. We might recognize St Paul as an exponent of this method, and this authoritative pedigree prompts many of the latest 'fresh expressions' of Church[38] to see Church Planting into a culture as the most effective style of mission. This approach insists that the Good News is an unchanging message and cultures are convenient letter boxes into which the message can be posted. The theologian's task, according to this model, is to distil the essence of the message from the context of first-century Palestine, and then to think of ways that the receiving culture can hear that message and believe. Many speak of taking the essential core of the gospel out of the first-century cultural husk that presently contains it, and re-planting it into new soil. There is inevitably some disagreement among theologians of this genre about what the essential core precisely is – be it allegiance to the Lordship of Christ, the fall and salvation of humanity, the Church, the Trinity, or a specific teaching of Jesus – but once the core is decided upon, the next stage, according to this model of theology, is to search the receiving culture for an appropriate story or situation in which this core of the Gospel can be rewrapped. As Pope John XXIII said, 'the substance of the ancient doctrine of the deposit of faith is one thing, and the way in which it is presented is another'.[39] The faith was deposited, in this view, as a revelation from God, and as such remains culture-free.

iv. God in the mix

Many will believe that God is not simply locked up in culture but they will also feel that God does not have to be introduced into culture like a seed into a virgin plot. They will want to acknowledge that God can indeed be in a culture and that God will be also in the traditions of the faith and, that by giving rapt attention to both, and holding them in tension, each will learn a great deal from the other. Some have called this a 'synthetic' or 'cross-pollination' model. An interesting feature is that this style of theology does not consider that only one context or culture should be considered – there is always an attempt to see a situation from as many perspectives as possible. So, for example, a passage from the Bible may be looked at from the woman's perspective and also from the man's point of view. When they then cross-check to see how each cultural perspective has impacted upon the text and how that text impacted upon them, then a conversation takes place to the benefit of all. New discoveries are made and fresh policies decided upon as a consequence – but the two perspectives remain valid and distinctive.

The way this is all achieved can be quite complex, Robert Schreiter being the most well-known exponent of this theological style.[40] His method is to enter a culture and listen carefully to it, using all the tools of sociology, and particularly picking up on the signs and symbols of meaning within the everyday experience of people in that culture. He then suggests that this 'thick description' of which we spoke earlier, will elicit basic themes that run through the heart of the particular culture. As this happens, so the traditions of the faith which are held in the cultural community begin to surface and are investigated to see what basic theological themes emerge. Once the themes from the culture and from these local theologies are focused, then they are brought side-by-side so that a wonderful theological conversation can take place between the two. In this conversation, the cultural themes and the local theologies are never allowed to lose their distinctiveness – both are respected for what they are and they learn from one another without one taking control or having precedence over the other. It is a model very suited to our post-modern age where multiplicity is understood to be of importance in itself, and compromise and false unity are not believed to do justice to the evident reality of diversity. It is a relational model of theology, where the themes from different cultures relate with one another, but the relationship itself is respected and maintained rather than dissolved into 'sameness'.

Kosuke Koyama, in his book *Waterbuffalo Theology*,[41] describes a theology 'from below' as he speaks out of his Thai experience of sticky rice, chickens, villages and farms. He immerses himself in that experience with his people and then interprets the biblical text and allows the culture to open it up in new ways, just as the text opens up the culture. So he tells us that local Thai religion will know about the 'cool' enlightened Buddha and will see Christ as the 'warm' impassioned one. The first is a picture of non-involvement, the second, one of passionate engagement. Koyama does not disregard the Buddhist cool way, while yet, as a Christian, he acknowledges that there is also, within the Christian heritage, the cool, self-emptying of traditional Christian devotion. But while making this observation about Christianity, he also asks that the Buddhist should warm up a little. His style of theology asks that the two cultures speak the truth in love to one another.

v. The praxis model

So, we eventually return to the spiral model of action–reflection theology which is at the heart of this book. As we can now see, it is a methodology which is distinct from other forms and yet in so many ways it tries to encompass the best of the other methodologies, being open to various human temperaments, to the various roles that theology must play, and open to the various understandings of culture.

First, it offers opportunity in the various phases of the Doing Theology Spiral process for the different gifts and temperaments of all those involved to be engaged – for the introvert to bring personal poems and reflections from their heart, for the activist to engage in social analysis, for the extrovert to perform or act out the Word in society, for the academic and the manual worker both to play their part.

Second, whatever the role one wants theology to perform, it is an appropriate method which is available to all – it is there for Church leaders, for those who are concerned that their own group should find a voice, for those who are engaged with world issues, and for individuals who meditate on their own walk with God.

Third, it accepts that some aspects of culture are the very antithesis of the Kingdom and yet it also sees the very presence of God in the heart of all things, and seeks to engage culture in as realistic and purposeful a way as possible. It understands its role, not so much as a matter of convincing the minds of non-believers, as seeking where God is at work in the world and getting alongside God in that *Missio Dei*.

At its heart, the spiral theological method is designed to enable radical social change in God's world. But the change for which it strives is not simply a superficial healing of the structures of this or that society. It certainly seeks to make an impact on the 'principalities and powers'[42] – the forces at large in society which disfigure the quality of our social interrelationships – but it strives for something deeper too. This method calls for a deep repentance in all those who are involved in the issue being considered. The New Testament word for 'repentance' is *metanoia* – which means a complete turn-around in understanding and way of life. This *metanoia*, literally 'new-mindedness', is the expected outcome for each participant as each seeks to respond to the divine light shining into their lives from their theological engagement. We would hope, too, for this *metanoia* in the lives of those involved in the issue we are addressing, for as our responsive action touches upon the situation, we hope that it will raise consciousness for all those involved and point to the transformation required in us and in others by the Kingdom of God.

Four criticisms

The different theological models that are described in this chapter do raise significant questions of our own action–reflection model and they deserve to be addressed briefly here.

First, we may feel that our model can learn from those who concentrate on the inner journey of the soul in meditation, and we may wish to build more opportunity for this sort of personal prayer into our work. We might be accused of having produced a model which is so activity- and society-centred that the interior life is not given sufficient scope to be touched by the holiness of God. However, as we will emphasize in the final chapter, a deep spiritual awareness is called for from all those who undertake this work seriously. If the spiral is thought of as a hamster-wheel of frantic activity, then the wrong impression has been given altogether. There is much to be done when one does theology but every part of it must be completely underpinned by prayer and worship, together and in the confines of our private devotions. But, unlike the first alternative method we discussed – the 'Personal Walk with God' – our prayer also will have practical outworking. Our prayer should be modelled on the Lord's Prayer, which begins and ends in adoration of the Holiness of God, but acknowledges that that adoration will issue in concern for daily bread, mutual forgiveness and community. If we believe that our experience of God is confined to the back seat of the chapel, we will not understand why the incarnate God becomes so embroiled with the Jewish and Roman authorities of his day. As with Jesus, so with us, our prayer life, like our theological work, should be an interweaving of reflection and seriously committed action.

Second, some might suggest that some of these other models of theology benefit from having less reliance than our own upon group work. Surely, we might ask, there must be a place for the lone traveller, especially since we know that God can find us in the solitude of our own room. Two things might be said in reply. First, it is to be hoped that all who take part in our theological group bring to it their own personal prayer life too. We might compare it with how, on Sundays, we gather together to worship with the whole Eucharistic community, but that Sunday worship is all the better when each participant brings to it the riches drawn from their personal devotions through the week. A Christian should not think to function with only public worship or private devotion, but with both informing each other. Likewise, the theological group benefits from the input from each individual's theologizing. How much more, however, does the individual benefit from membership of the group – the Body of Christ. Second, I believe it is indeed possible to utilize the Doing Theology Spiral, even if we are by ourselves. It is better done with a group, just as I have, in the main, described it. But I confess that when I am having to make personal decisions or think through an issue, it is to the Doing Theology Spiral that I look, even in the privacy of my own home.

Third, when comparing our approach with that of others, it may occur to us that our theological method is rather too dependent on clinical, logical progression round the circle, rather than a more free-flowing spontaneity. Must we really go through the steps of the spiral in such regimented fashion? It seems to make theology into a programmed syllabus, as if our own hard work will bring us salvation! In reply, I must say that as I look back over what I have written, I too have that concern. But I know that in describing the process I have had to try to write logically and thoroughly, whereas my long experience of actually doing theology this way feels nothing like a programmed and routinized process. The reality has an organic and relaxed feel about it – probably aided by the friendships and recreation that naturally flow from the meetings. In any case, I would warn against any harsh regimenting of the process. Go with the flow, but make sure we don't leapfrog over any of the crucial phases here described.

Fourth, some would argue too that this method is not sufficiently strident about the privileged authenticity of the gospel message. Perhaps it allows too much 'hermeneutical suspicion' about the text and the motives of the powerful. Would it not be more 'faithful' to accept the Bible and the Tradition of the Church without so much recourse to human probing? All I can say in reply is that, as an Anglican, I very much believe that part of the genius of Anglicanism is that at the Reformation it determined that it was proper to put alongside

Tradition and Scripture the noble and God-given virtue of Reason. Suspicion of un-reasonable authority has long been a mark of the Anglican because, through our history, we have seen how text and social structure can be marred by human beings. Our martyrs have died for the gospel, but not 'without reason'.

A Rule of Life

However, having offered the Doing Theology Spiral model of theology in this book, and having argued for it as good practice, I am the first to become excited when I see other methods being used with success. And so my prayer is that reading this book will prompt the reader to think carefully about their own style of theologizing and to try various methods until they can own one that really works well for them. I would also commend an idea which Judith Thompson suggests in her book, *Theological Reflection*.[43] She offers a list of questions from which the reader is invited to create a Rule of Life for themselves as a theologian, and I set out just a few of her helpful questions here, for you to consider.

- Which model of theology will you take as the basis for your own approach?
- How will you adapt it to make it your own?
- How will your patterns of prayer and your theological model be related?
- What will you do to enrich your knowledge of Scripture and Tradition?
- What group will you do theology with, and when will you use the model alone?
- How will you monitor how you're doing?

Notes

1   Tracy, D. (1981), *The Analogical Imagination: Christian Theology and the Culture of Pluralism*. New York: Crossroad.
2   Lonergan, B. (1972), *Method in Theology*. New York: Herder & Herder, p. 293.
3   Killen, Patricia O'Connell and de Beer, John (1994), *The Art of Theological Reflection*. New York: Crossroad.
4   See for example, Young, R. J. C. (2003), *Postcolonialism: A Very Short Introduction*. Oxford: Oxford University Press. Also see Keller, C., Nausner, M. and Rivera, M. (eds) (2004), *Postcolonial Theologies: Divinity and Empire*. St Louis: Chalice Press. Also, go online to the Postcolonial Network on 'Facebook' at www.facebook.com/group.php?gid=23694 574926.
5   See for example Moore, S. D. and Segovia, F. S. (eds) (2005), *Postcolonial Biblical Criticism. Interdisciplinary Intersections*. London: T & T Clark.

6 Morton, Nelle (1985), *The Journey Is Home*. Boston: Beacon Press, p. 128.

7 Loades, A. (1987), *Searching for Lost Coins: Christianity and Feminism*. London: SPCK.

8 See Elisabeth Schüssler Fiorenza (1983), *In Memory of Her: A Feminist Theological Recon-struction of Christian Origins*. New York: Crossroad.

9 Farley, E. (1983), *Theologia: The Fragmentation and Unity of Theological Education*. Philadelphia: Fortress Press.

10 See Kinast, Robert (2000), *What Are They Saying About Theological Reflection?* New Jersey: Paulist Press, p. 16.

11 Whitehead, James and Evelyn (1980 & 1995), *Methods in Ministry – Theological Reflection and Christian Ministry*. Lanham: Sheed and Ward.

12 Forrester, D. (2000), *Truthful Action: Explorations in Practical Theology*. Edinburgh: T & T Clark, pp. 26–7.

13 Tracy (1981), *The Analogical Imagination*, pp. 405–21.

14 See Veling, Terry (2005), *Practical Theology*. Maryknoll: Orbis, p. 205.

15 See Ballard, P. and Pritchard, J. (1996), *Practical Theology in Action*. London: SPCK. Also, the *International Journal of Public Theology*, published since 2007 by Leiden & Boston: Brill.

16 See Ryle, G. (1949), *The Concept of Mind*. London: Hutchinson.

17 Geertz, C. (1973), *The Interpretation of Cultures: Selected Essays*. New York: Basic Books, esp. pp. 3–30.

18 Wink, Walter (1981), *Transforming Bible Study*. London: Abingdon.

19 Kolb's initial findings were developed further by Honey, P. and Mumford, A. (1986), *Using Learning Styles*. Maidenhead: Peter Honey Publications.

20 See Keirsey, D. and Bates, M. (1978), *Please Understand Me: An Essay on Temperament Styles*. Del Mar, CA: Promethean Books.

21 Graham, Elaine, Walton, Heather and Ward, Frances (2005), *Theological Reflection: Methods*. London: SCM.

22 *The Confessions of St Augustine* (trans. F. J. Sheed) (1944), London: Sheed and Ward.

23 Schwartz, H. (1998), *Reimagining the Bible: The Storytelling of the Rabbis*. Oxford and New York: Oxford University Press.

24 See Green, Laurie (1987), *Power to the Powerless: Theology Brought to Life*. Basingstoke: Marshall Pickering, where the construction and purpose of the Parables are discussed at some length, pp. 50–64.

25 Quoted in Dych, William, SJ (1999), *Anthony de Mello*. Maryknoll: Orbis, p. 9.

26 Hughes, Gerard (1996, new edition), *God of Surprises*. London: Darton, Longman and Todd. Also see Fleming, Daniel L. (1978), *The Spiritual Exercises of St Ignatius*. St Louis: The Institute of Jesuit Sources.

27 Bonhoeffer, Dietrich (1954), *Life Together* (trans. John W. Doberstien). New York: Harper and Row.

28 cf. Boff, Leonardo (1986), *Ecclesiogenesis. The Base Communities Reinvent the Church* (trans. Robert Barr). London: Orbis/Collins. Also Marins, José, Trevisan, T. M. and Chanona, Carolee (1989), *The Church from the Roots*. London: CAFOD.

29 See especially Tillich, Paul (1968), *Systematic Theology* (combined volume), Welwyn: James Nisbet.

30 Snyder, Richard T. (1988), *Once You Were No People*. Bloomington: Meyer-Stone Books.

31 Graham, Walton and Ward (2005), *op. cit.*, p. 201.

32 See Schreiter, Robert (1985), *Constructing Local Theologies*. London: SCM Press, p. 2.

33 Bevans, Stephen B. (1992 & 2002), *Models of Contextual Theology*. Maryknoll: Orbis.
34 Cited in the Introduction to *Six World Faiths*, W. Owen Coles (ed.) (2004, new edition). London: Continuum.
35 Mercado, Leonardo (1972), 'Filipino Thought', *Philippine Studies*, 20/ 2, 54–8.
36 Newbigin, L. (1989), *Gospel in a Pluralistic Society*. London: SPCK.
37 See Wink, Walter (1986), *Unmasking the Powers: The Invisible Forces that Determine Human Existence*. Philadelphia: Fortress Press.
38 Log on at www.freshexpressions.org.uk.
39 'Pope John's opening speech to the Council', in Abbot, W. M. (ed.) (1966), *The Documents of Vatican II*. New York: Herder and Herder, p. 715.
40 Schreiter, R. (1985), *ibid*.
41 Koyama, K. (1974), *Waterbuffalo Theology*. London: SCM.
42 Wink, Walter (1986), *op. cit.*
43 Thompson, Judith with Pattison, Stephen and Thompson, Ross (2008), *SCM Studyguide to Theological Reflection*. London: SCM, p. 114.

9

Spirituality –
Where Will We Find God?

A holy and spiritual person is one who becomes so open to the transforming presence of God at the very heart of their experience that other people sense that same transcendent presence of God when in their company. When others see this, they themselves become hungry for God. By this reckoning, spirituality itself is not so much a thing, as a way of doing and being. I believe that a welcoming encouragement to follow this liberating path to a fuller spirituality must be part and parcel of the theological enterprise and, in my submission, the quest cannot even be called theology without this spiritual dimension being in its every fibre and at its very heart.

Such spirituality at the heart of the theological enterprise will make our doing of theology into an opportunity for addressing the Divine presence within the contemporary situation, hearing the challenge of it, and responding in courage and humility. So the essential and pivotal question of spirituality is 'Where do we meet the Divine?' This becomes the essential question for those who would 'do' theology.

A Rabbinic story

For some years now I have been living with an old rabbinic story that continues to fascinate and intrigue me, and I suspect that it will help us to appreciate the subtle mystery with which our spirituality question tries to grapple.[1]

A man was going from village to village, everywhere asking the same question: 'Where can I find God?' He journeyed from rabbi to rabbi, and nowhere was he satisfied with the answers he received, so he would quickly pack his bags and hurry on to the next village. Some of the rabbis replied, 'Pray, my son, and you will surely find him.' But the man tried to pray and knew that he could not. Some replied, 'Study, my child, and you shall find him.' But the more he read, the more confused he became, and the further he seemed from God. And some replied, 'Forget your quest, my child, God is within you.' But the man tried to find God within himself, and failed.

One day the man arrived, very wearily, at a very small village set in the middle of an enormous forest. He went up to a woman who was minding some chickens, and she asked whom he could be seeking in such a small place; however, she did not seem surprised when he told her that he was looking for God. She showed him to the rabbi's house. When he went in, the rabbi was studying, so he waited a moment; but he was impatient to be off to the next village if he could not be satisfied, so he interrupted, 'Rabbi, how do I find God?' The rabbi paused, and the man wondered which of the many answers he had already received he might be told this time. But the rabbi simply said, 'You have come to the right place, my child. God is in this village. Why don't you stay a few days? You might meet him!' The man was puzzled. He did not understand what the rabbi could mean. But the answer was unusual, and so he stayed. For two or three days, he strode round and round, asking all the villagers where God was that morning, but they would only smile, and ask him to have a meal with them. Gradually, he got to know them and even helped with some of the village work. Every now and then he would see the rabbi by chance, and the rabbi would ask him, 'Have you met God yet, my son?' And the man would smile, and sometimes he understood, and sometimes he did not understand. For months he stayed in the village, and then for years. He became part of the village and shared all its life. He went with the men to the synagogue on Fridays and prayed with the rest of them, and sometimes he knew why he prayed, and sometimes he did not. And sometimes he really said prayers, and sometimes he only said words. And then he would return with one of the men for a Friday night meal, and when they talked about God, he was always assured that God was in the village, though he wasn't quite sure where or when he could be found. Gradually, too, he began to believe that God was in the village, though he wasn't quite sure where. He knew, however, that some-times he had met God.

One day, for the first time, the rabbi came to him and said, 'You have met God now, have you not?' And the man said, 'Thank you, Rabbi, I think I have. But I am not sure where I met him, or how, or when. And why is he in this village only?' So the rabbi replied, 'God is not a person, my child, nor a thing. You cannot meet him in that way. When you came to our village, you were so worried by your question that you could not recognize an answer when you heard it. Nor could you recognize God when you met him, because you were not really looking for him. You were only looking for an answer. Now you have stopped pressuring and persecuting God, you have found him, and now you can return to your own town if you wish.' So the man went back to his own town, and God went with him. And the man enjoyed studying and praying, and he knew that God was within himself and within other people. And other people knew it too, and sometimes they would ask him, 'Where can we find God?' And the man would always answer, 'You have come to the right spot, God is in this place. Why don't you stop a while? You might meet him.'

This story intrigues me because it gives some clues to our search for an incarnational spirituality by addressing that crucial question for theology: Where do we meet God? In our spiral model of doing theology we have attempted to pay due attention to the here and now, the contextual situation in which God has placed us, and this paying of attention to context is not merely some methodological trick of theology, but hopes to be nothing less than a journey into God. For calm, committed reflection in the community of believers, surrounded by worship, celebration and work is a way to meet God, and must be at the very heart of our theological life. Over the years, my own involvement in the Doing Theology Spiral has brought home to me many ways in which God is to be encountered within the theological process, and it may be helpful to mention just a few of those here.

Finding God where you are

First, the rabbinic story forcefully reminds me to be attentive to my own contextual situation and let my natural faculties alert me to God's presence there. Christians often speak of finding God in nature, but the first fifty years of my life were deeply urban and I found the countryside very remote and my ideas about it were romantically unreal. By starting from where I am, however, I can find the presence of God in my own urban experience rather than having to go outside it. I can find what I might call an urban sacramentalism. As I now drive home at night along the urban motorway, I wonder at the city and its iconic forms, its orange glowing factories and stunning floodlit building sites. I sense there the majesty, energy and power of God and our solidarity with that creativity – of belonging with God in the fascinating experiment of industrial production. I am delighted by a sense of wonder that we have been given the gifts to work with such complexity and find comradeship, worth and identity in that communal endeavour.

When I stroll round the city centre I glory in the variety of architectural spaces and buildings, and I am impressed by the Council House where so many men and women have, over the years, worked through their political parties to devote their lives to getting our city right – working the democratic process in order to help all its citizens. In the back offices, city planners try to make sure that the very fabric of the houses, shops, cinemas and amenities are well planned and constructed and that God's people in the city are surrounded by a stable and decent environment.

I walk into the centre of the banking and commercial district, and am intrigued at people's attempt to create the good life. The expertise and the vigour of wealth creation are impressive. And the service industries that support a city are, for me, another place in which to see sacraments of God's presence. Hospitals, shops, sewers, dustbin collection – all gifts in their fascinating complexity. And with each and every one of these gifts I sense too the challenge, the anguish, even the terror when we get it wrong. When industry becomes unjust, when political parties seek their own aggrandizement, when wealth is created for only the few, when social services are badly resourced, then I can still feel God within it, but this time yearning and suffering with us all. Working the Doing Theology Spiral has helped me once again to feel spiritual resources flowing up from the pavement – God's presence, even in my own urban backyard.[2] Where will I find God? – right here, wherever I am!

Finding God in servanthood

Second, in the rabbinic story, the man stayed around the village and found God by forgoing the burden of his status and helping where he could. Working with the Doing Theology Spiral has reinforced in me the conviction that God is to be found in servanthood. During my university and college training in England, I was seduced into thinking that I was learning a whole system of theological 'answers' which I could then impart to 'my' laity when ordained. I now realize that my experience of God is so partial that I need to be a fellow learner with God's laity so that together we may discern God's presence and God's will. For an ordained person such as myself, becoming the true servant of a lay theological group has required of me over the years a profound conversion to a diaconal style of relationship with my fellow Christians. Despite all the fine words I heard during my ministerial 'formation' at college, the overall package I was sold did not truly speak of servanthood and sacrifice. I now try to distinguish clearly between what it is to have 'expertise' and what it is to be an 'expert'. The first makes one a servant; the second, a trapped status-seeker.

Finding God at the edges

Third, it is very evident to me that we meet God in the ordinary encounters of life with other people, and especially in the poor and marginalized – those whom the old Prayer Book referred to as the 'heavy laden'. Many times during the process of following round the theological spiral I have had to acknowledge that its concern for the poor is much more than just a human social concern. In the parable of the sheep and the goats, which is recorded for us in St Matthew's Gospel, Christ actually locates himself in the body of the oppressed. He does not simply enjoin us to be of service to the poor as a moral outcome of following a just God, but he states quite plainly that it is *in* them that he himself is to be met. 'In as much as you did it to one of these, you did it to me' (Matthew 25.40). This is not altogether surprising if we look at the circumstances of his birth, his life and his death, for each point out to us God's intention to be present with the poor and lowly. Time and again, when we are living with the poor, they will smile and say they can't always say exactly when or where God can be found, but they do know God to be in there among them. If we don't honour this, then our theological work will be sadly lacking.

Finding God in the issues

Fourth, the theological cycle makes us address life's issues as opportunities for finding God. Racism, ageism, sexism, politics, ecology, education, housing – challenging and burning issues such as these take on a new spiritual dimension when we put them alongside our Christian traditions. We may, for example, look at the tradition of the Magnificat (Luke 1.46–55), in which Mary sings of how she, the lowly handmaid, can now sense God's justice being worked out in her life. 'He has scattered the proud in their conceit. He has filled the hungry with good things and the rich he has sent away empty.' We can sing the Magnificat and, with Mary, begin to sense God's presence with us in the challenging issues of our own situation. The difficulty is usually that conventional theology, while agreeing with Mary in theory that God 'puts down the mighty from their seat', has in practice wanted it to happen so gently that the mighty would not even feel the bump.[3] But participation in the divine transformation of the issues of society offers us an experience of being touched by the transparent closeness of God, for in this God is truly Mary's incarnate Immanuel – 'God with us'.

Finding God in repentance

Fifth, the theological cycle helps the theologian, perhaps surprisingly, to critique the traditions of theology by what is learnt of God from present experience. Jesus consistently held the Torah Law traditions of the Hebrew

Scriptures up to the light of the suffering world, accepted the critique of the present and broke the law accordingly (e.g. Luke 6.1–11). During the Reflection phase of our cycle, as we seek to let this happen, we too will find that the old traditional wineskins may not always be able to contain the new wine, but new wineskins will have to be fashioned in order that God's presence may be perceived even more transparently in the world (Matthew 9.17). The moment when we appreciate the fuller implications in our own lives of Jesus' teaching that the Sabbath was made for human beings and not the other way around, can prove to be for us a '*Kairos* Moment' – a moment of new revelation.

We know, for example, that many have experienced anguish in the past because of the masculine slant of our English language. Taking the issue around our theological spiral leads us to Explore that old wineskin, the English language, and to find that it is largely pagan in origin – not essentially a Christian language at all. We then turn to theological Reflection and realize that our male-oriented theological language has blinded us to many of God's other, more feminine, attributes. It is not easy of course to take our mother tongue and acknowledge its limitations and prejudices in this way, because our language is so much a part of who we are, but our openness to God in our theological work will demand that we look at it again, this time with repentance and a new spiritual perspective. This repentant frame of heart and mind will change us and our relationship to others and to God. We will find that, as we engage in this struggle to find ways to redraft our language according to Gospel principles, so we find ourselves on a spiritual journey in which we are confronted by the presence of the Divine. Like the man in the rabbinic story, we meet God in our own repentant transformation.

Finding God in the ordinary

The old rabbinic story also brings home to us the simple truth that God is there in the spiritual and sacramental nature of every detail of our lives. For centuries, monks and nuns have sworn vows of chastity, poverty and obedience, attempting to treat as spiritual the three basic issues of sex, money and power. For what were these three vows of chastity, poverty and obedience if not an honest attempt to make an offering to God of their money, their sexuality and their power? Following in that perceptive tradition, modern-day religious have a great deal to teach us about seeing spirituality as a complete and very physical commitment. The ancient Christian heritage they represent, and still live out in their own lives, proves to us that we can meet God even in the hard-edged questions of sex, money and power – and not only through abstinence. Our monks and nuns do their theology from their everyday monastic experience, teaching us to meet God in the spiritual sacraments of our everyday lives.

The rabbinic story reminds us of one more thing. When the rabbi eventually returns to the man, to find that he has finally met God, he explains to him that he was so absorbed by his question and his quest that he had not given himself space to hear the answer in the midst of all that was already around him. If our theological work is truly to lead us to God then it must be shot through with prayer and spaciousness. There must be times of relaxation and times of celebration, as well as meditative moments. Sometimes solitude will allow us to listen or, in the group, times of meditation with music, a picture or a candle will still our hearts and make us more attentive. To be still is as much a part of the dynamic of the spiral as is the rush and bustle of information gathering. Indeed, the imagination, upon which the theological spiral so much depends, is often opened to the creative assistance of the Holy Spirit in times of quiet contemplation when our mind is allowed to stray from the issue at hand and work unconsciously, guided and directed not from within, but from beyond.

Joys and sorrows in the Spirit

When God speaks to Moses at the burning bush, God's command to Pharaoh has two facets. God says, 'Let my people go, so that they can hold a feast in my honour in the desert' (Exodus 5.1). The call is both to freedom – 'Let my people go', and to celebration – 'a feast in my honour'. It is a vocation to salvation, which is both liberation and celebration; an awareness of the need for freedom into our full identity and, at the same time, the celebration of the fact that our God is so very near and present with us. In like manner, engaging our Doing Theology Spiral offers, I believe, an opportunity for a spiritual encounter with the Divine, where we may have a real experience of seeing people freed and released from what holds them back, and at the same time it offers a chance to celebrate the experience with feasting, fun, games, adoration and thanksgiving in God's presence.

What Moses and the Hebrew people had to learn – and the story is told in the long book of Exodus – is that the journey to the Promised Land demands self-sacrifice and struggle. Let us therefore, before turning to consider celebration, attend to how the Doing Theology Spiral will alert us to that inevitable struggle and pain.

Theology demands self-sacrifice

My experience has been that there is always struggle involved in committed theological activity, just as there is always an element of struggle in all creativity – but it is within that struggle that we can in fact meet God.

First, the cyclic process of theology which we have described expects there to be a committed involvement and confrontation with an issue experienced in real life, and this issue can sometimes be quite worrying or daunting. Trudy Cox had been working as a nurse for many years in Basildon, Essex, when her Christian faith led her to realize that she and a small band of helpers simply had to build a hospice for the dying. The frustration at the Health Service's poor provision for the dying and the bereaved was matched only by the anguish engendered by the daunting task that lay ahead. It was a long and painful struggle – which, I'm glad to say, led to a glorious resurrection on the opening day of St Luke's Hospice. But Trudy will witness to the fact that she met God in the struggle, frustration and self-sacrifice. Despite all our committed action, as we do theology together there will remain the realization that, of ourselves, we are unable to solve the great problems that underpin the issues confronting us. The realization that we as yet participate in the Kingdom of God only through our powerlessness can be a cause of great anguish and frustration. The disappointment, the fears of honesty and inadequacy, and the realization of being so small and powerless amid such crushing problems, can all be very painful when the reality of it strikes home. Yet within all that, we sense God's presence with us, deep in the anguish.

Related to this is a second frustration and disappointment to which our theological method introduces us. We have frequently had to come to the conclusion during the course of this study that theology can only be provisional, that there are no easy answers, and no authoritative body of theological knowledge to which we can lightly turn. Answers do appear from time to time after rigorous engagement and hard theological work, but even then they can only be provisional answers that serve us for our present situation. Tomorrow will require new answers, because God and God's world will already have moved on to new things. This faithful living with provisionality has always been part of Christian experience (Hebrews 11.1 ff.) for, although our repeated spiral of theological learning will amass experiences of God's abiding love and convince us that God's character is, and always will be, that same unfathomable love, even in that we will be trusting in a love that is a dynamic and relational process, forever in motion. God is not a fixed and unmoved abstraction. Einstein's remarkable discovery reminds us that things still make sense even though everything is in a state of relativity. We know this too from the Christian doctrine of the Holy Trinity, which speaks of God as a unity of dynamically interrelating persons, rather than one unmoved and immovable reality. But we human beings do not like to 'let go and let God', and instead we cry out for firm answers and simple explanations. Jesus, though, offered his followers no simplistic answers to their problems, but instead taught them to ask their own questions and become creative learners, learning on the road the appropriate ways of loving and living at the threshold of the Kingdom. The freedom and liberation that God brings is a freedom into the desert of provisionality, so that our questioning may be completed in faith.[4]

May I share one other thought about theology as self-sacrifice? The current political glorification of upward mobility is very difficult to square with St Paul's hope for us that we should pattern ourselves after the mind of Christ, who 'emptied himself, taking the form of a servant' and 'being found in human form, he humbled himself' (Philippians 2.6–11). Jesus invited his first disciples to make a journey downward with him[5] and he may also expect that downward social journey of us. Such downward mobility will require of us that we learn the languages of the people, and especially the language of the streets, so that we may properly participate in and learn from the experience of those who are at the margins. So it was that when the great theologian Martin Luther was preparing to translate the Old Testament into German in 1524, he first stood in the marketplace in Wittenberg for two weeks, in all weathers, just listening silently to the peasants as they went about their business. He did this so that he could use the people's language and not his own in his translation of the sacred text. To do any other would have wrecked his theological quest. If we want to enter into a theological investigation of who Jesus was and is, it is no good contemplating his healing miracles without ourselves visiting the sick. It is dishonest to meditate on his cross without seeking to serve until it hurts. In Madurai in south India, the syllabus of the Tamilnadu Theological Seminary requires its students to live, during their studies, for a whole year with their family, in the dreadful slums of the city. We may not have the courage to go that far, but the study of theology will eventually confront all of us with Jesus' words to his disciples: 'Follow me!'

We have considered just a few aspects of the sacrifice that may be expected of those who engage in our model of theology, but Jesus also makes it plain that those who are prepared to take such risks and follow him, will also find cause for exhilarating joy and celebration.

Celebration within the struggle

Our emphasis upon the concerns and problems of the world should not blind us to the beauties of the world's potential and to the joys and playfulness of creation. Whenever I see a painting of Mary with the Christ child, and see in the child's hand an orb symbolizing the world, I am reminded of Moltmann's words, 'Not Atlas carries the burdens of the world on his shoulders, but the child is holding the globe in his hands.'[6] It is as if the world has been created as a beautiful gift for Christ the Son of God. For God has created the world not of necessity, but for sheer joy and companionship. Even the strictest Puritans had to admit that humanity's 'chief end' is not to work and be useful, but 'to glorify God and *enjoy* Him for ever'.[7] So it is that theology is more than a tool or a method, it is a joy in itself – a celebration of God and an opportunity to play with ideas and creative actions in response to encountering God within our experience.

It is as if theology itself has to undergo a Copernican revolution and stop centring in so much upon sin, evil and the Fall, and instead start where God starts – for we are told that, as God was creating the world, at each phase he stopped, looked, and saw that 'it was very good' (Genesis 1.31). It is, after all, love, joy and peace that are the fruits of the Spirit, so a theological group should revel in thanksgiving and celebration by making its central focus the glory and wonder of God, and from this all manner of good things will come. The Christian Church is the Eucharistic community, and the word *eucharisto* means, 'I give thanks!' So, if the theological group has a joyous atmosphere, that will give it a little glimpse of heaven which in itself will be a reminder of why they struggle to see the Kingdom of Heaven on earth. Celebration can so easily unite a group, helping them to rejoice as equals before God with all the normal human hierarchies suspended amid the fun and festivity.

The group's atmosphere of celebration will welcome people from all walks of life and with all manner of difference. It will affirm many different gifts too, for cookery, dance, song, drama, poetry, fashion, all manner of talent and giftedness come together to make the joy of the party and the thanksgiving. And to cap it all, the laughter and song of the community has a mysterious power to convert fear into courage. How joyously the Civil Rights Movement sang freedom songs and spirituals together to lighten their spirits and give them courage and the solidarity they needed so much. With Jesus as Lord of the Dance, his joyous disciples can become as little children, even while engaged warily in the struggles with the powers of darkness. We can see this in the life of Annie Mawson – a Christian Cumbrian harpist and singer. She and her partner Michael have surrounded themselves with children and adults who have profound learning difficulties and have introduced them to the joys of making music together. Tourists visiting the English Lake District go along to an advertised concert, only to find themselves being swept up in the joy and celebration of music made by people who radiate the joy of finding God's miracle happening in their lives – lives which usually appear so limited and frustrated by 'disability'. They call themselves the 'Sunbeams'.[8] Many attending these concerts have come expecting to hear only professional musicians and, at first, the tension is palpable, as anger at hearing 'second-rate' amateurs strains the atmosphere. But as the concert progresses and the Sunbeams radiate their joy, so angry faces are transformed and something akin to a deep repentance changes the frowns to tears of joy.

Mary, the mother of Jesus, looks down upon the Christ child and weeps, but her tears are as much tears of sorrow as of joy. She senses the sorrow of all the world's suffering in her child, born in a stable, but she celebrates the birth of her first-born who is here to save us all from ourselves. We find God with us in joy and in sorrow, and find God there in our own experience opening the pathway to our own destiny. Theology exists to help us find God and open ourselves that God may find us.

Worship and prayer

Any theology of worth should be able to bear the title 'spiritual theology', just as did the earliest theology of the Church. Deeply woven into the process of the Doing Theology Spiral there will, therefore, be both worship and prayer. Indeed, Christian groups who take up this challenge of actively doing theology have commented that their worship has come alive in a remarkable way. Their Eucharist is no longer merely a re-enactment of a liturgical rite but a clear participation in God's present action. For in these communities one becomes aware that the issues of ecology, schooling, ageing, health and so on, begin to be perceived aright as 'spiritual' issues, and therefore become the focus of the community's prayer and sacramental action. When, in the Eucharist, the words 'do this in remembrance of me' are heard, there is an awareness that Jesus is not simply referring to the community's need to share bread and wine together, but is imploring his disciples to engage themselves in the committed and transforming actions in the world of which the Eucharistic actions are yet sacramental signs.[9] When he says 'do this', he is telling us to re-enact the loving self-sacrifice of his own life. In this way, the community's theology, born in the cradle of worship, puts us directly in touch with God's present life in the world.

The practice of prayer is equally essential to any theology worthy of the name. In the book of Job, Job himself is in deep anguish and trouble and his so-called 'comforters' share with him their pre-conceived theologies of suffering. But while they talk abstractly *about* God, Job's predicament moves him to talk directly *to* God in prayer. The theologian who is personally engaged – as our spiral method engages – with the reality of the issue, is always moved to this direct encounter with God.

Job's prayerful encounter with God enlarges his awareness. He sees now his own suffering as participation in the suffering of the world. Then, in his prayer, God makes Job aware of a profound truth – that creation exists, not in order to be useful to human beings, but because of God's overwhelming and creative love for creation itself. Job's comforters were presenting to Job the picture of a God who was simply not big enough to cope with Job's own suffering experience. But his direct and forthright prayer with God shot Job into an awareness of a greater dimension.[10] But Job's prayer is not a gentle rehearsing before God of his likes and dislikes – as much superficial prayer can be – but engages argumentatively with God about the world's suffering. Job's prayer is focused and forthright.

This Jewish tradition of faithful argumentation with God continued even into the camps of the Holocaust. It is reported that at Buchenwald, Auschwitz and other concentration camps, the prisoners held theological meetings where God was put 'on trial' and found guilty of callous injustice regarding his gassed and tortured people. But after the trials, the prisoners gathered together once again, to worship and pray to God as before.[11] This totally faithful discipleship is echoed in the New Testament in many passages. Jesus despairs of God on the cross as he cries, 'Why hast thou forsaken me?' (Mark 15.34). He pleads with God in the Garden of Gethsemane until his sweat is like drops of blood (Luke 22.44). He teaches his disciples to ask, seek and question God in sure faith that they will receive, find, and the door shall be opened to them (Luke 11.9–13). Life's agonizing is part and parcel of prayer, and should not be separated from it as if the moment of prayer were too holy a place to allow our real concerns to surface. To bring our whole self before God in prayer is to bring the tears of our agonies and sorrows, as well as our tears of joy. It is for this reason that the thorny issues and tangled problems which crystallize during the spiral of theology can and should become the raw material of our prayer life. We will often find ourselves bemused and confused amid the questions that we encounter on our way round the theological spiral, and we will need to take these things before God in prayer if we are to rise above our own inabilities to understand them.

Each phase of the cycle of theology, if taken seriously, will be an attempt to live faithfully in the world without blinkers on; and having its own discrete integrity, each phase will require prayer, spiritual sensitivity and courage. Since spirituality is a practical matter, it may be helpful here to talk once again in very practical terms, and describe a method of group prayer that I learnt from José Marins, a Brazilian priest of great insight and experience. José works within Basic Christian Communities, which is a movement of ordinary Christians who are intent on the transformation of their society to conform with the Kingdom of God.[12] The style of group prayer that he describes is very reminiscent of our Doing Theology Spiral, even to the extent that it has a diagram to go with it! José's prayer groups begin with conversation about the ordinary but important events of life that are touching the group members. José speaks of this conversation as the 'Word about Realities' – we may call it simply, 'our concerns'. He draws a big circle and writes or draws into that circle something to represent the concerns they have named. At this point the group searches for anything within the Christian traditions of Bible, church, hymns, psalms and Christian history, that resonates with the experience that has been described. How similar this sounds to the Reflection phase of our Doing Theology Spiral. As a certain word or phrase from the Bible story, hymn or psalm is experienced as especially pertinent to their concern, so that word or phrase is repeated just a few times quite meditatively around the group and is written into a second circle of the diagram. Then in silence the group lets this Christian word or phrase 'echo' in their hearts and minds. Those who wish to make a brief comment may do so, although this is done prayerfully and is not intended to develop into a discussion or Bible study.

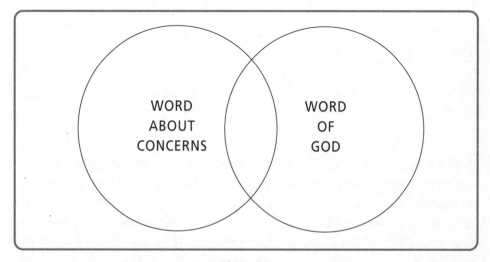

Figure 9.1

The third element in this prayer process is what José calls 'Our Word'. This is the moment, well on in the meeting, when the group may break into more common and traditional ways of praying in order to give some expression to the feelings, hopes and fears that have been generated as the two circles have come together. Spoken prayers and the singing of appropriate hymns, chants or choruses may follow, together with any other expression with which the group feels at ease. José draws a diagram of three connecting circles to represent the process to his groups, and then he draws across the diagram two long lines in the shape of a cross.

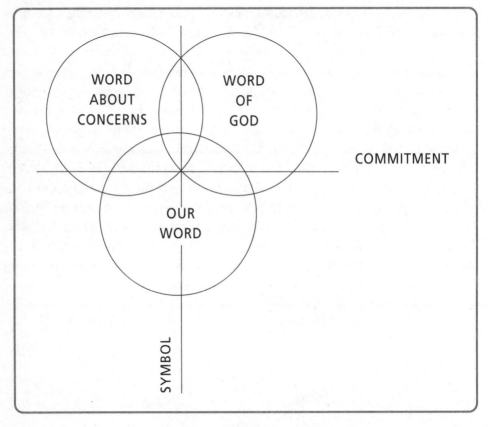

Figure 9.2

The first of the two lines is the line of commitment. The group decide what action or commitment should follow from their experience together. How similar this is to the response phase of our own spiral diagram. The second, vertical line is to remind the group to fasten upon a symbol to represent the prayer session and their resultant commitment. It may be a simple knot in a handkerchief, or something more thought-provoking, like a seed or a stone.

Each group member tries to keep that symbol by them until the group meets again; this is to remind them of the content of the session, but also acts as a symbol of their fellowship and shared commitment.

Prayer like this helps the group to remember that the theology they are creating is a spiritual theology, intended to help them become adept at seeing heaven on earth – the breaking in of the Kingdom even amidst the thorny issues and concerns of their life.

Converting the Church

To speak of theology and spirituality in the way that I have, is essentially to claim that God is at the heart of all our experience and that the old distinction between the sacred and the secular really does no justice to God's intimate concern for the world. This may sound a very mild and obvious statement, but in fact it is a subversive and dangerous claim. For if the curtain that divided holy things from secular things in the Jerusalem Temple really was torn from top to bottom at the death of Christ (Matthew 27.51), then the conclusion we must draw is that Christ died not only for a holy religion, nor even for the Church, but for the whole world. But the Church has not found it easy to accept such a breadth in God's generosity, and instead has wanted to claim God as its own private possession. Its theology has, at times, therefore tended to be inward looking, keeping itself to itself, and it has not been allowed into the hands of those who are engaged at the margins, or outside the institutional Church, in the cut and thrust of society.

My concern throughout this book has been to expand our thinking about the nature of theology, to release it from those who believe that they are its guardians, and allow it across the boundaries and into the hands of common folk. To enable this to happen, there has to be a change in the culture of theology, and we are certainly beginning now to see that happening. But that conversion of theology is being hampered by the inward-looking stance of the Church itself.

The Church as a privileged instrument of the Kingdom

The Church has a mission that will sometimes require it to stand over against prevailing cultures and be prophetic of them, but also, our Doing Theology Spiral teaches the Church to push back the boundaries of its expectation and look for God's presence already there in the world's cultures, even where we might least expect to find it. It is instructive, for example, to notice that some writers have shied away from Jesus' use of the term 'Kingdom', preferring to use a word with fewer sexist and monarchical associations, such as 'Reign' – they do not expect to find a truth hidden in such an 'obscene' word as Kingdom. But in doing this they have failed to grasp that Jesus would have been even more aware of the oppressive provenance of the word than we are – he was, after all, tortured and murdered by the association of two 'kingdoms', the Roman and the Jewish. He nevertheless takes this hated word, deconstructs it and reinvents it, to mean an altogether different society in which the God of love reigns supreme here on earth as in heaven. He takes a hated word from his context and turns it inside out until we can see God's possibility within it – and in re-constructing the language in this way, he gives his teaching the cutting edge and the tough reality that marked the whole of his life and teaching. Jesus makes us stare at even the crudities and vulgarities of incarnation and find God there – and he starts the process in a stinking stable. Doing theology in the way we have presented it, asks the Church to search for God's unexpected, even in the everyday and the mundane. For the element of surprise that is manifest in Christ's birth in a stable is to be experienced time and again in so many of the manifestations of his gracious love, and as evangelists of the gospel of love we must push back boundaries, and look in the most unexpected places till we find God's steadfast love already at work there. Our missionary task is to witness to that love in action and join it there wherever and whenever we may find opportunity. Our theological method is designed to assist precisely this.

Our problem, however, is that at present the Church runs the risk that it will only enter into mission that is pleasant and self-enlarging, and prefers to spend its time looking to itself, its own concerns and well-being. My dear friend, Sister Carolee Chanona, is a radical theologian in Belize and she has shared with me a challenging picture of the institutional Church. In her picture, the Church is represented as a wonderful car which belongs to a family who live in a lovely town house with a large attached garage. In the garage, the family keep their very splendid car. Every day the father of the family goes with two of his well-behaved children to inspect the car, cleaning its wheel-trims, waxing the bonnet, inspecting the oil gauge, even polishing the interior upholstery. But such a lovely car, the family are convinced, should never be taken on to the dangerous and dirty road. And for that reason the car is kept snug and dry in the garage, and the family think it best to come and observe it there instead of bringing it out into the open. Each Sunday the whole family pack their sandwiches and go out to the garage and sit together in the car. They eat their meal together there and sing very lovely and sentimental songs about journeys, roadway dangers and the beauties of the car. Sometimes things get so emotional that the family cry together a little because they are very nice people and love their car. They love it so much that once or twice a year the family invite all their neighbours to come along to a special gathering in the garage. The neighbours especially enjoy all the present-giving that accompanies these big annual festivals. The family are very pleasant people, much-loved and respected by all their friends and neighbours. But the fact remains that the car has never been out of the garage. It is a great pity, but all the neighbours know that the family has actually gone mad.

The Church is a precious vehicle for the Kingdom of God. It is a means to an end, and for that reason it should always be out there on the dangerous road. When the institutional Church gives itself to this transforming focus it becomes the privileged instrument of the Kingdom; but if it denies this calling, then the institutional Church may be very far from being the true Church at all. It will simply be playing mad games in the garage.

In the Acts of the Apostles we learn that it was the Jewish St Peter who first recognized that the non-Jewish Cornelius and his fellow Gentiles were also being inspired by the Holy Spirit (Acts 10). At first sight we are apt to read this story as an account of the conversion of the first Gentiles, but we are prompted to wonder whether in fact the story is rather an account of the conversion of Peter himself to a more expansive appreciation of the Kingdom. God is already out on the road, motoring into areas of the world where our theologically pre-conceived understandings of God dare not take us. It is the Church which needs conversion towards God's world, and a radically open method of doing theology can help in that transformation. In the Gospels, we see Jesus time and again helping ordinary people to examine their own surroundings and situations so as to encounter the Spirit of God within their experience. In this way he transforms them and the situations that entrap them. If we can convert theology so that it may help ordinary people to do a similar thing together, then it will be a transforming and spiritually potent theology indeed.

Notes

1 I have made many unsuccessful attempts to trace the origin of this story. It reads like many a Hasidic story, but one typed script had the name Jeffrey Newman appended.

2 For a full exposition of urban theology using this theological methodology, see Laurie Green's (2003), *Urban Ministry and the Kingdom of God*. London: SPCK.

3 I am grateful to the Revd Ken Leech for sharing this phrase with me, which, he tells me, can be attributed to the wit of Conrad Noel.

4 I am not here thinking so much of the 'Vale of Soulmaking', as the experience akin to the desert experience of Exodus and of Jesus' own temptations in the wilderness.

Compare the work of Harry Williams (1968), *The True Wilderness*. Harmondsworth: Penguin, and (1983), *True Resurrection*. London: Fount, and the as yet unpublished Cadbury Lectures of Juan Luis Segundo.

5 Mark 10.28 etc. See John Vincent (1986), *Radical Jesus*. Basingstoke: Marshall Pickering, especially section 20.

6 Moltmann, Jürgen (1973), 'The First Liberated Men in Creation' in *Theology and Joy*. London: SCM, p. 40.

7 Quoted from the *Westminster Catechism* (1647).

8 To learn more about Annie Mawson and the Sunbeams Music Trust, log on to www.sunbeamsmusic.org.

9 For a full explication of this notion, see Gorringe, Timothy (1986), *Redeeming Time: Atonement through Education*. London: Darton, Longman and Todd, p. 157.

10 See Gutierrez, G. (1987), *On Job*. Maryknoll: Orbis, esp. pp. 16–88.

11 Wiesel, Elie (1974 & 1984), *Souls on Fire*. Harmondsworth: Penguin, p. 111. See also the unpublished doctoral thesis by Jeni Parsons, 'Modern Jewish Attempts at Theodicy, with Particular Reference to the Holocaust', Cambridge University, 1990.

12 See for example Marins, José, Trevisan, T. M. and Chanona, Carolee (1989), *The Church from the Roots*. London: CAFOD. See also Boff, Leonardo (1986), *Ecclesiogenesis: The Base Communities Reinvent the Church*. Maryknoll: Orbis/Collins.

Appendix:
A Survey of 'Conventional Theology'

I present here what can only be an outline sketch of some of the areas included in 'theological study' as conventionally understood. This survey is included to give those readers who may be new to the subject an idea of the vast array of disciplines usually studied within a theological course – and these are only a few of the 'treasures of the Christian heritage' to which I have constantly referred in my description of the Doing Theology Spiral. They will help us to do theology, especially at our 'check-out' stage, but *they are not in themselves what doing theology is all about*.

There is simply no room to include here the more contextual strands of theology, such as feminist, black, urban, or postcolonial theology, which are referred to in the body of this book, and which are radically affecting how we understand theology, but I hope that the following selection will offer a reasonable overview of the subject fields.

1. Biblical studies

The Bible is rightly recognized as a very authoritative foundation document of the Christian faith. In order to understand it better the scholars look intently at the Bible and bring to bear upon it many tools of discovery. The word 'criticism' is often used in this connection to indicate that the scholars' attitude will be one of exploration and digging down to find the truth. There is a whole range of approaches that lead into the overall discipline of biblical criticism, and I attempt below to sketch something of the landscape.

Getting the right biblical text at which to look

i. Textual criticism

We have no biblical text actually from the hand of the authors. The oldest Old Testament fragment that has so far been discovered is from the third century BC, and the earliest New Testament manuscript is a fragment of St John's Gospel, dating from the second century AD. Many minor alterations were made either intentionally or unintentionally by copyists, and this means that although we have lots of copies to choose from, each fragment or manuscript may present a text that is slightly different from the next. Textual criticism tries to determine which variants are the most authentic or reliable. This is the arduous business of the textual scholar and is sometimes called 'lower' criticism.

ii. Translating the language

The Old Testament, or to use better terms, the *Tanach* or Hebrew Scriptures, are written in the old Semitic language, Hebrew. The New Testament is written in a particular type of Greek, *Koine* Greek – the common language of the Roman Empire. Jesus probably knew both these languages, but his mother tongue was almost certainly Aramaic, a Syrian Semitic language similar to Hebrew in many respects. The grammatical critic will attempt to recreate the thought forms and linguistic frame of reference that the original writers may have been using when the texts were written. This will help us to understand a little more what the text may have originally meant. It is notoriously difficult, however, to capture the feelings and thoughts of one language by translating it into another, especially when ordinary words are used in special 'theological' ways by the original authors. The use of lexicons, dictionaries, biblical wordbooks and concordances will help us to gain some insight into the meanings of particular words, but the linguistic critic will also need to search after the ways in which words worked together syntactically in the original languages. Even if we begin to appreciate all the nuances of the Greek New Testament, we will then need to get back to an understanding of what Jesus may have meant in his own Aramaic tongue. And it is not simply a matter of literal substitution of an English word for a Greek or Aramaic one, for each language has its own conceptual system and is a world in its own right. So the academic theologian will need a thorough grounding in the original languages of our Scriptures in order to get over some of these initial hurdles.

Getting behind the text

i. Historical criticism

Nothing in the Bible was written in a vacuum, but each book and each passage within it came out of a particular historical context. If we are to understand what was written in the Bible, we must investigate what was going on around the authors at the time. The scholars will therefore need to know the cultural background and the expectations of the original audience if they are to help us understand it. The second concern that the historical critic will have, is to help us to appreciate the historical background of the events and stories actually described in the text itself. In all this, Bible atlases and geographies will help us locate the happenings, while contemporary manuscripts from other religions and cultures will provide helpful parallels. Archaeological digs and sociological analysis will also provide a certain degree of background information, and in the last ten years this area of research has led us radically to reappraise previous assumptions about the meaning of many texts.

ii. Tradition criticism

Behind many of the written sources that were used by the writers or editors, lay long traditions of storytelling, worship forms, hymns, songs and so on. These oral sources also had a history of development within the community that cherished them, and the way in which these oral traditions grew, and how they were crystallized into the forms that have come down to us, has to be understood by the scholars.

iii. Source criticism

Biblical writers used written sources as well as the oral traditions of the people, to such an extent that some biblical writers are better described as editors than authors. When they took written sources to work from, they made certain decisions about the incorporation of this material into their work. The scholar looks at these written sources and enquires about their origins and the processes of this incorporation. We sometimes also refer to it as 'higher' criticism.

Asking how the text was used

i. Form criticism

This sub-discipline classifies the literature into types or genres, and then associates those genres with the social realities that would have pertained at the time of their composition. The psalms were among the first of the biblical writings to receive this sort of attention, but in the New Testament too, the text divides into all sorts of genres. In the Gospels alone, there are miracle stories, pronouncement stories, parables, birth stories and so on. If scholars should find that a particular section of text seems to have its origin in worship, or in preaching, or in early Christian instruction classes, it will be easier to understand what the words themselves were trying to say.

ii. Redaction criticism

Once the other disciplines have reconstructed the pre-history of each section of text or oral tradition, the redaction critic can then set about discovering why these separate sections were sewn together in a particular way to form a coherent whole. As each author made their editorial decisions, so he or she must have utilized certain criteria that guided their choice of material and determined how they were to position each section within the framework of their whole text. To find out the nature of these criteria and the process of editing, scholars study and explore the background, cultural expectations and situations of each editor (redactor) or editorial group. The redactor will have had his or her message to get across, and the way in which the stories and sections are used will help us discern the redactor's own message and theological insights.

iii. Literary criticism

This phrase can describe a vast array of concerns, but I use it here more specifically to allude to the way in which the various biblical editors or authors have structured the work that they have produced. This discipline is very similar to redaction criticism, but it concentrates particularly on matters of style, rhetoric and structure, and looks upon the Gospel or biblical book more as a work of art, using those approaches to the work that we might find operating upon Shakespeare's plays or Milton's poems in the world of artistic literary criticism. The shape of the whole work and the literary style of the author figure large in this type of interpretation, and philosophical structuralism is often strongly related to the discipline.

iv. Canonical criticism

Many early books, gospels and writings that we still have, were not eventually included in the Bible, and the choice of what to include gave the Bible the shape it has today. The Bible is now more than just the sum of its parts, and one of its books is often taken to interpret another. One is felt to reflect another and often there is cross-referencing and quotation within the Bible as a whole.

This final literary form of the whole text has prompted certain interpretations through the ages, and the Church has invested authority in each book of the Bible only in so far as it takes its rightful place within the whole. This has to be firmly understood and studied by the scholars if we are to appreciate how the texts have been interpreted by the Church through the centuries. The word 'canon', by the way, means Church 'rule' by which writings were included, or omitted if they were not sufficiently authoritative.

v. Reliability

Most of the biblical investigation that we have outlined above can be undertaken without asking whether or not we are getting to the 'truth'. However, when it is realized that in the New Testament, for example, the Acts of the Apostles and St Paul's letters differ in what they say happened at the Jerusalem Council, or when we discover that Matthew's description of the Pharisees at the time of Christ is inaccurate, or when we find varying accounts in the Hebrew Scriptures of certain historical happenings, we are bound to want to ask where the truth lies, now that we are beginning to see the text in a clearer light. By bringing the insights of all the biblical sub-disciplines together, we may find ourselves making sense of some of these complexities. We will then have to make choices about whether we are to read a passage as symbolical or as historical, and in what sense we might do either. It is at this point that we realize that God does not seem to have handed revelation to us on a plate in the Bible, but God has presented us with something that demands that we bring our reasoned critique, integrity and faith to bear upon the material in order to understand it.

2. Church history

The people of God have experienced God's presence through the ages, even amid the tough realities of politics and the rise and fall of civilizations. An appreciation of this story must form an integral part of the process of conventional theology. It was particularly the early centuries of our Church's history that saw the development of central Christian beliefs, Church organization and worship. For an understanding of the forms that are recognizable today, those early years must be scrutinized as accurately and perceptively as possible. Especially important to those early Christians were those groups who had very different understandings from their own about the nature of Jesus and his relationship with God and humanity. The big question for them at that time was whether, in Jesus, God was just pretending to know what it is like to be human, or whether Jesus was so much a man that really he was not God at all. Scholars study what the Church did about these early doctrinal deviations, and they help us realize that a lot of those old heresies are not dead but are around within the Church and society, even today.

There have been many great turning points in the long history of the Christian Church, the most notable being the great schisms and reformation periods that sent the world into such turmoil and split the Church into various denominations. An understanding of the causes and disputes that led to these upheavals will help us appreciate the intricacies of the questions that were at issue, and will also lead to a more reasoned appreciation of the nature of the Church as it is today. We may even be led to a concern to work for more acceptance and understanding between denominations once something of the history is better understood.

Church history will also focus on more recent events, trends and personalities in the life of the Church so that we can more readily appreciate current features and issues that demand our faithful attention.

A very careful study of cultural, political and economic factors through the ages will help us to understand the story of our Christian Church; and by knowing what has gone before, we will be in a better position to understand the present, and plan for the future.

3. Christian doctrine

Here we seek to 'systematize' the major themes of our faith, like the nature of the Trinity, the personhood of Christ, the nature of salvation or redemption, and work out in detail what we really believe about each of them. We then see if they make sense separately and together.

The problem that we immediately encounter here is the problem of authority, for in some quarters of the Church it was strongly feared that this critical approach to such sacred matters was at least dangerous, if not blasphemous. The Roman Catholic Church has feared that independent minds may mislead the faithful if human reason be brought to bear upon some of the teachings of their Church. Pre-Vatican II Catholics tried to get around the problem by differentiating 'dogma' (unquestionable fact as expounded by Church authority) and 'theology' (tentative critique based upon those facts). In this way it was made clear what was 'authoritative' and what was not, and the Church hierarchy could still determine for the faithful those dogmatic aspects of Church doctrine which, in their opinion, were simply not open to theological question. A similar approach has been used by some evangelicals to shield certain matters of belief from over-critical scrutiny. They have taken their lead from such thinkers as Karl Barth, who stressed that God cannot be the object of human inspection, but is rather the Subject which gifts us with such revelation as God chooses. In this way, Barth could say, like the Roman Catholic hierarchy, that there are revealed 'givens' from which we can move into theology, but which themselves are not to be questioned. The problem with such approaches as these is not simply that they are discordant with that enquiring spirit that has given birth to our culture, but also that there seem to be such profound disagreements among Christians about what is included within this dogmatic, unquestionable revelation and what is not. Doctrinal studies try to find a way through this impasse by applying to these great themes of our faith the criteria of reason, biblical authority, inner coherence and so on.

4. Philosophy of religion

In the thirteenth century, Thomas Aquinas argued brilliantly that reason was the gift from God that provided a validating principle by which we could often judge a doctrine to be true or heretical. Reason was also, in his submission, a means by which human beings are able to form a sturdy substructure of understanding upon which Christian revelation could then build its fuller doctrines. He therefore set about using reason to construct what he felt to be sound rational arguments for the existence of God. Anselm had earlier argued that if we define 'God' as the ultimate thing that we can conceive, then, according to a prevailing philosophy of his day, such a thing must exist – whatever its attributes might turn out to consist of. An easier notion for our century to grasp, perhaps, was Aquinas' thought that since everything is caused by something else, surely there must be a first cause upon which all else relies, this cause being not only chronologically before all else, but also logically prior to all else. One of Aquinas' arguments has been especially foundational for later philosophy, namely, his assertion that the reasonableness of creation requires that it must have a designer. But as reasonable as they are, such arguments lead in turn to other philosophical problems, for many feel that they leave us with the challenge of explaining why evil and sin could exist if our world is derived from such a wonderful designer. Indeed, centuries later, Pascal commented that these logically based philosophical arguments give the impression that God is rather cold and aloof. He felt that there was a clear difference between the 'warm' God of Abraham, Isaac and Jacob, and the clinical God described by the philosophers. Others have felt that philosophical argument about God's existence or the possibility of miracles, and so on, seems at best presumptuous, as if reason were asking God for credentials. In response, later philosophers of religion have tried to speak more of the warmth, vulnerability and relatedness of God, and they themselves have lately been more tentative than arrogant about their claims; pointing out that reason does indeed have obvious limitations. They have added, however, that those limitations are no greater than the limitations which Scripture and Tradition share, given what scholarship has revealed about them.

Some philosophers of religion and other spiritual thinkers have therefore suggested that in order to do justice to the holiness and otherness of God, it is best to speak only of what God obviously is *not*. This is the Apophatic or Negative Way. Other philosophers believe, however, that there is much that we still feel pressed to claim about God that is positive. Philosophers usually do this by using language in special ways, for example, by the use of analogy, symbolism, or poetry; while others will find it best to speak of God in the language of story or myth – 'myth' being a specialist term for an imaginative story used by a community or culture to express some underlying truth or characteristic of its life in relation to God.

Some syllabuses of the Philosophy of Religion will include the study of the other great faiths – Islam, Hinduism, Judaism, Buddhism, Sikhism, Taoism and so on. This comparative study of religions is a growing and increasingly relevant enquiry into the texts, cultures and beliefs of other seekers after God. A deeper appreciation of the current ideologies and philosophical understandings of society will be important too, for we will not understand religion, its roots or its implications, if we are not alert to such factors as post-modernism, globalization, imperialism, secularization, and so on.

The Philosophy of Religion will therefore help us to understand what we are doing when we talk about God, and will help us do that with the integrity of reason.

5. Ethics

Human beings are constantly called upon to make moral decisions, to distinguish what they consider to be right and wrong, and to act upon those decisions in particular circumstances. Christians are often understood to be under certain moral obligations to act in a 'Christian' manner in personal relationships and in society – but can such specifically Christian virtues, values and policies actually be formulated and agreed? Such will be the concerns of the Christian ethicist. It is possible to discern within the Hebrew Scriptures and the New Testament certain frameworks of ethical decision-making which may or may not be felt to have application or relevance to present ethical issues. Words such as 'sin', 'grace' and 'forgiveness' all have biblical roots, but have been variously interpreted and understood during the intervening centuries of Christian ethical study. Some major theologians of the past such as Augustine, Calvin and Luther have played substantial roles in the history and development of the discipline, and scholars have to study their work carefully. Many Christian ethicists seek to determine what the foundational ethical principles should be and search the Scriptures, creeds and other traditions to arrive at those principles. Other thinkers, such as Joseph Fletcher, propose that each situation is so distinct that a more experience-based ethic for each situation has to be framed.

Christians are not, however, the only human beings confronted by ethical challenges, and so the ethicist will investigate secular concepts such as goodness, value, duty and so on, and the work of secular philosophers or theologians of other faiths will also be considered in order to see what their explorations have revealed.

This sub-discipline attempts to be more than theoretical and generalized, and often addresses specific issues very carefully in order to understand the complexities and implications of our ethical challenges in the realms of law and justice, war and peace, medicine, industrial and ethnic relations, marriage, sexuality and so forth.

6. Spiritual theology

Many human beings seek a relationship of some sort with the divine ground of our being, and an understanding and description of the varieties of this activity has been variously termed 'mystical theology', 'spirituality' or again, 'spiritual theology'. Our relationship with God influences the way we live our lives and it also deeply influences some societies, especially in the eastern and southern hemispheres. This sub-discipline may therefore find itself ranging quite widely in its attempt to understand both the nature and the implications of prayer. There are many 'schools' or styles of prayer, often with great teachers or saints of the past figuring centrally in each. There are great classics of spirituality to be read and assimilated but, more important still, scholars will attempt to move deeper themselves into understanding how it might be that humankind finds itself able to come close to God and find itself accepted there.

7. Liturgy

Worship is such a central feature of Christian faith that the issues and challenges of worship and liturgy will arise in relation to many of the sub-disciplines we have already described; but the study of worship will warrant attention in its own right. In fact, it is often remarked by scholars that it is worship that precedes doctrine and theology, since human beings naturally set about giving praise, adoration and devotion to God before they formulate why it is that they are doing so. The historical development of worship, its shape, particular practices and deeper meanings, will all be of great concern to the liturgist, who will attempt to make sense of the immense variety of different styles and understandings of worship, both formal and informal.

There is a growing concern that worship, although a natural human function, is no longer a vibrant and vital experience for many in our contemporary cultures, and much revision and reformulation is at present occurring. The liturgist will play an important role in helping the Church to stay true to its liturgical traditions, while at the same time giving contemporary expression to its faith in rite, ritual and worship.

8. Vocational training

Many theological courses also include a large number of modules specifically designed to assist the minister or minister-to-be in playing their full part in the Church's work. This will be in addition to all the above, and will be geared specifically towards active service. How to preach (homiletics); how to communicate in today's society; how to care for the needy – also known as pastoralia, which may include training in counselling, community development, and so forth; missiology, which will look at the many styles of Christian outreach; all these will have their place. In addition there will be courses in leadership and group work, administration, fund raising and ethnicity awareness. There will be many other areas where the trainee minister will need to acquire skills, and all this will be in addition to study of the more conventional theological disciplines that we have described above.

Bibliography and Contact Addresses

Adult education and group work

Ball, P. (1988), *Adult Believing*. London: Mowbray.

Bates, P. and Smith, L. (1991), *Understanding Groups – A Study Course in Five Sessions*. St Alban's Diocesan Board of Ministry. Download from www.cofe.anglican.org/info/education/lifelong/sharedresources/resources/understandinggroups.

Baumohl, A. (1987), *Grow Your Own Leaders*. London: Scripture Union.

Boud, D., Keogh, R. and Walker, D. (eds) (1985), *Reflection: Turning Experience into Learning*. London: Kogan Page.

Craig, Y. (1994), *Learning for Life*. London: Mowbray.

Douglas, T. (1978), *Basic Groupwork*. London: Tavistock.

Freire, P. (1972), *Pedagogy of the Oppressed*. Harmondsworth: Penguin.

Green, L. (1987), *Power to the Powerless: Theology Brought to Life*. Basingstoke: Marshall Pickering. Available from www.lauriegreen.org.

Honey, P. and Mumford, A. (1986), *Using Learning Styles*. Maidenhead: Peter Honey Publications.

Hull, J. (1985), *What Prevents Christian Adults from Learning?* London: SCM.

Kindred, M. (1987), *Once Upon a Group*. M. Kindred, 20 Dover Street, Southwell, Notts NG25 0EZ.

Kolb, D. (1984), *Experimental Learning: Experience as the Source of Learning and Development*. New Jersey: Prentice Hall.

Purnell, A. P., SJ. (ed.) (1987), *To be a People of Hope*. London: Collins.

Rogers, J. (2007, 5th edn), *Adults Learning*. Maidenhead: Open University Press.

Staley, J. (1982), *People in Development*. Tonbridge Wells: Search Press.

Todd, N., Allen, M., Green, L., Tytler, D. and Parsons, J. (1987), *A Thing Called Aston: An Experiment in Reflective Learning*. London: Church House Publishing.

Wren, B. (1977), *Education for Justice*. London: SCM.

Group resources

Brandes, D. and Philips, H. (1982), *Gamester's Handbooks I and II*. London: Hutchinson.

de Mello, A. (1984), *The Song of the Bird*. New York: Image.

Dych, W., SJ (1999), *Anthony de Mello*. Maryknoll: Orbis.

Grigor, J. (1980), *Grow to Love*. Edinburgh: St Andrew Press.

Hope, A. and Timmel, S. (1999), *Training for Transformation* (series of four books). Rugby: ITDG (originally Gweru: Mambo Press).

Keirsey, D. and Bates, M. (1978), *Please Understand Me: An Essay on Temperament Styles*. Del Mar, CA: Promethean Books, Inc.

Raudsepp, E. (1980), *Creative Growth Games* New York: Putnam Perigee Books.

Schutz, W. C. (1967), *Joy: Expanding Human Awareness*. New York: Grove.

Thompson, J. with Pattison, S. and Thompson, R. (2008), *SCM Studyguide to Theological Reflection*. London: SCM.

Warren, Robert (2004), *The Healthy Church Handbook*. London: Church House Publishing.

Contacts

Iona Community
Music and worship and other resources. www.ionabooks.com

Unlock
An Urban Theology resource which produces, for free download, masses of good material, largely based on the style of theology offered in this book. The author worked with Unlock in its earliest days and the same aims and style remain. www.unlock-urban.org.uk.

Bible study and method

The Contextual Bible Study Development Group (no date), *Conversations: The Companion*. Edinburgh: The Scottish Bible Society. Available from www.scottishbiblesociety.org.

Crossan, J. D. and Reed, J. L. (2001), *Excavating Jesus: Beneath the Stones, Behind the Texts*. London: SPCK.

Davies, J. (2002), *Only Say the Word: When Jesus Brings Healing and Salvation*. Norwich: Canterbury Press.

Davies, J. D. and Vincent, J. J. (1986), *Mark at Work*. London: Bible Reading Fellowship.

Dodd, C. (1989), *Making Scripture Work*. London: Geoffrey Chapman.

Fiorenza, E. S. (1983), *In Memory of Her: A Feminist Theological Reconstruction of Christian Origins*. New York: Crossroad.

Hollenweger, W. (1982), *Conflict in Corinth*. Mahwah, NJ: Paulist Press.

Malina, B. J. (2003), *Social-Science Commentary on the Synoptic Gospels* (second edn). Minneapolis: Fortress.

Meeks, W. (1983), *The First Urban Christians*. Yale University Press.

Moore, S. D. and Segovia, F. S. (eds) (2005), *Postcolonial Biblical Criticism: Interdisciplinary Intersections*. London: T & T Clark.

Strong, D. (2003), *Complete Guide to Godly Play* (Vol. 5). Denver, CO: Living the Good News. (Vols 1–4 by Berryman are available from the same publisher.)

Vincent, J. J. (1986), *Radical Jesus*. Basingstoke: Marshall Pickering.

Weber, H-R. (1981), *Experiments with Bible Study*. Geneva: World Council of Churches.

West, G. (2007), *Doing Contextual Bible Study: A Resource Manual*. Download from SORAT, University of Kwazulu-Natal at http://www.ukzn.ac.za/sorat/ujamaa/ujam 123.pdf

Wink, W. (1981), *Transforming Bible Study*. Nashville: Abingdon (new edn 1990). London: Mowbray).

Contacts

The Bible Society
Very wide range of scripture resource materials. www.biblesociety.org.uk.
Also see www.scottishbiblesociety.org.

Scripture Union
Non-denominational biblical resources. www.scriptureunion.org.uk.

Churches Together in Britain and Ireland
Especially good at offering materials for special seasons and ecumenical projects across UK. www.ctbi.org.uk.

The nature of theology

Boff, C. (1987), *Theology and Praxis: Epistemological Foundations*. Maryknoll: Orbis.

Boff, L. (1986), *Ecclesiogenesis. The Base Communities Reinvent the Church* (trans. Robert Barr). London: Orbis/Collins.

Fraser, I. M. (undated), *Reinventing Theology as the People's Work*. London: USPG.

Sedmak, C. (2002), *Doing Local Theology: A Guide for Artisans of a New Humanity*. Maryknoll: Orbis.

Segundo, J. L. (1977), *The Liberation of Theology*. Dublin: Gill and Macmillan.

Derek Winter (ed.) (1980), *Putting Theology to Work*. London: British Council of Churches.

The different styles of theology

Bevans, S. (1992 & 2002 revised), *Models of Contextual Theology*. Maryknoll: Orbis.

Graham, E., Walton, H. and Ward, F. (2005), *Theological Reflection: Methods*. London: SCM.

Graham, E., Walton, H. and Ward, F. (2007), *Theological Reflection: Sources*. London: SCM.

Killen, P. O. and de Beer, J. (1994), *The Art of Theological Reflection*. New York: Crossroad.

Kinast, R. (2000), *What Are They Saying About Theological Reflection?* New Jersey: Paulist Press.

Thompson, J. with Pattison, S. and Thompson, R. (2008), *SCM Studyguide: Theological Reflection*. London: SCM.

Whitehead, J. and Whitehead, E. (1980 & 1995), *Methods in Ministry – Theological Reflection and Christian Ministry*. Lanham: Sheed and Ward.

Practical and contextual theology

Atherton, J. (2000), *Public Theology for Changing Times*. London: SPCK.

Bailey, E. (2006), *Implicit Religion: An Introduction*. London: Middlesex University Press.

Ballard, P. and Pritchard, J. (1996), *Practical Theology in Action*. London: SPCK.

Graham, E. (2007), 'Power, Knowledge and Authority in Public Theology', *International Journal of Public Theology*, 1.1.

Marins, J., Trevisan, T. M. and Chanona, C. (1989), *The Church from the Roots*. London: CAFOD.

Reader, J. (1994), *Local Theology: Church and Community in Dialogue*. London: SPCK.

Veling, T. (2005), *Practical Theology*. Maryknoll: Orbis.

Contacts

The Contextual Theology Centre
CTC in East London combines grass-roots engagement and links with international centres of academic excellence. www.theology-centre.org.

Institute for Urban Ministry
Students from across Southern Africa. Radical training in context. www.tlf.org.za/ium.htm.

Urban Ministry & Theology Project. Newcastle, UK.
Lives out a style of Christian ministry, community and training. www.umtp.org/.

Urban Theology Unit. Sheffield, UK.
Offers courses in theological education and training – a Community of Study and Commitment, based in the inner city. www.utusheffield.org.uk/.

Tamilnadu Theological Seminary. South India.
A pioneering institution, of contextual theology and social concern. Has championed Dalit Theology. http://tts.org.in.

New York Theological Seminary
An impressive, pioneering and engaged syllabus, even training in prisons and the cross-cultural city. www.nyts.edu.

Examples of doing theology

Amirtham, S. and Pobee, J. (eds) (1986), *Theology by the People: Reflections on Doing Theology in Community*. Geneva: World Council of Churches.

Bailey, E. (ed.) (1986), *A Workbook in Popular Religion*. Bristol: Partners Publications.

Ballard, D. (2005), *Explorations in Computer Mediated Theological Reflection*, MTh thesis (unpublished), Cardiff University.

Beckford, R. (1998), *Jesus is Dread: Black Theology and Black Culture in Britain*. London: Darton, Longman and Todd.

Bonino, J. M. (1975), *Doing Theology in a Revolutionary Situation*. Minneapolis: Fortress.

Cone, J. H. (1975), *God of the Oppressed*. Minneapolis: Seabury.

De Gruchy, J. (1966), *Theology and Ministry in Context and Crisis*. New York: Harper and Row.

Donovan, V. J. (rev 1982), *Christianity Rediscovered: An Epistle from the Masai*. London: SCM.

Fraser, I. M. (undated), *Reinventing Theology as the People's Work*. London: USPG.

Fraser, I. M. and O'Brien, J. E. (eds) (1982), *A Theology for Britain in the 80s*. Leeds: ATFB.

Green, L. (1987), *Power to the Powerless: Theology Brought to Life*. Basingstoke: Marshall Pickering.

Green, L (2001, 2nd edn), *The Impact of the Global: An Urban Theology*. London: BSR Church House, Westminster & Sheffield: UTU. Available from www.lauriegreen.org.

Green, L. (2001), 'Global Urbanization: A Christian Response'. Douglas, I. T. and Kwok Pui-lan (eds) (2001), *Beyond Colonial Anglicanism: The Anglican Communion in the Twenty-First Century*. New York: Church Publishing Corporated.

Green, L. (2003), *Urban Ministry and the Kingdom of God*. London: SPCK.

Green, L. and Baker, C. (eds) (2008), *Building Utopia? Seeking the Authentic Church for New Communities*. London: SPCK.

Hazelhurt, B. and Chapman, C. (2006), *The Do It Yourself Kit for Estate Ministry and Outreach*. Available from www.nationalestatechurches.org and www.lauriegreen.org.

Leech, K. (2006), *Doing Theology in Altab Ali Park*. London: Darton Longman and Todd.

Reddie, A. G. (2008), *Working Against the Grain: Black Theology in the 21st Century*. London: Equinox.

Contacts

The William Temple Foundation
Ongoing societal and theological research for a just and inclusive society. www.wtf.org.uk.

Quaker Peace and Social Witness
Translating Faith into Action. www.quaker.org.uk.

Culture

Barber, B. (1992), 'Jihad vs. McWorld'. *The Atlantic Monthly* and reproduced in (1996), *Jihad vs. McWorld: How Globalism and Tribalism are Reshaping the World*. New York: Ballantine Books.

Davie, G. (2007), *The Sociology of Religion*. London: Sage.

Douglas, I. T. and Kwok Pui-lan (eds) (2001), *Beyond Colonial Anglicanism: The Anglican Communion in the Twenty-First Century*. New York: Church Publishing Corporated.

Geertz, C. (1973), *The Interpretation of Cultures. Selected Essays*. New York: Basic Books.

Keller, C., Nausner, M. and Rivera, M. (eds) (2004), *Postcolonial Theologies: Divinity and Empire*. St Louis: Chalice Press.

Koyama, K. (1974), *Waterbuffalo Theology*. London: SCM.

Kwok, Pui-lan (2005), *Postcolonial Imagination and Feminist Theology*. London: SCM.

Mercado, L. (1972), 'Filipino Thought'. *Philippine Studies*, 20/2.

Schreiter, R. (1985), *Constructing Local Theologies*. London: SCM Press.

Social analysis

Arbuckle, G. A., (1990), *Earthing the Gospel. An Inculturation Handbook for Pastoral Workers*. London: Geoffrey Chapman.

Cameron, H., Richter, P., Davies, D. and Ward, F. (eds) (2005), *Studying Local Churches: A Handbook*. London: SCM-Canterbury Press.

Holland, J. and Henriot, P. (1983), *Social Analysis: Linking Faith and Justice*. Maryknoll: Orbis.

Lovell, G. (1995), *Analysis and Design*. London: Epworth.

Shorter, A. (1988), *Toward a Theology of Inculturation*. London: Geoffrey Chapman.

Contacts

Centre for the Study of Implicit Religion and Contemporary Spirituality
Many publications, conferences and study courses. www.implicitreligion.org.

USPG
Anglicans in World Mission. Training and support across the globe. www.uspg.org.uk.

Spirituality

Andrews, D. (2006), *Compassionate Community Work: An Introductory Course for Christians*. Carlisle: Piquant Editions.

Elliott, C. (1985), *Praying the Kingdom: Towards a Political Spirituality*. London: Darton, Longman and Todd.

Ford, D. (1977), *The Shape of Living*. London: Fount.

Gutierrez, G. (1984), *We Drink from our own Wells. The Spiritual Journey of a People*. London: SCM & Maryknoll: Orbis.

Gutierrez, G. (1987), *On Job*. Maryknoll: Orbis.

Hughes, G. (1996, new edition), *God of Surprises*. London: Darton Longman and Todd.

Addressing social issues

Church Urban Fund (2006), *Community Value Toolkit*. London: CUF.

Freire, P. (2005), *Education for Critical Consciousness*. London: Continuum.

Illich, I. (1973), *Celebration of Awareness: A Call to Institutional Revolution*. Harmondsworth: Penguin.

Finneron, D., Green, L., et al. (2001), *Challenging Communities: Church Related Community Development and Neighbourhood Renewal*. London: CCWA & CUF.

Green, L. (2001, 2nd edn), *The Impact of the Global: An Urban Theology*. London: BSR Church House, Westminster & Sheffield: UTU. Also available from www.lauriegreen.org. (also in Tamil, Japanese and Portuguese.)

Green, L. (2003), *Urban Ministry and the Kingdom of God*. London: SPCK.

Green, L. and Baker, C. (eds) (2008), *Building Utopia? Seeking the Authentic Church for New Communities*. London: SPCK.

Messer, N. (2006), *The SCM Studyguide to Christian Ethics*. London: SCM.

Primavesi, A. (2000), *Sacred Gaia*. London and New York: Routledge.

Wallace, J. (2005 revised edition), *The Call to Conversion*. San Francisco: HarperOne.

Wogaman, J. (1988), *Christian Perspectives on Politics*. London: SCM.

Contacts

For my own website of resources and writing, see: www.lauriegreen.org.

CAFOD
Expresses and enacts human dignity and social justice. www.cafod.org.uk.

CARE
A mainstream Christian charity providing resources and helping to bring Christian insight and experience to matters of public policy and practical caring initiatives. www.care.org.uk.

Christian Aid
The UKs ecumenical aid programme campaigning to challenge the causes of poverty. www.christianaid.org.uk.

Church Action On Poverty
UK ecumenical social justice charity, committed to tackling poverty in the UK. www.church-poverty.org.uk.

The Church of England Mission and Public Affairs Division
Advises in social and public affairs; mission and evangelism.
www.cofe.anglican.org/about/archbishopscouncil/mpa.html.

Church Urban Fund
Faith in action, especially in UK urban settings. Raising money and offering consultancy, support and advice. www.cuf.org.uk and CUF-Exchange for sharing ideas at www.cufx.org.uk.

Estate Churches Network
Ecumenical network for clergy and laity working on housing estates and projects. www.nationalestatechurches.org.

Faithworks
A network for engagement in local and national issues with a helpful website at www.faithworks.info.

Rural Issues:
Training and resources on rural issues: www.arthurrankcentre.org.uk.

Urban Issues:
A mine of information, *Urblog*: based in UK but international in interest. http://www.urblog.typepad.com.

Index